# The Language of Russian Peasants in the Twentieth Century

# The Language of Russian Peasants in the Twentieth Century

## A Linguistic Analysis and Oral History

Alexander D. Nakhimovsky

LEXINGTON BOOKS
*Lanham • Boulder • New York • London*

Published by Lexington Books
An imprint of The Rowman & Littlefield Publishing Group, Inc.
4501 Forbes Boulevard, Suite 200, Lanham, Maryland 20706
www.rowman.com

6 Tinworth Street, London SE11 5AL, United Kingdom

Copyright © 2020 by The Rowman & Littlefield Publishing Group, Inc.

*All rights reserved.* No part of this book may be reproduced in any form or by any electronic or mechanical means, including information storage and retrieval systems, without written permission from the publisher, except by a reviewer who may quote passages in a review.

British Library Cataloguing in Publication Information Available

The hardback edition of this book was previously catalogued by the Library of Congress as follows:

**Library of Congress Cataloging-in-Publication Data Is Available**

ISBN 978-1-4985-7503-4 (cloth)
ISBN 978-1-4985-7505-8 (pbk)
ISBN 978-1-4985-7504-1 (electronic)

*To my children, who never cease to amaze me
(не перестают меня изумлять).*

# Contents

| | |
|---|---|
| Preface: Transcription, Formatting, and Other Conventions | ix |
| Acknowledgments | xi |

**1  The Language of Russian Peasants as a Social Dialect** — 1
  1.1  Introduction: The Language of Peasants — 1
  1.2  Peasant Language before 1917 — 9
  1.3  Examples from Bogoraz, Tenishev — 11
  1.4  An Initial Generalization: The Peasant Language Profile — 16
  1.5  A Longer Story from 1925 — 18
  Conclusions — 22

**2  The Impact of the Revolution** — 25
  2.1  Bolsheviks and Peasants — 25
  2.2  Letters to Power: Long History Pre-1905 — 26
  2.3  The Revolution of 1905 and New Kinds of Letters — 32
  2.4  Linguistic Background: Phraseology, Formulaic Language — 35
  2.5  Revolution and Civil War, 1917–1921 — 37
  2.6  Bolshevik Innovations and Peasant Attitudes — 40
  2.7  Available Peasant Materials, 1917–1921–1928 — 46
  2.8  Directions of Change — 54
  2.9  Categories and Examples — 55
  Conclusions — 64

**3  Personal Letters, 1939–1940** — 67
  3.1  The Source and the Background — 67
  3.2  Letters to the Army and Peasant "Moods" — 73
  3.3  Personal Letters as a Genre: Tradition, Structure, and Formal Elements — 75

|  |  |  |
|---|---|---|
| | 3.4 The Source and the Historical Background | 81 |
| | 3.5 Examples of Letters 1: Three Generations | 89 |
| | 3.6 Examples of Letters 2: Old People | 97 |
| | 3.7 Examples of Letters 3: Recent Peasants and Some Success Stories | 101 |
| | 3.8 The Defining Features of Peasant Letters | 108 |
| | 3.9 On Literacy and Letters from Schoolchildren | 110 |
| | 3.10 Discourse and Pragmatic Features | 113 |
| | 3.11 Overlap and Interpenetration with Other Social Groups | 114 |
| | 3.12 Vocabulary, Syntax, Phraseology | 123 |
| | Conclusions | 129 |
| 4 | Scholars and Narratives from the 1950s to Today | 133 |
| | 4.1 A Longer Timeframe, the Endangered Language | 133 |
| | 4.2 Biographic Narratives as Historical Testimony | 146 |
| | 4.3 Examples, Grouped by History | 149 |
| | 4.4 The Linguistics of Peasant Narratives | 185 |
| | Conclusions: The Unity of Peasant Language | 198 |
| Bibliography | | 201 |
| Index | | 209 |
| About the Author | | 213 |

# Preface

## *Transcription, Formatting, and Other Conventions*

The book contains many Russian names, Russian language examples, and quotes from Russian scholars. Except for well-established names (Gorky, Tolstoy), all Russian texts, if transliterated, follow the Library of Congress transliteration system. However, much Russian is left in Cyrillic on the assumption that the readers will either know the alphabet or will not be able to read Russian in any shape or form. Given the nature of our examples, most of which deviate from standard orthography, morphology, and syntax, reading them in transliteration would be an unnecessary strain on the reader. The bibliography is entirely transliterated. In those rare cases when the *sound* of Russian is important, the phonetic transcription (IPA) is provided.

Formatting closely follows the Chicago Manual of Style, 17th edition, except that Russian text within an English paragraph is left in Cyrillic. All examples are in block quotes and most of them consist of three parts: the Russian original, translation, and comments. Each example is followed by two subsections, one for the English translation and one for commentary.

Examples are numbered by chapter (N1) followed by the number of the example within the chapter (N2); the two numbers are separated by a period. If an example is too long to be presented as a single unit, it is broken into numbered parts: 4.15.1, 4.15.2, 4.15.3. Conversely, if several shorter examples are grouped together, they are given alphabetic subscripts, e.g., Example 4.23 may contain 4.23a, 4.23b. In Chapter 3, where the main source is a collection of pieces of mail, each of which can include separate letters written by family members, each individual letter gets a subscript.

Each chapter introduces a list of sources for the examples used in that chapter. The sources are frequently anthologies of documents that are numbered in the source. A reference to a document in such an anthology would include both the number of the document in the present book and its number in the source collection. If relevant, the date of the document is also provided. In the autobiographical narratives of Chapter 4 two dates are given: the respondent's date of birth and the year when the recording was made.

In Chapter 2, sources are referred to by abbreviations explained in the chapter. An abbreviation used throughout the book is RNC, for "Russian National Corpus" (Национальный Корпус Русского Языка).

# Acknowledgments

I am grateful to the wonderful people who read substantial chunks of the book and gave valuable commentary: Wayles Browne, Irina Paperno, Kira Stevens, Robert Chandler, Slava Paperno, Boris Dralyuk.

Several people recommended important materials and otherwise pointed me in the right direction. Olga Blinova in Petersburg is very knowledgeable about academic networks and helped identify and sometimes procure essential texts. Alla Zeide brought to my attention the invaluable and under-appreciated book by Zenzinov. Irina Viktorovna Lukka of the Helsinki library compiled long bibliographies and, with perfect timing, had an essential 1923 book scanned for me minutes before I had to go to the airport. Vera Knorring, formerly of the Russian National Library in Petersburg, filled in a multitude of important details for Chapter 3. Anatoly Nakhimovsky was and remains the quintessential presence in St. Petersburg, an expert in elaborate library research and tracking down out-of-print books in out-of-the-way places.

Irina Bukrinskaia and Olga Karmakova of the Russian Language Institute of the Russian Academy generously sent me their important papers and shared their vast dialectological expertise. Anastassia Ryko, a dialectologist at St. Petersburg University, helped work through several important texts and examples. Elena Markasova provided important background on the subject of *sel'kory*. Valerii Vingradskii in Saratov, a consummate collector of peasant interviews who himself became a competent all-around peasant in the process, shared his vast local knowledge as well as his books, photographs, and videos.

At several moments along the way, invaluable support and advice came from Olga Borisovna Yokoyama, Leonid Leonidovich Kasatkin, and Teodor Shanin.

Closer home, I had essential technical help from Dr. Tom Myers, a friend and co-author of many years, a man of creative mind and incomparable programming skills. For this book, he created several pieces of software that made certain tasks possible that would not otherwise have been done. Also on technical side, Olga Blinova was outstanding in completing an intricate task that greatly simplified the process of searching 266 letters for every minute detail.

Colgate University, in its many manifestations, provided essential support for this book as well as for much of my entire career, through generous travel and research grants. I had additional much appreciated support from Colgate's Center for Freedom and Western Civilization (Robert Kraynak, Director). Colgate's Library and Information Technology services are not only impeccably professional but also humanly supportive. In the library I was especially dependent on Lisa King, the head of the Interlibrary Loan program. In a small liberal arts college in a small village in upstate New York, she was the window on the vast world of library resources outside, and she was able to bring very rare items to Colgate and negotiate their extended use. Some of the sepia-colored pages of the 1920s Soviet books that Lisa obtained presented challenges for scanning but Rich Grant in Information Technologies expertly overcame them all.

Another indispensable presence at Colgate is Distinguished Professor of Russian and Jewish Studies Alice Stone Nakhimovsky. As always, she supplied professional copy-editing skills, psychological support, and sustenance. Nothing would have been accomplished without her.

*Chapter 1*

# The Language of Russian Peasants as a Social Dialect

## 1.1 INTRODUCTION: THE LANGUAGE OF PEASANTS

This book is about the language (strictly speaking, the social dialect) of Russian peasants in the twentieth century. At the century's beginning, there were close to 100,000,000 Russian peasants, by far the largest single demographic in Europe. Their language clearly separated them from other social groups: the vast majority of peasants spoke very differently from the vast majority of non-peasants. It is all the more remarkable that their language was not recognized as a distinct social dialect until the late 1990s, and even then that recognition was incomplete, came with reservations, and was strictly confined to dialect studies.[1] This book argues that the language of peasants was indeed a social dialect with identifiable linguistic features that transcend the divisions of local and regional dialects. It was a spoken language that shared some features with other varieties of spoken Russian, but also had features that were uniquely its own. A flourishing dialect early in the century, by the 1990s, when most available recordings were made, it was *severely endangered*—a term indicating that there were no more children speaking it natively, and no more native speakers of child-bearing age. By the beginning of the twenty-first century the language was gone, with no speakers left. This book aims to be an analysis, a historical record, and a tribute.

Why is it that a social dialect of such scope was not recognized as such until so late? The reasons have changed over time. Before the Revolution, they were internal to linguistics: there was as yet no sociolinguistics, and theoretical involvements in syntax, phraseology, and discourse organization were far into the future. The language of peasants was studied by dialectologists, who were interested in local differences, not underlying unity. They saw the language of peasants as a big conglomerate of dialects and groups of dialects—a "dialectal language," to use a later term from Avanesov (1964) and others. They mostly studied phonetics and morphology, the categories in which the differences were the most pronounced. This was acknowledged by the noted Russian dialectologist Nikolai Karinskii (1873–1935) who toward the end of his life wrote: "Scholars of Russian dialects mostly studied phonetics and morphology. Some scholars and collectors compiled local dictionaries. [ . . . ] We have almost no studies of lexical material or the syntax of Russian dialects" (Karinskii 1935:160).

In simple terms, for a dialectologist if a speaker uses the sound [ts] instead of [tʃ] (*цай* instead of *чай* [tea]); or says *он ушедши*, instead of *он ушел* (he left); or uses the local word *подкрадальня*—not registered in any dictionaries—to refer to a *маленький лужок, заросший молодыми березами* (a little meadow overgrown with young birch trees) (Filin 1936:138) then this person is a peasant, speaking his or her local dialect, and this is the essence of the language of peasants. The notion that there may be something in common to all peasant dialects—in word formation, syntax, phraseology or organization of discourse—is completely alien to this attitude. The attitude still persists, now blended with the historical knowledge of urbanization that destroys dialects and creates a more homogeneous language of the city.

Consider the following quote from a recent standard textbook of dialectology. It opens with the lament (55 years after Karinskii 1935!) that dialectal syntax had not yet been adequately studied. It continues in the most revealing fashion:

Quote 1.1 On dialectal syntax

Because of the as yet insufficient knowledge of dialectal syntax, it is not always possible to determine whether a given syntactic feature is varied by region and serves to distinguish dialects or whether it represents an element of *prostorechie* that is a layer between dialects and the literary language. (Kolesov 1990:147)

Here *prostorechie* (literally SimpleTalk) is a term in Russian linguistics that refers to the social dialect of less-well-educated urban speakers who do not speak the standard language. It is worthy of note that the Russian term for standard language is "the literary language," the language of literature. The entire space of Russian language is hierarchically organized in layers, with peasant dialects at the bottom, literary language at the top, *prostorechie* in the middle. There is no English term corresponding to *prostorechie*—the terms "colloquial," "informal," "slang," and "non-standard" do not refer to social dialects—and in no other language do linguists postulate the existence of a cross-regional urban dialect defined solely by the educational level of its speakers. But then no other country experienced the same level of internal migration and mixing of populations as the Soviet Union in the 1930s–1970s.² In Chapter 4, in the context of general discussion of today's Russian social dialects, the term "Urban Vernacular" will be used for *prostorechie*.

The Kolesov quote says that if a common feature is observed in peasant dialects then this feature is no longer "peasant" or "dialect" but rather rises up to the next layer, the result of the leveling of dialects in an urban environment. In this view, that goes back to the early twentieth century dialectology, as long as peasants remain in their villages, what they are speaking is a local dialect, and to describe their language means simply to describe how their dialect is different from other dialects and from the standard language.

Post-1917 Marxist linguists effortlessly integrated this hierarchical understanding of peasants' language into the historical-materialist scheme in which both peasants and their language were a relic of the rapidly disappearing past, not really worthy of scholarly attention. Ivanov and Iakubinskii (1930) provide a clear summary:

Quote 1.2 Ivanov & Iakubinskii 1930

[...] языку крестьянства свойственна значительная пестрота, унаследованная им от феодализма. [ ... ] Пролетаризующееся крестьянство приносит с собой на фабрику и на завод свои различные местные крестьянские говоры с их произношением, грамматикой и словарем [ ... ] самый характер рекрутирования рабочих из крестьян и подвижность рабочего населения порождают другой процесс: ликвидацию крестьянского наследства путем сглаживания особенностей местных говоров. На развалинах крестьянского разноязычия в условиях развивающейся крупной машинной индустрии как бы создается качественно новая единица — общий язык рабочего класса [ ... ] капитализму присуща тенденция к созданию общегородского разговорного языка данного общества.

The language of peasants has a motley diversity inherited from feudalism [ ... ]. On its way to becoming proletariat peasantry brings to the factory and the industrial plant their local peasant dialects with their phonetics, grammar and vocabulary [ ... ] the very process of recruiting workers from peasants and the mobility of worker population generate another process: the liquidation of peasant inheritance by way of leveling the particulars of local dialects. On the ruins of peasant multilingua, in the context of developing heavy industry, a qualitatively new entity can be said to emerge—the general language of the working class [ ... ] capitalism has the tendency of creating the general urban language of a given society.

Consider the following mental experiment: remove all Marxist terminology from this quote and replace the names of classes with the names of speech varieties—e.g., replace "the general language of the working class" with *городское* просторечие "uneducated urban speech." What you will get is something like the excerpt below, published fifty years later and still considered current in the twenty-first century:

### Quote 1.3 Zemskaia 2004

> Most speakers of просторечие are people who are not urban dwellers by birth but who have lived in a city for a long time [ . . . ] Просторечие is closely related to dialects, but it lacks narrow regional features. [ . . . ] There is an all-Russia nucleus of просторечие that is found in different cities that can be geographically distant. (Zemskaia 2004: 355)

In this quote "people who are not urban dwellers by birth" are, of course, peasants, who spoke dialects. This is why dialects are "closely connected" to the просторечие of the city. However, urban просторечие (just like the language of the proletariat in the preceding quote) is said to possess an "all-Russian nucleus," and the scholarly purpose is to identify and describe it. Do peasant dialects possess such a nucleus? Zemskaia, like Iakubinskii, does not seem to think so; in any event, the question is not even posed.

At the same time, some non-linguists clearly believed that some such nucleus exists. Here are two twentieth century testimonies. The first is from a 1926 newspaper article by Dmitry Stonov, eventually a well-known writer and journalist. (He was twenty-eight in 1926 but lived long enough to be arrested in 1949 in connection with the Jewish Anti-Fascist Committee trial and serve time in the camps.)[3]

### Quote 1.4 Stonov 1926

> [Я]зык деревенский - красочный, яркий и образный деревенский язык - портится. Поговоришь со стариком, - сердце радуется. Речь искрится, цветет, - настоящая земляная речь. Послушаешь молодого, - удивляешься. - "Постольку-поскольку", "в общем и целом", "констатируем", "явный факт" и прочая ненужная бессмыслица. А как обращаются с иностранными словами! К заседанию совета учительница принарядилась. Председатель сказал: - Анн Степановна сегодня в полном бюджете!

> The language of the village—that colorful, bright and imaginative village language—is deteriorating. Speak to an old man, and your heart fills with joy. His speech sparkles and blossoms, the real speech of the soil. Listen to a young man, and you will be surprised: "Insofar as," "in sum total," "ascertain [mispronounced—AN]," "explicit fact," and other such unnecessary nonsense. And the misuse of foreign words! There was a meeting of the Soviet, and the teacher came dressed up. The chair said: "Anna Stepanovna is today in her complete budget!" (*Izvestiia*, 16 May, 1926)[4]

The second testimony is from Maxim Gorky's speech of 1933. Gorky strongly disliked peasants. In 1919, at a meeting of the publishing house *Всемирная литература* (World Literature) he shared this opinion:

Quote 1.5 Gorky 1919

I was recently at the Congress of the Committees of Village Poor—10,000 mugs—the village and the city are headed for a confrontation, the village feels animal hatred towards the city, we will be like an island, the people of scholarship will be under siege, it's not even a struggle—it's like two different races. (Chukovskii 2012:244, diary entry of March 26, 1919)

Yet in his speech addressed to a gathering of sel'kory (syllabic abbreviation for селькоры СЕЛЬские КОРреспонденты—village correspondents) he said:

Quote 1.6 Gorky 1933

Вы будете работать в среде людей не очень грамотных, людей, круг мышления коих все еще весьма узок [ . . . ]. Но эти люди имеют некоторое и немалое преимущество пред вами: они мыслят конкретно, реалистически, в грубой зависимости от явлений природы (in a primitive dependence on events in nature), и они говорят между собою образным, весьма ярким и метким языком. (Gorky 1953:26)

You will be working among people who are not very literate, whose range of thinking is still very narrow. [ . . . ] However these people have some advantages over you: they think in concrete terms, realistically, in direct dependence on events in nature, and they talk among themselves in a in a language that is creative, very imaginative, and precise.

One could dismiss such effusions as the romantic infatuation of the educated elite with the exotic and oppressed народ (folk). However, neither Stonov nor Gorky quite fit the type: both experienced real hardship, traveled widely around the country, and heard many different dialects. What did they mean when using those admittedly vapid adjectives like яркий, меткий and образный (bright, apt, imaginative/metaphoric)? What are the precisely defined linguistic features that they refer to? The goal of this book is to identify those features and trace their evolution over the course of the twentieth century.

The book will follow the path that was recognized but not taken as early as 1925 by the remarkable linguist and psychologist Isaac Shpil'rein, from the prominent Shpil'rein family.[5] Shpil'rein had a modern understanding of what constitutes reliable data: transcripts of conversations and verbatim-typed letters. He also provides a great number of useful statistical tables, e.g., on the relative frequency of parts of speech for different language genres and groups of users. Unfortunately, his subject matter was specifically political discourse in the Red Army, so his recorded conversations are between soldiers and the political officer (politruk), and all the letters are addressed to the стенгазета (wall newspaper of the unit). Shpil'rein himself understood and at times regretted these limitations. In one of his passages, anticipating later ideas of Bourdieu and psycholinguistics, he writes about the letters:

Quote 1.7 Shpil'rein 1928

В общем можно найти среди текстов градации от девственного крестьянского языка, характеризующегося короткими предложениями, живостью и внезапностью перехода от косвенной речи к прямой и обратно, до языка газет и формального языка воинских рапортов. Можно предположить, что стиль языка в некоторых случаях вызывается целью письма – получить н еобходимую справку или разъяснение от редакции газеты. Возможно, что некоторые красноармейцы насилуют присущую им манеру выражения для того, чтобы придать своим корреспонденциям более импонирующий вид. В этом смысле, конечно, более характерными были бы письма частного характера – на родину, но их использование противоречило бы цели нашей работы – исследованию языка, употребляемого в общественной только жизни. (Shpil'rein 1928:40)

In general, the texts range from *virgin peasant language* [emphasis added-AN] that is characterized by short sentences, liveliness, and abrupt transitions from reported to direct speech and back—to the language of newspapers and military reports. One can suppose that in some cases the style of expression results from the purpose of the letter, which is to receive some information or explanation from the newspaper editors. It is possible that some soldiers distort their natural manner of expression in order to "dress up" their correspondence. In this sense, private letters to people back home would certainly be more typical, but their use would contradict the purpose of our work, which is to study exclusively language used in social contexts.

There is much that is remarkable about this passage. Shpil'rein recognizes that some genres of writing are better than others in reflecting speech, and that private correspondence among family and friends is better than public letters across some social distance. He recognizes that social pressure and aspirations for prestige can distort the language—cf. in this respect Bourdieu's observations on the language of petit-bourgeoisie in Bourdieu 1991:52. And finally, this rigorous linguist who associated statistical data with genres and registers does not hesitate to talk about "virgin peasant language" and identify some of its linguistic features. Both the letters in Yokoyama (2008) and our materials of Chapter 3 (peasants' personal letters from 1939–40) show precisely what Shpil'rein meant by "sudden transitions from reported to direct speech and back."

### 1.1.1 Periods and Sources

For much of the twentieth century, spoken peasant language has to be studied from written sources. Not all written sources are equally suitable for the task but the scholarly opinion has converged on this fairly intuitive hierarchy of genres (based on Schneider 2013:171).

*Hierarchy of Sociolinguistic Sources*

1. Reliable records of speech: interviews, conversations, narratives, trial transcripts.
2. Personal letters to family, friends. Some diaries.
3. Letters across some social distance, e.g., petitions, letters to officials or newspapers. The Russian term is письма во власть (letters to power).
4. Separated by time: memoirs.
5. Formal speech events: sermons, folklore, rituals.
6. Prose fiction.

In some cultures and historical periods, local court proceedings are also a reliable record of speech. However, this does not seem to apply to the proceedings of Russian волость courts. (Волость was the smallest administrative division in the Russian empire.) Court scribes were not trained stenographers: they summarized, and for a small fee they would slant the records in favor of the fee provider. Fenomenov (1925 vol.1:240–255) cites multiple selections from the archive of Rozhdestvenskaia Volost, Valdai District for the year 1869: they may be of great interest to a historian but of limited interest as a language record.

The pre-1990 twentieth century left relatively little material for studying peasant language. Table 1.1 lists the main sources for the first three chapters of the book, categorized by historical period and genre. Sources for the last chapter are too numerous to include here; they are listed in Table 4.3, Chapter 4. Most of the sources have never been used in a linguistic study before. Complete references can be found in the bibliography section. In broad outline, this chapter is based on genres 1 and 2; Chapter 2 on genre 3; Chapter 3 on genre 2; Chapter 4 mostly on genre 1.

Before launching into detailed discussions, I would like to present one compact example: the use of the Instrumental case to indicate the domain of the verb's action.

Table 1.1 Genres of Written Records. Compiled by the Author

| | 1. Records of Speech | 2. Personal Letters | 3. Letters "to power" |
|---|---|---|---|
| pre-17 Ch.1 | Bogoraz 1905. Tenishev multiple volumes. Fenomenov 1925. | Yokoyama 2008. Ushakin&Golubev (eds.) 2016. | Kriukova 2001. Sokolov 1998a. Orlov&Livshin 1998b. |
| 1917–28 Ch.2 | Samples in Iakovlev 1923, 1924, Shafir 1923, Selishchev 1928, Bogoraz multiple, Meromskii 1930. | | Kriukova 2001. Sokolov 1998a. Orlov&Livshin 1998b. |
| 1928–53 Ch.3 | Samples in Kushner 1958 quoted in Alymov 2006. | Zenzinov 1944. One letter in Danilov et al. 1999. | Orlov&Livshin 2002. Sokolov 1998b. |
| Post-1990 Ch.4 | Multiple recordings of autobiographical narratives. | | |

- In 1906, a group of peasants from the Voronezh province write in their petition: Мы, крестьяне, *стеснены землею*, – земли у нас совсем мало. (We, the peasants, are confined in terms of land—of land we have very little.) (Senchakova 1999:273)
- In 1939, a peasant woman in the village of Manturovo, Kostroma province, writes to her husband in the army: Леня *дровами плохо*. Дров я не купила, бьюся кое-как. (Lenya, with firewood it's bad. I didn't buy foreword, get by somehow.) (Zenzinov, 1944:284)[6]
- And in 1992, a peasant from the village of Chezhevo, Tver' province, reminisces about 1918: Хлеб у нас тогда был, *хлебом не бедствовали*. (We had bread then, bread-wise we were not in need.) (Kovalev, 1996:47)

This use of Instrumental was preserved exclusively in peasant speech from much older times, fourteenth to sixteenth centuries (Borkovskii 1978:354). It could not be found, and would be totally out of place, in urban speech, whether educated or not. This points to one reason why peasant speech persevered unity across local dialects: speech habits and patterns stayed around longer.

## 1.2 PEASANT LANGUAGE BEFORE 1917

The rest of this chapter uses available data to develop a linguistic profile of the peasant social dialect that comports well with the admittedly impressionistic but well-informed beliefs of such observers as Bunin, Gorky, Stonov, and others. The main features of the profile are: concrete vocabulary; economy of means; lexical creativity; and frequent use of formulaic expressions. Economy manifests itself both in syntax and in word formation. In the syntax of simple sentence, there is a tendency to use transitive verbs, avoiding prepositional phrases. Complex sentences have few conjunctions, relying on intonation to clarify syntax. Conjunction-less subordinate clause are also common in the spoken language of the educated, but, as documented in this chapter, there are variations that are found only in peasant language.

### The Sources for Chapter 1

Data for this chapter comes from three important records of peasant speech that have not yet attracted linguists' attention. The first is N. A. Tan's journalistic account of events of the 1905 revolution, Tan (1905). N. A. Tan is a pseudonym of the famous ethnographer Vladimir Bogoraz, itself a pseudonym for Natan (hence N. A. Tan) Mendelevich Bogoraz. Bogoraz was a *narodnik*, a populist (pro-peasant) revolutionary who spent his many years of Siberian exile doing groundbreaking ethnographic work on the language and culture of Chukchis.[7] This being Tsarist Russia, his work was published while he was still in exile, and at the request of the Russian Academy Bogoraz was allowed to do ethnography full time, first in an Academy-sponsored expedition, and then upon his early return to Petersburg. He soon received an invitation from Franz Boas to join the Jesup expedition studying peoples of the North on both sides of the Bering Strait.[8] Bogoraz spent several years in the United States, including a stint as the Curator of Ethnography at the Museum of Natural History in New York. In 1905, he went back to Russia to observe and document the revolution. His travels in the Saratov province in the summer of 1905 resulted in a book that contains a fair amount of linguistic material, including peasant stories and speeches. As a world-class ethnographer, he can be assumed to have produced reliable records of local speech, even though his interest was not linguistic. Bogoraz was a journalist recording stories, conversations, and speeches about current events, which is why his book is so useful for studying syntax and phraseology.

Another outstanding source are the materials from Prince Tenishev's Ethnographic Bureau (1897–1900). Tenishev is another oversized personality whose work preserved the language of peasants. He was an engineer and an entrepreneur nicknamed "russkii amerikanets" (the Russian American) for his business acumen. He built several factories and became fabulously rich. He was also a talented cellist, an amateur composer, and an important educator: in 1898, he founded the famous Тенишевское училище (Tenishev School), a secondary school in Petersburg whose alumni include Mandelstam and Nabokov among many others. However, Tenishev's real passion was ethnography. Also in 1898 he founded his Ethnographic Bureau. Working with professional ethnographers, he developed a list of topics and an extensive questionnaire that covered both traditional ethnographic interests and the social and economic aspects of peasant life. He hired a small army of "correspondents" from the local intelligentsia in several provinces, trained them well, and paid them good money for each page of collected materials that passed editorial review. In three years Tenishev's correspondents collected a huge amount of material. His plan was to write a fundamental book about the life of Russian peasants, but he suddenly died from heart disease in 1903. The collection spent a hundred years in archival boxes, was partially damaged during the Siege of Leningrad, and became available to scholars only after 1956. (See, e.g., Pomerantseva 1971.) It was published in its entirety—fourteen massive folio volumes—only in the twenty-first century.[9] Although language was not among Tenishev's central interests, the sheer extent of the collection is such that even his tangential interest yields a great deal of valuable data. The collection includes some observations specifically about peasants' language, but, even more importantly, it offers stories, legends, and snippets of conversation that can be assumed to be reliable records of peasant speech.

Materials for Chapter 1 also include a post-1917 publication: a story by a peasant woman published in 1925 by a remarkable ethnographer, Mikhail Fenomenov (1925 vols.1–2). We will see throughout this book that peasant women were less literate and less traveled than men, and thus preserved their language better. The story, one of several, shows no signs of revolution whatsoever, either in its language or content. Next to Bogoraz's recordings that reflect the excitement of revolutionary times, this story serves as a useful corrective, showing how powerless and abused young women could be in the Russian village.

In a different genre, Yokoyama (2008) presents a wealth of material on a peasant family's archive of correspondence from 1881 to 1896. The letter-writers are two parents and three of their five children, two sons and a daughter; the addresses are the remaining two sons. In addition to publishing all the letters, Yokoyama provides rich cultural background and a meticulous linguistic analysis of the texts. Some of her analysis concerns the genre of personal letters and specifically peasant letters, which had a tradition of their own. (This material will be included in Chapter 3 as a historical background to the collection of letters from 1939 to 1940 that constitutes the main subject matter of that chapter.) Unfortunately for the historical linguist, the family did very well: The brothers became successful entrepreneurs, and the daughter finished gymnasium, continued her education, and became a school teacher. She also became "the best represented author in the later part of the collection" (Yokoyama 2008, vol. 1:3). With rising literacy, those later letters became less reflective of peasant speech. For instance, Yokoyama (2008, vol. 1:400) notes that the orthography of loan words is becoming normalized over time, losing the phonetic features of spoken language.

The next section presents several data samples that illustrate the main features of peasant language. Each example, naturally, illustrates more than one feature. The final section is organized by features, each referring back to the examples for clarification and elaboration.

## 1.3 EXAMPLES FROM BOGORAZ, TENISHEV

### Example 1.1 An argument between peasants and an estate owner Kroshin. (Tan 1905:31–32)

Этот Крошин будет Матвей Филиппьевич, а отец его – Филипп Матвеевич, а дедушка – опять Матвей Филиппьевич. Так этот допрежний Матвей у нашего общества закосил луг. Тому прошло 60 лет невступно. Закосил и только. ничего поделать не могли. Тогда, сам знаешь, суды были тихие. Теперь, как пошло в народе беспокойство, стали наши общественные барина скучить: "отдай луг назад!" Приезжает к нам все начальство. "Есть ли у вас бумаги, документы например?" – "Документов, говорят, нету, а есть свидетели-старички, которые помнят: Лазарь Косой, это я то есть, да Фифа Антипьев".

Я-то еще не столько стар, мне семьдесят девять лет, а Фифе в позапрошлом году сто минуло. Когда волю давали, у него уж внуки были. [ . . . ] А барин говорит: "Они слабоумные, чего их и слушать." А я ему ответ дал: "Если я слабоумный, давай на пятьсот рублей об заклад биться. Вынимай деньги. Буде я не сосчитаю, – вся ваша правда. а буде я пересчитаю, да в карман положу, и ты тогда походи за мной". – А наш-то воин, земский начальник, говорит: "На что самоуправничать, отчего вы не жаловались?" – "Кому, говорят, жалиться. К тебе двери открыть – четвертной билет, закрыть – сотельная. У нас, мужиков, кишок не хватит". Так прямо и сказали, да.

*Translation*

That Kroshin would be Matvei Filipievich, and his father Filipp Matveevich, and his grandfather again Matvei Filipievich. That previous Matvei mowed a meadow from our commune. It's been sixty years, almost. Mowed, and that's it, we couldn't do anything. At that time, you know, the courts were docile. Now, as the folks got restless, our progressives started nagging the master: 'Give back the meadow!' A lot of big shots descended upon us: 'Do you have any papers, like documents?' 'No documents,' they said, but there are some old-men witnesses who remember: Lazar Kosoi—that's me—and Fifa Antip'ev."

Myself, I am not that old, seventy-nine, but Fifa turned one hundred year before last. When we got freedom he already had grandchildren. [ . . . ] So the master says: 'They are imbeciles, why listen to them.' And I gave him an answer, I said: 'If I'm an imbecile, let's have a bet on 500 rubles. Take the money out. If I can't count it—your truth in the whole thing. But if I count and put in my pocket, and it'll take a lot for you to get it back.' And our brave soldier, the district boss, says: 'Why act without authorization, why didn't you complain?' 'Complain to whom?'—they said. 'Just to open the door to you is 25 rubles, and to close—a hundred. We, the muzhiks, don't have enough stomach for this.' Exactly they said, yes."

**Example 1.2 Peasant women argue for their rights. (Tan 1905:13)**

Мы тоже не обсевки в чужом поле [ . . . ] Чего тут бояться? Нам тоже надо права и слободу! А если мужик хороший, то и баба по нем. Худая баба по худом муже. А другая баба умней всякого мужика.

*Translation*

We're also part of it, not like *obsevki* in somebody else's field. [ . . . ] What's to be afraid of? We also need rights and freedom. If a *muzhik* is good, his *baba* will follow. A baba is bad if her man is bad. But some baba may be smarter than any muzhik.

*Comment*

The key metaphor in this passage is in the word обсевок, (literally "a Plant-Around")—a small piece of somebody else's land in the middle of a peasant field, the result of land redistribution within a village. Women are not like обсевки, the speaker says, but part of the common field.

Because of their importance for the argument, the words мужик, баба are left untranslated.

### Example 1.3 From a speech at a Zemstvo meeting. (Tan 1905:40–41)

Разумные люди должны жить в складку и помогать друг другу. Одинокое поле ржа выест.

*Translation*

Reasonable people should live jointly and help each other. A lonely field will perish from bugs.

*Comment*

The expression в складку in the meaning "jointly" is old and specific to peasant speech. It is found only in the two oldest entries in 8, both before 1840. After that it is only found it its literary-language meaning "with pleats," e.g., юбка в складку (skirt with pleats).

### Example 1.4 About cooperation. (Tan 1905:42)

Можно ли нам заводить общества? [ . . . ] Мы живем в невежестве, в разноту. Общества наши распадаются от нашей темноты. Друг другу нет доверия. Только оснуют, год простоит и развалится. Один другому на руки смотрит.

Мы упущенные, опозданные люди. [ . . . ] Надо хоть молодежь просветить, чтобы не были такие тумаки, как мы.

*Translation*

Should we be setting up co-ops? [ . . . ] We live in ignorance, in disunity. Our co-ops fall apart because of how dim we are. There's no trust to each other.

As soon as they set it up, it will hold for a year and fall apart. Everybody's watching each other's hands.

We are lost people, too late for us. [ . . . ] We should at least educate the young so they are not so dumb as we are.

*Comment*

The expression живем [ . . . ] в разноту is a syntactically identical antonym to жить в складку. RNC has only nineteenth-century examples of that expression. In the last one, the expression is in quotes to indicate that it is stylistically and socially alien to the rich Moscow merchant milieu of Boborykin's novel *Kitai-Gorod* (1882).

"Опозданный" is a dialectal Passive Participle form of the intransitive verb опоздать "to be late." It is very expressive, suggesting people for whom everything is too late because somebody or something (fate? history?) confined them to obsolescence. It does not seem to be registered in any dictionaries, but RNC shows two examples. Neither of them is about people. One is a proverb, "Часом опозданное годом не наверстаешь" (What's late for an hour takes a year to catch up with.) The other comes in a story from a not very literate character.

## Example 1.5 An old man and his pitchfork. (Тан 1905:36)

[ . . . ] умирать не страшно. А только перед смертью хотя бы я одинова кому-нибудь трехрожки в мягкое всадить.

*Translation*

[ . . . ] dying isn't scary. But I wish I could just once before death sink my pitchfork into someone's soft part.

*Comment*

This is lexically very "peasant:" одинова is a dialectal word but easily recognized by its literary cognate; трехрожки, literally "three-prong," is clear from the verb. The nominalized adjective "мягкое" literally "the soft," is a typical example of dropping the noun if the adjective and the rest of the context make it obvious. This contributes to the economy and energy of the language. More such examples are in Chapter 4.

## Example 1.6 An exchange from Tenishev. K – peasant, C – data collector. (Tenishev vol. 3:185)

К. Вы дайте мне еще 10 копеек, я как раз привезу вам мякины вдвое.
С. Как же ты сможешь за 10 копеек взять столько, сколько и за рубль?

К. А так разве там сам хозяин отпускает? Дам гривенник Гришке, он мне вдвое и насыплет.
С. Да ведь это воровство.
К. Не мы с вами крадем, не на нашей душе и грех.

*Translation*

P. Give me another ten kopeks, I'll bring you double the chaff forthwith.
C. How can you get for ten kopeks the same as for a ruble?
P. Easy—you think the owner himself measures it out? I'll give Grishka a dime, he'll pour me out double.
C. But this is theft.
P. Not you and I are stealing, not on our soul the sin. (literal translation)

*Comment*

Chaff was widely used to dilute animal feed in order to save grain.

### Example 1.7 A story from Tenishev

Мой [который–AN] теперь умер батюшка, от кого-то, не ведаю, дознал, что лежат клады в Черной горе. Срядился один, не бая никому, и пошел рыть. Рыл и дорылся, бает, до ящика. Обрыл – ан через Волгу переезжает человек. Я, бает батюшка, и поопасся его. Пришел домой, бает: "Ребята запрягайте лошадь, я обрыл клад, совсем только увезти". Приезжает – там ничего. Рыли-рыли, нет ничего, а увезти его некогда и некому.

*Translation*

My—now dead already—father learned from somebody, I don't know who, that there are treasures hidden in the Black mountain. He got his things together, without telling anybody, and alone went to dig. After some digging he hit a box. He dug all around it—but then there was a man crossing Volga. I (father said) got apprehensive of him, so he came home and said: "Guys, get a horse ready, I dug all around the treasure, now it's just to take it away." He arrived there—nothing. They dug and they dug, there's nothing, but there had been nobody and no time to take it away.

*Comment*

Several remarkable linguistic features of this narrative are discussed in the next section.

## 1.4 AN INITIAL GENERALIZATION: THE PEASANT LANGUAGE PROFILE

From these and other samples several generalizations emerge that can be treated as hypotheses to be tested on other data from other genres and historical periods.

1. Words: local, old, and invented (опозданный). Within the samples, there are many dialectal words with very narrow specific meanings, designating specific details of peasant life: ржа (бурый грибок на пшенице, похожий на ржавчину), обсевок (незасеянное место на пашне), допрежний (более ранний), закосить (скосить на чужой земле). A great number of such words are found in Tenishev, e.g., заполосок (a space at the end of a *polosa* that is not part of it and not included in its measure, used by peasants to turn their horse around and start the next furrow).

   The samples also have many old words or old usages of the kind that can be found in historical novels, Russian classics, or the Dahl dictionary.[10] In peasant texts such words appear quite alive: words like одинова (once); невступно (almost); допрежний (former, previous); трехрожка (three-pronged pitchfork); раздружба (quarrel); в разноту (separately, in disunity). Educated people know the phrase "как раз" (in the meaning of "soon, right away") from a famous Pushkin poem.[11] In 1.6 it is part of a business proposition having to do with buying chaff.

2. Word formation. Word formation within the samples is concise: in many cases when there are different forms in the standard language and peasant language, the peasant form is shorter: ржа-ржавчина; оскома-оскомина; срядиться-снарядиться, масленка-маслобойка. There are a number of monosyllabic nouns of the kind that Pushkin was so fond of: he used the phrase конский топ (clatter of horse hooves) three times in his poetry, twice on the same line with людская молвь (sound of voices). While Pushkin's examples are all names of sounds, our peasant examples are tools and utensils: *цеп* (a tool for threshing); *жом* (a press that is part of a churn).

   There are a few counter-examples but not many. One systematic counter-example is the use of diminutive suffixes, of which Russian has several: дом means "house" but домик is "a little house." These are more common in the dialects than in the literary language, and there will be many of them in Chapters 3 and 4. They frequently get attached to personal names, adding the connotation of emotional attachment or breezy familiarity, as in Grish-k-a, from Grisha, in 1.6.

3. Within the samples, there are few adjectives; appositive (i.e., purely decorative) adjectives are absent.[12]

4. In 1.1, the official says жаловаться, but the peasants say жалиться. The suffixes -ова- and -ыва- are uncommon in peasant speech, especially -ыва- in the so-called second imperfectives.[13] One of Tenishev's data collectors reports: "Вместо слова закусывайте повсеместно говорят закусайте." (Tenishev vol.3:576.) Even in the 1990s an old peasant woman recalls: "У нас потом сильно кулачили [ . . . ]. Меня самою кулачили." (Kovalev 1996:138,296.) This is shorter than the standard рас-кулач-ива-ть almost by half.
5. The verb ratio within the samples is high, and transitive verbs are frequent: закосить (луг), обрыть (закопанный ящик), поопаситься (незнакомого человека). In 1.1 even the usually intransitive скучить (whine) is used as a transitive verb (nag). The verb полегчить, typically used with a Dative, shows up as transitive: "Надо прибавить нам земли, **полегчить** народ." (They should give us more land, make it easier for people.) (Tan 1905:43)
6. The samples have few deverbal nouns; nouns with the Church-Slavonic suffixes—ени(е)/–ани(е)/- ити(е) are extremely rare. Even the deverbal noun from the verb пилить in its metaphorical meaning "nag, scold," comes out as пилка, not пиление, as one would expect: "Ох и много же я **пилки** вытерпел от женского элементу." (Quite a bit of scolding did I have to endure from the female element.) (Tan 1905:53)[14]
7. The samples have few abstract nouns like участие "participation," and no phrases with semantically empty verbs like принять участие "take part."[15] There is a good example of this In Turgenev's novel *Новь* (Virgin Soil), 1877. The progressive Markelov tries to explain to peasants what "participation" in a collective means; they don't understand; he is indignant:

> [С]лово: участок им хорошо известно [ . . . ] а 'участие' [ . . . ] Что такое участие? не понимают! а ведь тоже русское слово, черт возьми!

> [T]he word 'участок' (meaning 'plot of land,' with the root meaning 'part') they know well [ . . . ] but 'participation' [ . . . ]. What's 'participation?' They don't understand! But it's just another Russian word, damn it!

But for peasants it is not a Russian word. After Markelov's lengthy explanation one of the peasants summed up with a proverb: "Была яма глубока [ . . . ] а теперь и дна не видать" (It was a deep hole, and now you can't even see the bottom.) The rest "испустили глубокий, дружный вздох" (gave a deep sigh in unison).
8. The samples have no present active participles or other Church Slavonic forms, which contributes to the stylistic profile and shortens the average word length.
9. The syntax of peasant speech, unsurprisingly, shares some features with the speech of educated classes as recorded in the studies of Zemskaia

and others in the second half of the twentieth century. One such feature is conjunction-less subordinate clauses. Karinskii (1935:170) reports: "В говоре отсталой части крестьян Ванилова сравнительно мало подчиняющих союзов, а в недавнем прошлом (по наблюдениям в начале XX века) их почти вовсе не употребляли." (In the dialect of the more backward peasants of [the village of] Vavilovo there are few subordinating conjunctions, and in recent past (according to observations of the early twentieth century) they were almost completely absent.)

There are features that are specific to peasant spoken syntax, e.g., a conjunction introducing the main clause after a conjunction-less subordinate clause: "Парохот-то ф Покшенгу-то первый пришол, дак фсе летя [ . . . ] парохот смотреть." ([When] The first steam boat came to Pokshenga, then all were running to look.) (Kolesov 2006:169)

10. Formulaic expressions of various kinds are very common in our data. Many are formally structured by a rhyme: пока рубль добуду, а дыра на полтора, (while I make a ruble, I get a ruble and a half hole) Tan 1905:43; or a syntactic parallelism (к тебе двери открыть--четвертной билет, закрыть--сотельная 1.1); Не мы с вами крадем, не на нашей душе и грех 1.6.).

There are many proverbs, and the definitive feature of peasant language is that proverbs are never used as a decorative quotation; the phrase "как говорится" (as it is said; as they say) is not found in our corpus. A Tenishev data collector confirms: "[П]оговорки крестьяне употребляют в разговорах как общие правила для обобщения и сравнения," (Tenishev 3:580). Example 1.3 is a good example: the proverb is part of a logical argument, and the proper frame for it would be "We all know that [ . . . ]." In today's Russia, the educated class learns proverbs in school or from Russian classics, and uses them self-consciously, while the *prostorechie* class does not seem to use proverbs at all: they are either forgotten or stylistically alien.[16]

This chapter concludes with a real-life story told by a peasant woman in 1925. It is included in this chapter because it bears no traces of the historical events or linguistic perturbations of 1914–1925. It is an excellent sample of the kind of new ethnography of the 1920s that studied current everyday life rather than traditional ethnographic subjects. As many other creative innovations of the 1920s it came to an end before the end of the decade.

## 1.5 A LONGER STORY FROM 1925

The last source for this chapter is Fenomenov (1925 v. 2). It contains the kinds of materials that are not found in our earlier sources or in any later literature until the 1990s: a record, in careful transcription, of a Russian peasant woman telling stories about recent events in her village. The story, the first of several, takes place in 1923. Because of its length, it is broken in two parts, Examples 1.7 and 1.8. The spelling, punctuation and capitalization are Fenomenov's.

## Example 1.8 A story about a young girl, told by U. M. Stukolova. Part 1

Парень Гришка гулял с девицей, по дням не гулял, а по ночам гулял. Она затежалела от его, все скрывалась от родителей и от людей. Ходила к нему навязываться, замуж чтобы взял, но он не взял: она бедная, а он хуть не очень богатый, а поправней ейного-то жил. Потом, когда отец ее узнал, что она в положении, он ее стал бить, выгонять стал. Она проживала кое-где: день сыта, а два дня голонная, потому что она не могла работать. Потом она, уже когда выгната была отцом, хотела она родить в роще и удушить ребенка; у нас есть роща така возле деревни, - в ней всё девки рожают да ребят душат; и она так хотела, да не удалось ей, народ тут все ходил, помешали. Тут кака-то женщина уговорила ею и увела в деревню в Скокова к себе - они двое со стариком жили, и она там родила. Они ею поили, кормили - батька недели три ее не брал, потом сожалелся, взял ею.

*Translation*

The young man Grishka hung out with a girl, during the day he didn't but during the night he did. She became pregnant from him, was hiding it from her parents and everybody. She would go to him to pressure him so he would marry her, but he didn't take her: she was poor, and he was though not very rich but surely better off than she was. Later, when her father learned that she was heavy with child, he started beating her and chased her out of the house. She lived here and there; one day she would have food, then two days would go hungry because she couldn't work. Then she, when already chased out by her father, she wanted to give birth in a little grove and strangle the baby—we have a grove like that near the village where girls would give birth and strangle their kids; so she also wanted like that, but didn't get a chance, there were people walking around, they were in her way. Then some woman persuaded her and took her to her village, Skokovo, she lived there with her old man, and she gave birth there. They gave her food and drink—the first three weeks or so her father wouldn't take her, then took pity, took her in his house.

*Comment*

The striking feature of this paragraph is that the entire history from 1914 to 1923 is absent. The episode is treated as commonplace, and described in a direct, precise, and dispassionate way, both in its cruelty and its kindness.

Linguistically, the text conforms well with the generalizations of the preceding section. The syntax is very simple. There are three subordinate conjunctions—"because" and "when" twice—otherwise connections are paratactic. The only adjectives are predicative: "poor," "rich," "better off." The descriptions are very economical ("она жила кое-где"). Syntactic parallelism is masterfully deployed: по дням не гулял, а по ночам гулял; день сыта, а два дня голонная (i.e., голодная. Transcriptions like this show that Fenomenov made an effort to show dialectal pronunciation.) There are several dialectal forms (хуть, поправней, ейного). The details are not important, but the presence of dialectal forms is, of course, typical.

The use of verbs contributes to the sense of the economy of narrative: some complements are often missing. The verb помешали is not followed by "to whom? to do what?" The verb уговорила is not followed by "to do what?" More such examples appear in Part 2.

### Example 1.9 The story, Part 2: Looking for justice

Потом когда она пожила у отца, ею научили подавать на его, на Гришку-то. Подала и все равно ничего не высудила: свидетели евонные ложно показали, что она гуляла с другим, имела она не одного, а несколько их, значит он не виноват. Показывали они так потому, что он побогаче, да еще он был староста [председатель сельсовета - комментарий Феноменова], упросит и покажут, а за ее никто не шол. Потом, покамест она судилась, ребенок помер. Теперь она в услуженьи. Ребенок жил полгода, и за полгода ничего не могли высудить ей.

Феноменов. Выйдет ли она замуж?

Конечно, выйдет. У нас это ничего: в нашем месте берут. На личико она хорошенька - молоденька (17 л.), ею возьмут с удовольствием.

*Translation*

After she lived at her father's for a while somebody taught her to sue him, Grishka. She did, but nothing came of it: his witnesses falsely testified that she hung out with another one, that she had several, not just Grishka, and so he is not guilty. They testified like that because he was richer, and also he was the village elder [chair of the village Soviet—Fenomenov], so he would ask and they would testify, but for her nobody would come. Then, while she was suing him, her baby died. Now she's a servant somewhere. The baby lived half a year, and in that half-year they couldn't get anything from court.

Question by Fenomenov: Will she get married?

Yes, sure. For us this is nothing, in our place [they] marry [such]. She has a pretty face, and young [17 - Fenomenov], somebody will be glad to marry her.

*Comment*

The only sign that a revolution had happened comes from Fenomenov himself. Stukolova uses the pre-revolutionary title for the elected village elder—староста—which Fenomenov corrects in parentheses to the Soviet title. Her own story continues with the same economy and precision. The phrase "подавать в суд" is abbreviated to just "подавать." The sentence "What he would ask them to say, so they would testify" is shortened to two verbs, "упросит и покажут." The sentence "Nobody would come to testify for her" is shortened to "за ее никто не шол," literally "nobody would go for her." About the girl's marriage prospects, a sentence with no subject or direct object is sufficient: "в нашем месте берут."

The tolerance reported in this example from the northwest of the country was far from universal. Vinogradskii (2012:13–14) quotes an old woman's interview that describes severe social punishments to young women who lose their "innocence" before marriage.

For lack of space, stories by other narrators with reminiscences of serfdom cannot be included here, but the same observations of simplicity and economy apply to them as well. Simplicity and economy are thus not U. M. Stukolova's individual style, but a common feature of peasant story-telling. Records of such story-telling were soon to disappear for several decades, until the end of censorship in the 1990s. The story-tellers were much older by then, but the economy and stylistic energy of their narratives remained the same. Chapter 4 presents multiple examples.

## On Fenomenov

Fenomenov was born in 1883, the son of a village priest. By 1905 he was already in prison as a socialist. Eventually he finished Moscow University and became an ethnographer. His 1925 book was his main achievement, earning him a medal from the Geographic society. It is fortunate that the book was published, and even more fortunate that Fenomenov was not arrested for it in the 1930s, especially in view of his criticism of Iakovlev's 1924 book *Наша деревня* (Our village). Iakovlev, an important Soviet official, is a major character in the next chapter. Fenomenov writes about his book:

Quote 1.8 Fenomenov on Iakovlev's Наша Деревня (Our village)

The author laments the failure to carry out the directive of the party congress to send, to every volost', 2–3 teachers, including a science teacher, a communist, who would spend a month and a half there. Obviously, the author did not count the number of volosts in the USSR, the number of educators who are communists, the number of science teachers who are not busy teaching, otherwise he wouldn't write things like that (рука бы не повернулась). The *real* implementation of such a measure would require more than the annual budget of *Narkompros* (the Ministry of Education).

This was, of course, accurate, and in the 1930s people were arrested for much less. It is probably significant that Fenomenov was very prolific in the 1920s but totally silent in the 1930s. In evacuation during the war he published two patriotic brochures before his death in 1944.

## CONCLUSIONS

The rest of the book traces the evolution of the profile just established in the language of peasants who were born between the end of the nineteenth century and the 1930s. The generalizations of Chapter 1 are confirmed by all pre-revolutionary materials. They also apply to the post-1990 peasant recordings, the subject of the last chapter. In between there are only letters, diaries, and prose fiction. These impose genre-specific and period-specific overlays on language that will be discussed in Chapters 2 and 3.

## NOTES

1. This was initiated by the "communicative dialectology" of Gol'din (1997), discussed in Chapter 4. The first extended study of specifically peasant language appeared only in the twenty-first century: Yokoyama, 2008. The standard textbook of sociolinguistics, Belikov and Krysin, 2017, does not even mention peasants.

2. Krysin (2003:53) writes: "*Prostorechie* is the most unusual subsystem of the Russian national language. If regional dialects and certainly the standard language have direct analogs in other national languages, prostorechie does not have any such analogs." The topics of migration and *prostorechie* are discussed in detail in Chapter 4.

3. This passage is quoted in Selishchev (1928:213) without the name of the author. Although it has been requoted a number of times, including in Nakhimovsky 2017, it has not been noted until now that the author is Stonov.

4. Stonov's article is quite long, spread over two consecutive Sunday issues, and contains remarkable material on how new "Sovietisms" penetrated the language of village youth. It will be revisited in Chapter 2.

5. The Shpil'reins—three brothers and a sister—all studied abroad, became accomplished scientists, and returned to the Soviet Union, where they occupied prominent positions in their disciplines. The three brothers were executed in 1937–38; the sister, Sabina, the most famous of the four (a psychologist; a patient and student of Carl Jung who also worked with Freud, Piaget, and Vygotskii among others and

published seminal articles) survived the 1930s by moving to the provincial city of Rostov, where she was killed in 1942 when the Germans occupied the city.

6. Zenzinov, Letter 2. Chapter 3 is based almost entirely on Zenzinov's remarkable collection of letters from families of Soviet soldiers.

7. Bogoraz was not alone: Johelson, Shternberg and others also became outstanding ethnographers in Siberian exile. Not all of them were Jewish, see on Zenzinov in Chapter 3.

8. Morris Jesup was a blue-blood Connecticut Yankee, fabulously rich and a major philanthropist, who in the 1880s was president of the New York Museum of Natural History. He hired Franz Boas as director of research and provided money for several Arctic expeditions. See, e.g., Freed et al. 1988.

9. The volumes are numbered 1 through 8 but several volumes have subscript numbers: 4a, 4b, etc. There are fourteen volumes altogether.

10. Vladimir Dahl was a great nineteenth century Russian lexicographer whose 4-volume dictionary remains a definitive record of old dialectal language. Vladimir Nabokov, in his early years of emigration, resolved to read 10 pages of Dahl's dictionary every day, to preserve "the only thing I had salvaged from Russia—her language" (*Speak, Memory*, 13.4.1).

11. Пора, мой друг, пора [ ... ] а мы с тобой вдвоем // предполагаем жить // и глядь - как раз - умрем.

12. On the distinction between appositive (non-restrictive) and restrictive relative clauses and adjectives see, e.g., rusgram.ru/относительные_придаточные#31. A canonical example of appositive-restrictive ambiguity is Chomsky's "The industrious Chinese dominate the economy of Southeast Asia." Chomsky 1965:217, meaning either that all Chinese are industrious [appositive] or that only the industrious ones dominate the economy [restrictive, suggesting that the less industrious ones do not do that].

13. E.g., писать (Imp.)—подписать (Perf.)—подписывать (Second Imperfective). There are, in fact, three distinct uses of this suffix: one as just mentioned; another to form verbs from other kinds of words, frequently foreign borrowings, e.g., арест-арестовать; and finally one that forms new verbs from imperfective verbs, to indicate frequent action, e.g., жить-живывать (live somewhere frequently). This last usage is not uncommon in peasant language; we will see examples in Chapter 4.

14. This example shows that the word элемент (element) in the meaning "a category of people" predates 1917. The RNC shows a peak of its use in 1905–1907 but a twice-higher peak in 1918–1921. This word will be discussed in Ch. 2.

15. This is elaborated in the section on Lexical Functions of Chapter 2.

16. This requires further investigation; the observation is based on Matveeva (1995), Shalina (2011).

*Chapter 2*

# The Impact of the Revolution

## 2.1 BOLSHEVIKS AND PEASANTS

The main topic of this chapter is the impact of the Bolshevik language of the new Soviet state on the language of peasants.[1] Terminologically, I would like to avoid the discussion of whether the official language of the Soviet state, as it emerged after 1917 and evolved over the decades of Soviet rule, is technically a "language" (it is not), a social dialect, a register, a jargon, the "official language," or something else entirely. It does contain a cluster of prominent diagnostic features that evolved over time, and it is those features that are important for our subject. (You recognize it when you see it even if there is no formal definition.) It is stylistically helpful to have a single noun referring to that cluster of phenomena. I use the term СовЯз (SovYaz), a syllabic abbreviation for Советский Язык (Soviet Language), introduced in Nakhimovsky 2015.

The time frame of the impact is from 1917 to 1928. The end point is easy to justify: at the point of the "Great Rupture" (Великий Перелом), peasants became kolkhozniks and mostly went silent. However, the start point is a little arbitrary. As the 1917–1928 material builds on an older tradition, some preceding history is useful. It is also interesting in its own right.

The genre of available material is different from what we saw in Chapter 1. There are very few records of peasant speech: they disappeared completely during the years 1914–1922 (WWI, Revolution, Civil War, famine), and there are only small samples for 1923–1928, of which the most substantial one is Fenomenov 1925. For those years, the only abundant and persistent data comes from letters to Soviet leaders and Soviet newspapers. These letters continued the centuries-old Russian tradition of petitions to higher authorities about the iniquities committed by landlords and local officials. Following

Orlov and Livshin (1998a, 1998b, 2002) and others after them, I call these texts "letters to power" (письма во власть).

Each of the great Russian ruptures of the first third of the twentieth century had an impact on the language of letters to power. These historical breakpoints are reflected in the structure of the chapter: before the revolution of 1905, 1905–1917, 1917–1922, and 1923–1928.

The main sources for the chapter are listed below. They are given abbreviations in order to keep example headers more compact.

| | |
|---|---|
| GN | *Golos naroda* (Voice of the people) Sokolov, A.K. (ed.) 1998a |
| OV | *Obshchestvo i vlast'* Sokolov, A.K. (ed.) 1998b |
| KG | *Krest'ianskaia Gazeta* (The Peasant Newspaper) |
| KI | *Krest'ianskie istorii* (Peasant stories) Kriukova 2001 |
| PVV | *Pis'ma vo vlast' 1917–1927* (Letters to power) Orlov and Levshin, 1998b |

## 2.2 LETTERS TO POWER: LONG HISTORY PRE-1905

Letters to power go back to the genre of челобитная established in the late sixteenth century. Ivan the Terrible had a special department for processing them, Челобитный приказ (Department of Petitions). The etymology and the syntactic frame of the word is instructive. It is formed from the expression бить челом (hit [the ground] with your face), indicating the kneeling, face-down position of a supplicant. The format of a челобитная was carefully defined. The first sentence stated who the supplicant was, to whom the petition was addressed, and, if appropriate, against whom the complaint was lodged: бьёт челом Государю холоп твой Васька на Петьку (Petitions to Your Majesty your servant Vas'ka against Pet'ka).

In the more enlightened age of Catherine the Great, the expression бьёт челом was abolished, replaced with просит (begs) or приносит жалобу (brings a complaint). The document itself came to be called прошение (petition) or жалоба (complaint) (Senchakova 1994, vol. 1:15). At the same time, the right to petition directly to the monarch was confined to the nobility, with occasional restrictions and relaxations. Peasants' rights to petition were severely curtailed, especially for serfs. Even though they could and did complain against their owner, there were instances when the complaint was found accurate and acted upon but the peasant who initiated it was still punished for his audacity. (Senchakova 1994, vol. 1:18–19)

After the emancipation of 1861, new forms of peasant self-government were introduced, including the деревенский сход (village meeting). In addition to прошение, petitions adopted by a сход could be called наказ (instruction) or приговор (verdict, decision). (In literary Russian, the word приговор is only used in its legal sense: verdict, sentence.) Most of these petitions were written by a scribe who would be literate and have a reasonably good mastery of the language of imperial bureaucracy. To provide a historical perspective, Example 2.1 shows a прошение from 1899.

## Example 2.1 Peasant representatives to the Governor of the Moscow province. KI, #2, p.16

Прошение уполномоченных крестьян Игнатьевского сельского общества Серпуховского уезда Московскому губернатору от 8 августа 1899 г.

Землевладелец наш Семенкович с самого начала приобретения им у нас в селе нашем господской земли так стал притеснять наших крестьян, что становится вовсе от его притеснения нельзя жить в своем селе: 1) так, он уничтожил из нашего села проезд в деревню Секирино, перекопав его канавой, который существовал испокон веков, 2) окопавши все свое имение канавами, так стеснил, что не оставил из деревни ни одного выезда [ ... ] 3) постоянно судясь с разными людьми [ ... ] и вызывая иных мужичков в качестве свидетелей в суд и большей частью в рабочее время, тем самым отвлекает нас от крестьянских работ и причиняет большие убытки. [ ... ]

Доносим о сем вашему превосходительству мы от имени всего общества, имеем честь покорнейше просить ваше превосходительство, не найдете ли возможным принять какие меры против таких стеснительных действий г-на Семенковича и огородить нас, бедных мужичков, от его убыточных поступков [ ... ]

*Translation*

Petition from peasants' representatives of the Ignat'ev village commune, Serpukhov district, to governor of Moscow province, August 8, 1899

Our landlord Semenkovich, from the very beginning of his acquiring the estate land in our village started oppressing our peasants so badly that because of his oppression it is becoming completely impossible to live in our own village: 1) thus, he destroyed the road from our village to the village of Sekirino by digging a trench across, which [road – AN] existed since time immemorial, 2) digging trenches all around his estate he constrained us so that did not leave a single exit from our village. 3) constantly litigating with different people [ ... ] he summons some peasants to court as witnesses mostly during the work time, thereby distracting us from our peasant work and causes big losses.

We report this to your excellency from the entire community, and we have the honor to most obediently request your excellency to see whether you could take some measures against such constraining undertakings by Mr. Semenkovich and protect us, poor little peasants, from his detrimental actions [ . . . ]

*Comment*

In working with letters, especially letters to power, it is useful to separate the frame (opening and closing) from the body of the letter. In this example, while the opening is simple, the closing contains formulaic elements, such as "we have the honor to most obediently request" or "protect us, poor little peasants," that clearly indicate pre-1905 provenance of the letter.

Within the body there are features that are typical of the bureaucratic language of the Empire but, as we will see, also flourish in post-1917 Bolshevik material. Specifically, there is a fondness for deverbal nouns in -ание, largely absent from peasant language. A peasant would say: "Как он купил господскую землю, так сразу стал притеснять. . . . " (When he bought the estate land, he immediately started to oppress [ . . . ].) The letter says: "from the very beginning of his acquiring the estate land [ . . . ]."

Another typical feature is what I will call "vague adjectives." Consider the sentence: "Его поступки причинили нам убытки." (His actions caused losses for us.) The source and direction of causality are clearly indicated. Replacing the sentence with a noun phrase, его убыточные поступки (his detrimental actions) makes the text vague: detrimental to whom? This kind of vagueness will become more common in post-1917 times when both the adjective and the head noun of the phrase may be unfamiliar and imperfectly understood by the writer.

Both features have the effect of reducing the number of verbs while increasing the numbers of adjectives and deverbal nouns. Such loss of глагольность (verb-ness) became very typical in the post-1917 language. (See Vinokur 1929:34–52 for a definitive discussion.)

## Economics and Demographics

Example 2.1 shows quite clearly the "correlation of forces" (to use the Soviet term) between the peasants and the landlord. Theoretically the peasants could take the landlord to court, but in practice this was impossible. It was not always clear that the landlord had violated any laws. The peasants would need a lawyer, which was expensive. They would have to invest a lot of time, which they did not have. The court would most likely take the side of the landlord. (Remember the speaker of Example 1.1: "The courts were quiet.") So, in the old Russian tradition they pinned their hopes on the higher authority, the governor, who was ultimately under no obligation to consider their petition and no authority to order the landlord what he could and could not do on his own land.

The root cause of the problem was the way emancipation was carried out in 1861. Every peasant household was given an allotment of land out of their landlord's holdings. The landlords had a major say in what part of his lands went to peasants; unsurprisingly, they did not give away the best arable lands and pasture. For the land they received, peasants had to pay выкупные платежи (buy-out payments) to the government; the government, in turn, guaranteed fixed-interest payments for former landowners until the land was paid for in full—only at that point did the peasants receive complete ownership rights. Peasants' payments to the state were, in effect, a tax, the biggest of the many they paid; the state's payments to landowners were, in effect, a rent for their land. Both were set unreasonably high: by 1906, when those payments to the state had to be summarily canceled because of the revolutionary movement, peasants had paid much more than the fair value of the land they received.

The worst of it was that because of rapid population growth, there was not enough land. An allotment that was adequate in 1861 was miserably inadequate for an expanded family forty years later. The only ways to get more land was either to buy it, which few could afford, or to rent it from the landlord. The state did not regulate that market, and landlords demanded exorbitant rents, equivalent in monetary terms to forty to fifty percent of the peasants' harvest. (Nefedov 2011:345. All the statistics in this section are from Nefedov 2011:338–45.) A common practice was for peasants to rent land "исполу" (at-half), an arrangement in which the landlord allowed the peasants to work on a piece of his land in return for half of the harvest. Such rents, writes Nefedov (2011:345), "are typical for periods of overpopulation and agrarian crisis."

Another symptom of the crisis was shortage of pasture, which peasants had to convert to arable land so they could grow more food for themselves. The share of arable land grew rapidly, reaching eighty percent in some provinces, much exceeding the average share in France or Germany (Nefedov 2011:339).

This resulted in shortages of animal feed for horses and cows. "The average weight of a working horse [in Russia] was about 18 poods$^2$ while in America it was 40 poods and in England 55 poods." (Nefedov 340, quoting an official Russian document of 1903.) Pursuit of more arable land also led to deforestation, which resulted in ecological damage and loss of firewood. This created yet another line of dependence on the landlord. A peasant letter from 1905 (Example 2.2 later in this chapter) sums it all in once sentence: "У нас нет ни земли, ни лугов, ни дров, что будем делать - плохо." (We have no land, no meadows, no firewood, what can we do—it's bad.) (KI #25, 42)

Ultimately, the crisis of agriculture resulted in widespread hunger during the poor harvest years of 1873, 1880, and 1883. The next poor harvest, in 1891, was exacerbated by large grain exports over several preceding years.

In a sequence that would repeat in the 1930s, Russia was poor but had to industrialize, in particular to keep up with the military advances in the West. To pay for imports of technology it greatly increased exports of grain, depleting reserves. As a result, the poor harvest of 1891 became a major famine, in which hundreds of thousands, perhaps half a million, died. At least the Tsarist government immediately stopped exports and provided help. In the 1930s, Stalin's government did not, and the deaths were in the millions.

In retrospect, it may seem inconceivable that a country beset by such problems of economic development would start a war in the Far East, driven solely by imperial ambition. The Russo-Japanese war of 1904–1905 completely depleted the government's finances, and also went very poorly for Russia. This was a major cause of the revolution of 1905. Example 2.2, a direct letter from a group of peasants to a landowner, is from the time of the revolution, but it illustrates the contents of this subsection. Alternately desperate and threatening, its main point is that the peasants need more land, and they are willing to work исполу (which they misspell изполу), i.e., giving half the harvest as rent. Even under these conditions the landowner offers them too little; they ask for more, and also for firewood. To a great extent, this letter is a record of speech, much like the personal letters of Chapter 3 are. The sequences in boldface are clear reflections of spoken peasant language.

### Example 2.2. Peasants to landowner, 1905 (KI 42–43)

Письмо крестьян землевладельцу Юрию Владимировичу Трубникову при с[еле]. Буракове Спасского у[езда].

Многоуважаемый, Милостивый Государь, Юрий Владимирович. Мы просим тебя, пожалуйста, Бога ради, пожалей нас несчастных, **не дай нам между себя бунт вести** и вас беспокоить. **Нам время пришло тревожное**, так плохо, что **мы друг дружку не знаем - кто я**. Юрий Владимирович, послушайте пожалуйста, **что это за факт** - земли вы нам даете мало изполу, так мало, что жить нам нельзя на этой земле, вы нас только привязываете, как корабль к берегу. Время пришло, оторвемся. Вы дайте нам земли изполу 165 десятин. Нам будет хорошо и вам не плохо. Будем мы заутро зябить, как вам надо.

Ежели вы нам земли не дадите сколько мы у вас просим, то мы и земли не возьмем и зябить не пойдем, пускай пропадаем без земли. **Куда Бог нас поведет. У нас нет ни земли, ни лугов, ни дров, что будем делать - плохо**.

[ . . . ]И вот еще что, Юрий Владимирович, - топить нечем, ни соломы, ни дров и купить негде, дайте хоть кустов в деньги или под работу. **Недашь дров, тогда отведем сами кусты и будем рубить по расчету**, поведем свидетелей посторонних и вытребуем начальство. Сколько оценят куст, столько и заплатим. Ю. В. "давайте жить по-обоюдни," лучше будет дело.

Юрий Владимирович, как прочитаете--дайте нам записку, дадите нам чего мы просим Вас или нет.

*Translation*

Letter by peasants to landowner Iurii Vladimirovich Trubnikov [henceforth Iu.V.—AN] at the village of Burakovo of the Spassk uezd

Much-esteemed merciful Sir Iu.V. We beg you, please, in the name of God, have pity on us, the unfortunate, do not let us start a riot among us and cause you trouble. We have arrived at a troubled time, it's so bad we don't know each other anymore—who am I. Iu. V., please listen, what kind of fact is this--you are giving us little land at-half, so little that it is impossible for us to live from that land, you just tether us like a boat to the riverbank. The time has come for us to pull away. Give us 165 desiatina at-half. It would be good for us and not so bad for you, either. We'll start plowing tomorrow, as you need it.

If you do not give us as much land as we are asking, then we won't take the land, and won't plow, let it be that we perish without land. Wherever God will take us. We have no land, no meadows, no firewood, what can we do—it's bad.

[ . . . ] And also, Iu.V,—we have nothing for heating, no straw, no firewood, and no place to buy it, give us at least some bushes, for money or labor. If you don't give us firewood, we'll select bushes ourselves and start cutting keeping count; we'll bring outside witnesses and call in the authorities. Whatever they appraise the bushes, we will pay. Iu. V., "let's live supportively," it will work out better.

Iu. V, after you read this, send us a note—will you give what we're asking for or not.

*Comment*

This letter has beautiful examples of peasant speech. I will comment on three.

The expression бунт вести, lit. "conduct a riot," is not found in RNC. It is a peasant version, possibly formed on analogy with, e.g., разговор вести (have a conversation). This is the first of a line of examples collected in the section on Lexical Functions later in the chapter. The writer needed a verb to go with the noun бунт to form a verb phrase that denotes the action expressed by the noun—and he chose a verb that seemed appropriate to him. The resulting phrase is not found in the RNC. Standard Russian has the verb бунтовать (to riot), but, as mentioned in Chapter 1, section 1.4, such -ова verbs are uncommon in peasant speech.

The phrase Что это за факт illustrates a recent borrowing whose meaning had not yet been completely assimilated in the language. Such examples will multiply manifold in peasant letters to Bolshevik authorities who themselves sometimes used not-quite-assimilated foreign borrowings.

The sentence Недашь дров, тогда отведем сами кусты и будем рубить по расчету has a conditional clause without a conjunction: [If] you don't give us firewood [ . . . ]. Such conjunction-less clauses are common in other varieties of spoken Russian as well, e.g., Не сделаешь уроки, в кино не пойдем. ([If] you don't do your homework, we're not going to the movies.) However, only in peasant speech is it common to have a conjunction-less subordinate clause followed by a conjunction in the main clause: Не дашь [ . . . ], тогда отведем [ . . . ]. Similar examples from spoken narratives are discussed in Chapter 4.

In the same sentence, будем рубить по расчету is a very concise, peasant-kind way to say "we'll cut the bushes keeping track of how much we cut."

This 1905 example, in its contrast with Example 2.1, clearly shows the changed mood of the country.

## 2.3 THE REVOLUTION OF 1905 AND NEW KINDS OF LETTERS

The revolution of 1905 started on Sunday January 9 with an attempt by St. Petersburg workers to deliver a petition to the Emperor. It was organized by a charismatic priest named Gapon, and the participating workers thought of it as a religious procession. The other parties involved had different ideas. The Tsar chose not to be in town. The city was secured by regular troops. Gapon was in contact with revolutionary parties who were planning red flags, barricades, and an armed confrontation. The text of the petition included political demands such as a call for a for parliament elected by universal direct and secret ballot. On the day of the procession, the revolutionaries successfully provoked the troops, the troops started indiscriminately firing into the crowds, and hundreds were killed. A police general, summarizing the reasons for the massacre, lists "the provocations of the revolutionary activists and Gapon, the stupidity and inaction of the responsible authorities, and the people's faith in the Tsar." (Nefedov 2011:467) Gorky, extremely pleased, wrote about that day: "Our mood is rising—the prestige of the Tsar has been destroyed--this is the meaning of the day. The Russian revolution has begun, congratulations. Let us not be embarrassed by the dead--history can be repainted in new colors only by blood" (Gorky's Archive, v.5, Moscow 1955, p.148. Quoted from Nefedov 2011:466).

The outcry against the massacre was huge, and in February the Tsar announced the creation of an elected parliament (Duma), and granted a right to petition to all estates. There was an immediate outpouring of peasant letters to the Tsar, to cabinet ministers, and, once the Duma had been elected, to the Duma's representatives. The tone of the letters changed markedly. Recall the old man's story in Example 1.1, recorded in 1905, that mentions "progressives" who helped peasants with their petitions and court cases. These were either local intelligentsia or traveling revolutionaries, who helped with writing the petition or provided templates (Senchakova 1994, vol. 1:87–88). Some peasant petitions began to sound as if they had been written by two people, a village scribe and a political organizer. In Example 2.3 the split is on the word постановили (resolved) shown in boldface. In the translation, capitalization of the original is preserved to further indicate the split.

## Example 2.3 To the Governor of the Moscow province. KI #4, p.17

1905 г, ноября 5-го дня, мы, нижеподписавшиеся крестьяне тульской губернии [ . . . ] деревни алеексеевки быв сего числа на сельском сходе в присутствии нашего сельского старосты ефима Фролова макарова, выслушали высочайший манифест от 17 октября сего года, а затем имели суждение о своих нуждах, **постановили**: 1) что выборы наших представителей по положению о Государственной думе не могут обеспечить защиты наших нужд, при составлении законов в Государственной думе; 2) для удовлетворения же наших нужд необходим немедленный созыв учредительного собрания, избранного всеобщим, прямым и тайным голосованием. [ . . . ]

*Translation*

November 5, 1905, we, the undersigned peasants of the Tula province [ . . . ] the village of alekseevka having been on this date in the village gathering in the presence of our village elder efim Frolov makarov, listened to the Tsar's manifesto of 17 october, and then had a judgment about our needs, **resolved**: 1) that the election of our representatives according to the statute about the State duma cannot guarantee protection of our needs, in writing laws in the State duma; 2) for fulfillment of our needs it is necessary to immediately convene a constitutional assembly, elected by the universal, direct and secret ballot. [ . . . ]

*Comment*

The opening of the verdict contains the usual formulas of a peasant petition: "we the undersigned," "in the presence of our village elder." The capitalization is erratic. Starting with the verb "resolved," rather awkwardly attached to what precedes it, the language becomes completely standard, using correct political formulas. The elided remainder of the letter lists further demands: free universal education; the abandonment of estates and equality before the law; a single direct progressive tax; and the canceling of peasants' "buy-out payments." The letter is signed by 25 peasants from 13 villages in the Volokolamsk district.

There are also petitions that, while preserving the traditional formal frame, tell the story in simple language and thus can serve as a language record.

**Example 2.4 To court in Moscow, 1906. Two recent borrowings are in boldface. KI #6, p.18**

Приговор крестьян села Дальней Борщевки, Калужского уезда, Лущихинской волости.

Мы, крестьяне вышеозначенного села, купили луга у своего барина Ершова, но луга оказались потравленными с того времени, как отдали задаток. Когда мы пришли косить и осматривали побой, позвали управляющего и стали просить его по чести, чтобы он сбавил цену, но управляющий стал нас бранить матерным и **обнажил револьвер**, хотел всех перебить, а когда пришли к дому и стали просить все деньги назад, а луга отдать другому обществу, то он сам не показался, а дал два выстрела из окна. За это мы **сделали забастовку**, в чем мы и подписуемся, за неграмотных крестьян, а равно и за себя по их личной просьбе сельский староста Федор Кальянов

*Translation*

We, the peasants of the aforementioned village, bought meadows from our landlord Ershov, but the meadows turned out to be damaged since the time when we made the down payment. When we came to mow and inspected the damage, we sent for the manager and started asking him, in fairness, to reduce the price, but the manager started to abuse us in foul language and *pulled out his revolver*, wanted to kill us all, and when we came to his house and started asking for all the money back, and give the meadows to another community, he did not himself show up, but gave two shots through the window. For this we *made a strike*, in which we sign, for the illiterate peasants as well as for myself according to their personal request the village elder Fedor Kal'ianov [ . . . ]

*Comment*

Apart from "aforementioned" in the first sentence and "in which we sign" etc., in the last, we have a literate but simple narrative. The economy of syntax and word formation is the same as in the speech records of Chapter 1: "потравить луг" is a perfect match for "закосить луг" in Example 1.1, and "побой" (damage) goes together with "ржа" (Example 1.3) and "разнота" (Example 1.4). There are many verbs and no adjectives; матерное (obscene language) is a noun, a complement of the verb. The only abstract noun is in the formulaic expression по чести (in fairness). However, there are two borrowings in the letter, boldfaced in the original: *revolver* and *strike*. Their phraseological treatment gives the impression that they were recent and not completely assimilated. Since post-1917 letters contain many such examples, the next section introduces the concepts and terminology that are needed to state this impression with greater precision.

## 2.4 LINGUISTIC BACKGROUND: PHRASEOLOGY, FORMULAIC LANGUAGE

Formulaic language is a broad field of linguistics that studies how words are combined into idiomatic or high frequency phrases, including clichés. In the Russian linguistic tradition, this field has been called Фразеология, and the term made it into English as Phraseology. The precise boundaries of the field and the relationship between the two terms are beyond the scope of this study. I will use the term Phraseology for the entire field and concentrate on two subfields that are of direct relevance to our material: Lexical Functions and Conceptual Metaphors. Both develop meta-vocabularies for grouping together phraseological expressions based on their meanings.

### Lexical Functions (LF)

The notion of Lexical Functions was first introduced by Igor Mel'chuk, see Mel'chuk (1974). A lexical function answers the question of how some very general meaning is expressed in combination with some specific word W. The answer depends on W and can be said to be a function of W. For instance, how do we say that there was a lot of something, like rain? The answer is idiomatic and depends on language: in English it is "heavy rain," in Russian it is "сильный (strong) rain." For "very much darkness" the English is "pitch black," and the Russian is "кромешная тьма." The notion is useful in language teaching and dictionary making. If functions are given standard labels—e.g., Magn for "a lot of," then we could write, imitating mathematical notation, Magn (rain) = heavy. A list of such labels for Lexical Functions is included in the RNC;[3] for further discussion and English examples see Wanner (1996).

When a new word appears in a language indicating a new concept, many native speakers find themselves in the position of a foreigner who does not know the new word's Lexical Functions. They have to guess, and the result can be awkward, or funny, or sometimes unexpectedly poetic. In any event, it will often be unidiomatic. We find many examples of that in peasant letters, including Example 2.4. Consider a group of functions called "Caus," expressing the meaning of "bring about some condition or action:" "start/strike up a conversation" (начать/затеять разговор); "make/build campfire" (развести костер); "call a strike" (объявить забастовку). The verb объявить would be the most common to use with the noun забастовка. (RNC contains 155 examples with объявить, and only seven with сделать забастовку, as in Example 2.4). This is a common strategy in improvising Lexical Functions: use the most general word for the required range of meaning.[4]

Another common strategy is analogy. Consider the meaning "take out your personal weapon in preparation for use." This meaning is not very general—it applies only to weapons—so there is no LF label for it, but it is still expressed idiomatically depending on the weapon. For swords or rapiers Russian uses обнажить or оголить (literally "bare"). Faced with the new firearm, revolver, the peasant authors of 2.4 transferred the term for cold arms (оголил револьвер). The standard usage would be выхватить (pull out, whip out).

*Conceptual Metaphors*

Sometimes the value of a lexical function is suggested by a Conceptual Metaphor (Lakoff and Johnson 2003) A conceptual metaphor is not itself a metaphorical expression in the language but rather an abstract meta-label that groups together a number of such expressions, frequently so common that they are no longer perceived as metaphors. For instance, in many languages the notions of "up" vs. "down" are (metaphorically!) associated with ethical and socio-economic distinctions: high principles; low manners; upper vs. lower classes; high vs. low incomes; rising vs. falling incomes; incomes are going up/down. Schematically, the common underlying image can be described as "UP IS GOOD, DOWN IS BAD." This is an example of a conceptual metaphor. At the next level of abstraction, Lakoff and Johnson note that conceptual metaphors are frequently based on concrete sensory experiences that we know from childhood, e.g., "warm vs. cold smile" is one of many metaphors based on WARM IS GOOD, COLD IS BAD.

Since there are many idiomatic ways to say about something that it is "bad," one might want to posit a lexical function for this phraseological relationship, and indeed RNC posits one, calling it ANTIBON. (There is also BON for how to say idiomatically that something is good.) Some examples are: "weak student, boring book, oppressive atmosphere, crooked (or cold) smile." Clearly some of the values of this LF will be based on Conceptual Metaphors.

Suppose a speaker has learned a new abstract noun, положение (condition, situation) and wants to say that someone's condition is "very bad." He does not know the adjective "critical (condition)," so he uses a Conceptual

Metaphor and says "упадшее положение" (fallen condition: DOWN IS BAD). Meromskii (1930:103–4) actually cites such an example. This is what he writes:

> Quote 2.1 Meromskii on "critical" vs. "fallen"
>
> Next to a peasant who writes: "Я вижу его бедность и критическое положение" (I see his poverty and critical condition), there is another one in whose letter we read: "У нас на хуторе тут одно семейство в самом упадшем положении." (At our settlement here one family is in the most fallen condition). The word "critical" has not yet reached this sel'kor, and he uses his own home-made artisanal synonym. However much you value the freshness and expressiveness on the virgin peasant speech [ . . . ] you couldn't help but appreciate that "critical" is beginning to encroach on this sort of "very fallen," squeezing it out from the pages of peasant manuscripts.

Remarkably, Meromskii is talking about the language of peasants the way Gorky and Stonov do, calling it "fresh," and "expressive." And this point we can state precisely what he is talking about: using a Conceptual Metaphor to express a common Lexical Function. But in addition, Meromskii clearly articulates the party attitude: squeeze out this kind of "artisanal" expressiveness, replacing it with a foreign borrowing that does not mean anything to a peasant but is a common party-language cliché. As could be expected, peasants who did adopt "critical" as "VERY BAD" for situations and conditions, overgeneralized it to other nouns as well: "я оказался придавленным неподсильной нуждой и критической бедностью всего семейства" (I became pressed down by overpowering hardship and critical poverty of the entire family.) (Letter of Jan. 1925, KI 66)

This section was prompted by some peculiarities in a letter from before 1917, but as it developed, it had to cross over that threshold into the new sociolinguistic situation in which "peculiarities" became, in fact, regularities, actively promoted by the new ruling class. It has been noted by many linguists as early as the 1920s that much linguistic innovation of the time was present in a limited latent form before the revolution but greatly increased in breadth and intensity after it. The frequency of garbled Lexical Functions in post-1917 letters (see a later section) supports the accuracy of this observation.

## 2.5 REVOLUTION AND CIVIL WAR, 1917–1921

The revolution of February 1917 ended monarchy in Russia. Power passed to the Provisional government (Временное правительство) that organized elections to the Constitutional Assembly (Учредительное собрание). It was scheduled to convene in February 1918. In parallel to the government of ministers, there were also local councils (Советы, Soviets) that formed independent power centers. In Petrograd[5] especially, the Soviet of Workers and Soldiers Deputies (Petrosovet), wielded considerable power. Initially it was dominated by Mensheviks and SRs, but in September Trotsky became Chairman of the Executive committee, and under his leadership Petrosovet played a major role in the Bolshevik takeover.

After February 1917 there were no more constraints on who could write to whom. Letters became individual, and they frequently dispensed with formulaic openings and closings. This does not mean that they became more reflective of spoken language. During that time, the language of newspapers and public speeches became laden with social-democratic jargon. Millions in the army were exposed to it, especially from Bolsheviks, flush with German money to support their propaganda effort. This started the wave of linguistic innovations that is usually associated with the Bolshevik takeover. Consider Example 2.5, a letter from a soldier to the chairman of Petrosovet. (The chairmanship had just passed from Trotsky to Zinoviev.)

**Example 2.5 From a soldier to chairman of Petrosovet**

Товарищу председателю С[овета] р[абочих] С[олдатских] депу[татов].
    Решился я описать наше будущее, что перед нами предстоит.
    Мы, солдаты 177-го зап[асного] полка, как мы пробыли в армии четыре года, вооружены. А теперь, как мы видим, распускают с полка на родину без оружия. У нас между солдат выходит негодование, как мы читали резолюцию С[овета] р[абочих] Со[лдатских] де[путатов] [ . . . ], что все войска по силе окончания войны должны возвраща[ться] на свои места постоянного жительства с оружием в руках и снабженные боевыми припасами.
    А почему же у нас этого нет зато? Мы боимся о будущем нашего положения. Так что безоружные мы будем бессильны отстаивать свои права, потому что у нас казачество вооруженное. [ . . . ].

*Translation*

To comrade chairman of the S r S depu [Soviet of Worker-Soldier deputies].
    I have resolved to describe our future, what is awaiting us.
    We the soldiers of the 177 reserve regiment, as we have been in the army for four years, are armed. And now, as we see, we are dismissed from the regiment to our homes without arms. Among us soldiers indignation takes place, as we have read the resolution of S r So de [ . . . ] that all troops by

virtue of the ending of the war must return to their places of permanent residence with weapons in hand and provided by ammunition. Why is it not the case with us instead? We are afraid about the future of our situation. Therefore, as unarmed we will not be able to defend our rights because our Cossack population is armed. [ . . . ].

*Comment*

The letter is dated December 28, 1917, two months after Bolsheviks came to power, but its linguistic habits had obviously been formed before that. It stands in sharp contrast to the pre-1917 letters to power: it is written by a single person, not a group, and its opening is greatly simplified. The text in the body of the letter shows multiple deviations from the peasant profile of Chapter 1: it is verbose, influenced by various jargons, and occasionally garbled. Here are specific points:

- There are three deverbal nouns with -ание/-ение: окончание, негодование, положение. All three have problems.
- The first is used with cumbersome syntax: instead of "Since the war ended [ . . . ]" it says "By virtue of the ending of the war [ . . . ]." It also garbles the correct bureaucratic phrase "в силу" (because of, in virtue of) using "по силе" instead.
- The second deverbal noun, "негодование," is used with a wrong Lexical Function "у нас выходит негодование" (indignation [the grammatical subject—AN] comes out / results). The correct phrase would be "Это у нас, солдат, вызывает негодование" (this arouses/causes indignation [the grammatical object]).
- The problem with положение is that it is redundant: instead of "We are afraid about our future" it says "about the future **of our situation**." (Here and elsewhere, boldface will be used to indicate words and phrases that are the focus of current discussion.)
- The verb бояться is used with the wrong preposition, "бояться о чем-то." This use is found in the RNC only once, in an obscure document from 1820. The verb is probably conflated with беспокоиться (worry) that does use the preposition "о."
- There are bureaucratic phrases, probably copied from the resolution to which the letter responds: "with weapons in hand," "places of permanent residence."

Could this possibly be a peasant letter? Ninety percent of soldiers were peasants. The author was not from an urban area: there were Cossack populations around. Most importantly, peasant letters of the 1920s provide many similar examples of systematic deviations from the peasant language profile of Chapter 1. Example 2.5 is thus the earliest extant example of what can happen to the language of peasants after prolonged exposure to the new mode of expression, especially after it became the language of state power. Peasants in the army were early adopters. Example 2.5 will be revisited in later sections as the initial point of a widely followed trend.

## 2.6 BOLSHEVIK INNOVATIONS AND PEASANT ATTITUDES

Much of the rest of this chapter presents and dissects various systematic deformations of language. Some of them are awkward, some downright ugly, and some strangely poetic, but all of them show damage to the texture of simple, concise, and expressive peasant speech. Before getting into a classification and examples, this section presents the main strands of SovYaz, the new officialese of the Soviet state and the Bolshevik party. It should be kept in mind that SovYaz changed over time in its vocabulary, syntax, and mode of interpretation. The SovYaz of 1917–1928, which is the time frame of this chapter, is very different from the post-Stalin SovYaz of Khrushchev and Brezhnev times. The latter could be ignored most of the time, and if one wanted to engage with it there were stable and relatively simple rules of interpretation. Peasants in the 1920s could not easily ignore the language of the intrusive new power that was frequently backed up by a detachment of armed men. And the rules of interpretation for what the new power was saying were anything but simple. The central slogan of the revolution, Land to Peasants, did not really mean what it said, and its meaning kept changing. It took until 1923 for peasants to arrive at this understanding:

### Example 2.6 Peasant on Bolsheviks, taxes, and prices. Iakovlev 1923:68

Жить бы хорошо при Советской власти, кабы не драли двух шкур, а то земельку без аренды дали, а за это товарищи проналог берут и за пуд соли 3 пуда ржи.

*Translation*

Life would be good under the Soviets if they didn't skin us so badly; they gave us land without rent payments but in return the "comrades" take a tax in kind, and for a pood [16 kg—AN] of salt you have to pay 3 poods of rye grain.[6]

*Comment*

This thirty-word statement is, in effect, perfect, both conceptually and stylistically. It masterfully contrasts the official phrase при Советской власти with the colloquial metaphor драть две шкуры, literally "flay two skins." It injects his peasant attitude to land by inserting an affectionate suffix in the word for it, земелька. Using masterful economy of means it exposes the Bolshevik lie in the Bolshevik slogan "All land to peasants," which in fact means "All the land to the state, and we will lease it to you for free but will collect exorbitant taxes in kind." It registers the bitter irony of how the word "comrades" came to be a reference to state power. And it sees through the state policy of setting up a big gap between low agricultural "peasant" prices and high manufacturing city prices, the "scissors of prices," in Trotsky's phrase. Salt, in particular, was extremely important to peasants and thus a powerful tool for the Bolsheviks. Lenin, who understood well the value of both salt and Soviet money, gave these instructions in 1921, soon after the NEP (New Economic Policy) was adopted: "First, I recommend that you sell salt only for grain, and under no circumstances for paper money. Second, sell it only to those districts, villages or individual households who submitted at least 1/4 or 1/2 of their in-kind tax (продналог)."[7]

Note how the Bolshevik linguistic innovation продналог, a syllabic abbreviation of продовольственный налог (literally produce tax) was already in Lenin's speech and by 1923 in the speech of the peasant of Example 2.6.

## The Expanding Old and the Brand New

While some elements of SovYaz were genuinely new, much of it came from two earlier varieties of Russian that greatly increased in their spread and intensity after 1917: the language of imperial bureaucracy inherited by their Soviet successors, and the language of the revolutionaries who became the new ruling class. Two days after coming to power, Bolsheviks promulgated the decree "On the press," closing most opposition newspapers. Their language thus received a monopoly on public attention, and their linguistic innovations automatically acquired the imprimatur of state power and ideology. They also dominated the speech of "orators" and "agitators" who visited the villages to explain the policy and ideology of the new government. Selishchev (1928:27) writes:

> Quote 2.2 Selishchev (1928:27) on the language of
> "revolutionaries"

The differences between the language of the revolutionary period before 1917 and the post-October language lie in the degree of intensity and the breadth of spreading of some peculiarities of language. [ . . . ] After the revolution of

1917, the linguistic features of the speech of revolutionaries started spreading very intensely, penetrating wide layers of urban, industrial and to some extent village populations.

One of the conduits for spreading the speech of revolutionaries was the rapid growth of the party. The Bolshevik ruling class of Soviet Russia contained two distinct layers. The top consisted of those who were party members at the time of the February revolution. There were about 5,000 of them altogether, many—including Lenin, Trotsky and Bukharin—in emigration. They were mostly intelligentsia who spoke literary Russian with a strong admixture of the social-democratic jargon. Many of them, to use Selishchev's delicate description, "were related by their origin to the southwest region of former Russia. Their Russian language reflected some features of the speech of those areas" (p.26). What he likely meant was that they came from Ukraine and the Pale of Settlement.

A few months after the revolution, the party had 115,000 members, most of them from workers, soldiers, and the semi-educated urban population.[8] The party jargon expanded enormously, responding to the needs of expressing the new worldview, running the country, and indoctrinating its population. The less-educated did not have a perfect command of the new ruling-class language. In their linguistic aspirations they can be compared to petit-bourgeoisie as described in Bourdieu (1991:52): a class that is somewhat ashamed of its social status and manner of speaking, but tries to advance by imitating the upper class. Peasants, who came into contact with the government at the local level or listening to the visiting "agitators," mostly heard the defective Russian-Bolshevik language of the semi-educated class. Many imitated it out of unconscious conformism, or conscious strategy of survival and advancement, or, especially in the case of young people, infatuation with the new and "hip."

Stonov in his 1926 *Izvestiia* article notes that after the revolution there was a reversal of the traditional hierarchy in the village, with the young having a much greater say in public affairs. In the village he visited, they were passionately involved with amateur theater, which proved to be another conduit for linguistic innovation. Stonov went to see a play by a contemporary author. The main evil character is a former general, an emigre who came back from Paris to undermine the Soviet state.[9] He is recruiting a Menshevik—a member of a moderate Marxist party that was in opposition to Bolsheviks and in various ways suppressed after the revolution until completely destroyed in 1922. The following conversation ensues:

## Example 2.7 A general and a Menshevik. Stonov 1926

Генерал: Ты будешь богат и знатен, если я вернусь к власти. Постольку поскольку я опять сяду, ты будешь графом.

Меньшевик: Слушаюсь и очень буду проводить на практике, ваше превосходительство.

*Translation*

General: You will be rich and famous if I come back into power. Insofar as I take the seat, you will become a count.

Menshevik: Yes, sir, and I will very much put into practice, your excellency.

*Comment*

The expressions for "insofar as" (постольку поскольку) and "put into practice" (проводить на практике) are specifically elements of the bureaucratic jargon that proliferated in the language of the state. Here we see them entering the language of the village. In the same article Stonov notes "insofar as" and other "useless nonsense" in the language of village youth. (Quote 1.4 in Chapter 1.)

Turning to genuinely new elements of SovYaz, a good starting point are neologisms. One simple source for them was renaming: the new institutions of authority had to be named, and the old ones renamed. The new names were often long and cumbersome, and thus had to be abbreviated. For some reason, all abbreviations for the security forces were *initialisms*: Cheka (the names of letters ЧК), GPU, NKVD, MVD, KGB. These quickly became full-fledged words, from which other words could be formed: people working for Cheka became known as чекисты[10] (chekists), followed by гэпэушники, etc. Otherwise, *syllabic abbreviations* were the most common, e.g., волисполком—волостной исполнительный комитет—Volost' executive committee (of the local Soviet). The chair (председатель) of such a committee would be предволисполкома, with the Genitive ending preserved. A common variation was a syllabic abbreviation with the last component preserved as a complete word: партячейка - партийная ячейка - party cell (a small party organization in a village or within a single factory shop), and indeed продналог (prodnalog) from Example 2.6.

Some of Bolshevik abbreviations made it into English: Komsomol, Komintern, Agitprop (Agitation and Propaganda, referring both to a genre of political speech and the division of the Party Central committee in charge of it). Scores of others confronted Russians in newspapers, billboards, signs or the door, official speeches, and official documents. Among the documents, the most important ones were ордер (warrant for search, arrest, requisition) and мандат (credentials, authorization).[11] Armed with one of them one could walk into an apartment or a peasant house and confiscate what they want. Prishvin writes in his diary for 1919: "Today I beat back an attack by three armed men with a *mandat* for confiscating my telephone" (RNC). A common wisdom was "Не будь богат, а имей мандат." (Don't have money, have a *mandat*.) (Selishchev 1928:194). The writer Sollogub proudly told the story of how he was sitting on a park bench smoking; a homeless kid approached him and demanded a cigarette for himself; "Do you have a *mandat*?"—inquired Sollogub, upon which the boy immediately turned and ran away (Chukovsky 2012, vol. 2:43).

Apart from new names, there was a proliferation of abstract nouns designating current events and the key concepts of the new state ideology: socialism, dictatorship of the proletariat, bourgeoisie, intervention, ultimatum, separate peace, class solidarity. These were not new to the revolution but became difficult for peasants to ignore as they populated newspapers and speeches by visiting Bolsheviks who came from the district capital to a village to give a speech. They were known as ораторы, агитаторы ог инструкторы (speakers, propagandists or instructors)—all three words showing sharp spikes in the RNC for several years around 1920. "Speaks weird—must be a bolshevik"—this 1926 quote from *Рабочая газета* (The Workers' Newspaper), repeated in Selishchev 1928:55, certainly expressed the peasant attitude during the Civil War. It seems accurately recorded in Seifullina's 1923 novella *Перегной* (Humus) about how the Revolution and Civil War played out in a small village in Southern Urals. At some point a visitor arrives "in a wide-open urban fur coat, breeches, with a red star on his black leather cap and a fat black leather briefcase under his arm." He recognizes the chief Bolshevik of the village (recently back from the army) and speaks to him thus:

**Example 2.8. SovYaz in literature. Seifullina 1923:23**

Здравствуйте, товарищ! Я вас в городе видел, сразу же узнал. Вы, кажется, здесь предволисполкома? [ . . . ] Вот мой мандат. Это собрание ячейки? [ . . . ] Здравствуйте, товарищи, готовитесь к выборам в Советы? Какие планы у вас земельного распределения? [ . . . ] А где здесь меня чаем напоят?

*Translation*

Hello, comrade! We met in town, I recognized you right away. You seem to be the chair of the volost' executive committee here. [ . . . ] Here is my mandate. Is this a meeting of your party cell? [ . . . ] Hello, comrades, are you getting ready for the elections of Soviet deputies? What are your plans for land redistribution. [ . . . ] And who will give me tea?

*Comment*

A peasant character listening to this monologue delivered at high speed thinks: "He must have a little machine inside that pushes the words out. Never stops."

## Hard-core SovYaz

This brief section presents a strain within SovYaz that forms the party and government jargon for political and ideological discussions. Selishchev (1928) collects this material in the section "The Party. Reflection of its program and activity in language" (pp.97–115). Although many examples from that section "are abundantly present in the speech of Soviet citizens" (p.115) they have not penetrated peasant letters except those by *sel'kor*s, a syllabic abbreviation for сельский корреспондент (village correspondent). A section on *sel'kor*s later in the chapter provides an illustration. This section discusses several nouns and verbs, and their underlying metaphors.

Lenin's party from the beginning was a strictly hierarchical organization, that had a "верхушка" (top) and "низы" (bottoms), or "низовые организации" (bottom organizations), also known as "ячейки" (cells). The verb describing communication from the top to the bottoms was "спустить (директиву, инструкцию, информацию)" (send down a directive, instruction, information).

Another good verb is "поставить (вопрос на повестку дня)" (put a question / item on the agenda). A typical feature of SovYaz was to use the main transitive verb of a formulaic expression without its direct object. The sentence "Придется на завком поставить [ . . . ] дело серьезное." (Selishchev 1928:194) literally means "We'll have to put [it] on zavkom [ . . . ] it's a serious business." Here "zavkom" is the syllabic abbreviation for "заводской комитет" (factory committee of the *profsoiuz* organization), where "profsoiuz" is the syllabic abbreviation for профессиональный союз (trade union). In addition, "zavkom" is a synecdoche for "zavkom meeting."

A similar reduction of a common cliché to a single word happened to the noun "элемент" (element) in the singular. It belongs to the "inherited bureaucratese" part of SovYaz, as it first appears in RNC in the phrase "преступный елемент" (criminal element), in an 1886 example where the phrase is in quotes, indicating that it is a recently borrowed expression. (Nakhimovsky 2015:282) Bolsheviks started using the noun, both singular and plural, with class-based and revolutionary-struggle-based adjectives: bourgeois, capitalist, landlord, counter-revolutionary, anti-Soviet element(s). The next step was to use just the noun in the Singular to refer to one undesirable person or collectively to a group of such persons. Mokienko and Nikitina (1998:676) cite: органы очистят город от элемента ("the organs will clear the city of the element"),[12] where органы is also a reduction to a single noun of the phrase органы госбезопасноти (organs of state security), i.e., the Cheka or one of its successor acronyms.

The relevant point for us is that kind of hard-core SovYaz is not found in peasant letters except in letters by sel'cors, the subject of a forthcoming section.

## 2.7 AVAILABLE PEASANT MATERIALS, 1917–1921–1928

So far, there have been two examples for the period 1917–1921: 2.5, a letter to the Petrosovet with multiple SovYaz features, and 2.8, a speech by a character in Seifullina's novella. Prose fiction is hardly a reliable "record" of spoken language but it is the only record available for 1917–1921. This is not surprising. Linguists lived in cities. Their attention, apart from trying to get enough food, was completely consumed by the huge linguistic processes unfolding right before them in public speech, in interactions with the new government, and in newspapers and official documents. Travel in the countryside was dangerous in many parts of the country.

Even peasants' letters to power became very scarce. Although different in tone and format, these were still complaints to central authorities about local iniquities. Peasants had plenty to complain about in 1918–1921, but the situation was complex and confusing. On the one hand, in one of its first actions, the new state erased all peasant debt and gave official sanction for peasants to take over all landlords' possessions, including land. It also quickly concluded a separate peace with Germany, which brought home many peasant men. Building on these actions, state propaganda among peasants was quite successful, especially since its call for "socialism" was in harmony with peasants' traditional idea of social justice. On the other hand, the state's economic policy toward the peasants manifested itself in so-called War Communism, in which "communism" meant that everything that peasants had could be taken without compensation by the state or by whoever had a gun and claimed to represent the state. Requisitions of food and horses (according to established quotas but frequently exceeding them) were the law of the land.

A linguistic anecdote can illustrate this. In 1922 both the Civil War and War Communism were over, and millions of Red Army soldiers returned home. The bond these soldiers constituted between the state and the peasantry dissolved suddenly when they were replaced by young recruits who had not been properly indoctrinated. Realizing that it needed to establish a new line of communication with peasants, the Bolshevik government decided to rely on newspapers instead of ad hoc "agitators." It was not, however, obvious that peasants could read Bolshevik newspapers, so an effort was made to find out. Its main result was Shafir's *The Peasant and the Newspaper* (1923), a book about how peasants understood—or, more often, did not understand—the language of Bolshevik newspapers. One of Shafir's research methods was to give peasants a list of words and ask to explain what they meant. Many explanations were incoherent or amusing, based on folk etymology, but some were concrete and precise, confirming Gorky's idea about the language of peasants. Thus, when asked to explain the word "ultimatum" a peasant said: "It's when you say: pay the money, or give up your horse, or I will kill you.'"[13]

*The Impact of the Revolution* 47

The policy of War Communism provoked multiple peasant uprisings that were brutally suppressed. In 1921–1922 that policy greatly contributed to a famine in which millions died (and millions were saved by Western aid while the Soviet government was selling grain abroad). This combination (exporting grain during a famine) would be repeated in the famine of 1932–1933, in which more millions died. Andrea Graziosi (1996) aptly called the entire period from 1918 to 1933 "The great Soviet-Peasant war." By 1933 the war was over, the Soviets had won, and one of the consequences was that the habits and patterns of peasant speech were no longer transmitted to the next generation (D'iachok 2003:104). But in the meantime, the years 1922–1928 were a period of truce, and abundant letters to power.

## NEP Background

In 1921 War Communism was abandoned in favor of NEP (an initialism for New Economic Policy), whose main purpose was to make peace with peasants, restore agriculture, and feed the cities. Requisition quotas were replaced with taxes, and agricultural surplus could be sold and bought. By 1923 the situation had substantially improved. Peasant policy was actively discussed, and peasants' speech began to be recorded again, in small fragments, by government officials, newspaper professionals, and, briefly, ethnographers. Still, there was not nearly enough of it for a linguistic study. Selishchev (1928), the main linguistic treatment on the Russian language of the first decade after the revolution, has only a short section (pp.210–18) on the language of peasants. It opens with this passage:

> Quote 2.3, On language of peasants. Selishchev 1928:210
>
> How were the years of revolution reflected in the language of the village? What linguistic innovations have appeared there in recent years? To what an extent the language elements of the revolutionary period penetrated there together with the corresponding social changes? [ . . . ] Regretfully, these very important questions cannot yet be completely answered because we do not have adequate observations of the language of the village. We have only fragmentary observations related to these questions.

Most of Selishchev's peasant section relies on materials from Shafir (1923). It also includes the quote from Stonov's newspaper article of 1926, discussed in Chapter 1 and soon to be revisited.

## Sources for Recorded Speech

Data for the rest of this chapter falls into two unequal parts: small parcels of recorded speech and a great number of peasant letters to the new power:

newspapers and Soviet officials. The first part comes from these publications: Iakovlev (1923), already quoted, Iakovlev (1924); Shafir (1923), already noted; Meromskii (1930), first published in articles during the 1920s; Fenomenov (1925), presented in Chapter 1; and once again Tan-Bogoraz, whose 1905 book contributed greatly to Chapter 1. In the 1920s Tan-Bogoraz wrote introductions to three collections of student papers based on summer ethnographic expeditions (Bogoraz 1924a, 1924b, 1925). The expeditions were organized by Bogoraz and another prominent ethnographer, Iakov Shterenberg, both working at the Leningrad Geographic Institute, which would soon become the Geography Department of Leningrad University. The students were tasked with doing "new ethnography," recording the current processes and events in the village rather than old rituals and material culture. This new understanding of ethnography was ultimately inspired by Bogoraz's long association with Franz Boas and his approach to ethnography-anthropology. Since there were no textbooks for this kind of work, Iakovlev (1923) "was adopted as a methodological manual, almost as a textbook" (Bogoraz 1924a:6).[14]

Bogoraz, Shpil'rein and Selishchev were scholars; the rest were young Soviet functionaries. Of this group, Iakovlev was by far the most important, and in the most important position. Fitzpatrick (1998:349, note 52) writes about him: "Iakov Arkadevich Iakovlev (né Epshtein), 1896-1938, is an interesting and somewhat puzzling figure in the politics of the 1920s and 1930s who still awaits his biographer." Iakovlev's biography was indeed remarkable. He joined the Bolshevik party at seventeen and rose steeply through the ranks during the Civil War. By 1920 he was in Moscow, working in the Agitprop division of the Central Committee and continuing his steep rise, which culminated in 1929 in his appointment as the *НаркомЗем*, People's Commissar (Minister) of Agriculture. He stayed in this position until 1934, "and was thus the man directly in charge of agriculture during the worst excesses of collectivization. Yet his writings and speeches on peasant questions, both before and after this period, are notable for their pragmatism and common sense" (Fitzpatrick, 1998:349, note 52). Perhaps for this reason, or possibly for no reason at all, in 1937 he was arrested and executed.

Back in 1922–1924, Iakovlev was director of the Press section of the Agitprop. His mission was to organize a two-way communication between the party and the peasants, which, as noted above, had broken down after the massive demobilization at the end of the Civil War. The idea was to create a newspaper targeted at peasantry that would provide a combination of useful information and propaganda, and receive letters informing the party about the situation in the countryside. Agitprop's goal was to have at least a million subscribers.

As part of this project, in 1923 Iakovlev carried out a sociological study of Russian peasants that included field work, and published two books,

*Derevnia kak ona est'* (1923) and *Nasha derevnia* (1924). Like Bogoraz in 1905, he did not collect language data but simply talked to people about what was important to them. For linguistic purposes, this means that samples of peasant speech in his book are brief. They are nonetheless remarkable, as Example 2.6 illustrates. The entire book is a paragon of clarity in both argumentation and writing. It is not surprising that Bogoraz recommended it to his students. Soon after its publication, in the end of 1923, Iakovlev created *Krest'ianskaia Gazeta* (KG—The Peasant Newspaper) and served as its editor until 1929. The newspaper was a big success, receiving over the time of its existence millions of peasant letters. A remarkable sample of them was published, mostly from unpublished originals, in Sokolov (1998a) and Kriukova (2001). (Anything that was actually published would have been heavily edited both for content and language.) Together with Orlov and Livshin (1998b), these books are the main sources of peasant letters for the remainder of this chapter. Recall that they are abbreviated as GN, KI, and PVV, respectively.

## About Sel'kors

In addition to spontaneous letters from peasants to KG, an institution of "селькоры" was established. Meromskii (from Quote 2.1 above) was an official in charge of the education and training of sel'kors, while Iakovlev was the editor of the magazine Sel'kor from 1925 to 1930. This publication was very much unlike KG both in its intent and its language. One striking difference is that KG discouraged and did not respond to anonymous letters, while Sel'kor recognized them as practical necessity, because most of its mail was, in effect, denunciations of local deplorables and their misdeeds. A substantial number of sel'kors were physically assaulted and some of them murdered. The story is well told in Маркасова (2002).

With respect to our topic, sel'kors' language often contains slogans and SovYaz vocabulary, but the features of peasant language still persist, as in 2.9.

### Example 2.9 An anonymous denunciation of a local kulak. KI #70, p.94

Осадит[ь] Кулака Укрывателя хлеба

    Член Правления Ямановского кооператива быв.[ший] помещик кулак Глотов Леонид Петрович усиленно агитирует за здачу хлеба в кооперацию а свой собюственный хлеб задержаный несколько лет продает спекулянтам по 3 руб. за 1 пуд и выкармливает свиней по 12 пудов как спрашивается может ли кулак Глотов после этого убедить крестьян продавать хлеб в кооперацию [ . . . ]

Вот такой элемент нам в кооперации не нужен, да и лишон голосом он и все его родители лишены голосом потому что бывшии крупный помещики вон из кооперации такого типа
Селькор

*Translation*

Rein in the kulak Hoarder of grain

Member of the board of the Iamanov cooperative former landowner kulak Glotov Leonid Petrovich strongly agitates for handing the grain over to the coop but his own grain, stashed away for several years, he sells to speculators at 3 rub. for 1 pood and raises pigs at 12 poods—how, one may ask, whether kulak Glotov can after that convince peasants to sell the grain to the coop. [ . . . ]

We don't need this kind in our coop, and besides he was stripped of his vote and all his parents were stripped of their votes because former large landowners. Out of the coop that sort
[signed] sel'kor

*Comment*

The SovYaz elements of this anonymous letter almost drown out its peasant substrate. The title and the last sentence are "hortative," i.e., slogans. The signature is simply "sel'kor." The use of the word "элемент," without any attributes, to refer to an undesirable person was presented in "Hard-core SovYaz." In general, many sel'kors' language shows deliberate attempts to adopt the language of power, while peasant letters typically show unconscious adaptations. But elements of peasant orality persist even in this particular letter: the Instrumental case complement to the verb лишить; the contamination of two syntactic constructions in как спрашивается может ли; the phonetic spellings.

## A Simple Letter as a Record of Speech

Compared to pre-1917 examples 2.2–2.4, post-1917 letters show some striking changes, as 2.5 already illustrated. They are mostly written by a single person, not a group. Their formulaic frame is simplified and sometimes dispensed with altogether. And many of them show a strong impact of the language of the new ruling class, the Bolsheviks. Examples 2.5 and 2.9 exhibit all three of those features. But not all peasant letters are so affected. Unlike the soldier-author of Example 2.5, or the village youth absorbing "useless nonsense" from the modern play of Example 2.7, or the sel'kor of Example 2.9, the writer of Example 2.10 has the skill to convey his spoken word in a letter to the editor. Example 2.10

is written almost like a personal letter, including disregard for spelling, punctuation and capitalization. (Many such examples are presented in Chapter 3.) In the translation, a few commas are introduced to indicate syntactic divisions.

**Example 2.10 KI #37, p.62. Undated; archived May 31, 1924. Editorial tag: Ножницы (Scissors, a reference to Trotsky's term)**

В редакцыю Крестьянской Газеты
 Скоро ли подешевеет товар
 В селе Матреновки Матреновской волости [ . . . ] Воронежской Губернии все мужики стали горбатые а именно отчего да от таго что в селе Матренавки бувает каждую неделю базар по понедельникам и вот утром собираются на базар насыпают в мешки рож и приходится нести до базара на себе потому что лошаде нету в половине населения и пока дойдеш до базара приходится несколько раз отдыхать а за этот мешок ржи только и купиш на одну рубашку ситцу потомучто аршин ситцу стоит 45 копеек а пуд ржи 35 копеек.
 Когда же будем покупать по дешавой цене ситец.

*Translation*

**To the editorial board of the Peasant Newspaper**
 How soon will the manufacturing goods become cheaper?
 In the village of Matrenovka of the Matrenovka volost' [ . . . ] Voronezh province all the muzhiks became hunchbacks, and why exactly, well because in the village of Matrenovka every week there is a market on Monday and so in the morning they get ready to go to the market and pour rye grain in their sacks and have to carry to the market on their backs because half the population don't have horses, and until you come to the market you have to sit down to rest a few times, and for this sack of rye you can only buy enough chintz for one shirt because an *arshin* (about 70cm) of chintz costs 45 kopeks and a bag of rye 35 kopeks.
 When are we going to buy chintz for a low price.

*Comment*

This letter should be read in conjunction with a record of peasant speech in Example 2.6. As socioeconomic data, both complain about the unfair pricing on industrial products (salt in 2.6, chintz in 2.10). As records of speech, they present an interesting contrast. Example 2.6 is a direct reliable record of something actually said. However, the educated recorder (Iakovlev) who is not a linguist trained for field work wrote it down with all the commas and capital letters according to established orthography. Example 2.10, although a letter, is in fact the record of a story teller. It starts with something of a puzzle: "Everybody's become a hunchback." It continues with a narrative trope: "And why is that?—Well, because [ . . . ]." (This trope occurs in several personal letters of Chapter 3, from different parts of the country, indicating that it is a common trope of peasant story telling.) It proceeds to tell the story of peasantry's sorry condition (no horses, expensive manufacturing goods).

Literacy for this peasant mostly means learning the alphabet and establishing correspondences between letter shapes and sounds. Those correspondences are then used to record on paper a text that is quite similar to from what he would say in a conversation. To reconstruct the syntax of that text in the absence of the traditional orthographic handles, the reader has to articulate it. This results in a greater involvement in the process of reading than in Example 2.6. Chapter 3, based on a great number of personal letters, will have more to say about this subject.

Overall, peasant letters of the 1920s range in their language from Example 2.10 (most traditional) to 2.5 (most distorted). The general trend is that the closer the author wants to be to the new government, the further away he moves from the simplicity and conciseness of peasant speech. Example 2.11, from the middle of the range, presents three excerpts from a long letter: the opening, a passage from the middle, and the ending. While sharply critical, the letter shows a willingness to explain and work together.

The beginning and ending of the letter are reasonably clear in spite of all the solecisms. The middle passage is more of a challenge and therefore some punctuation has been added in square brackets. The translation has all word divisions, punctuation, and capitalization in place.

## Example 2.11 KI:61–62, No date; editorial stamp January 18, 1924

Прошу редакцию к-ой [Крестьянской] газеты паместить ниже написанную мною статейку о жизни крестьянина в обще и что зависит от Советской власти на первых порах чтобы улутьшить положение крестьянина

Как всем так и Советской власти не безызвестно, что крестьянин советской россии находится в самом критическом положении и влачит жалкое существование жизни. [ . . . ]

Производимый продукт крестьянина обесценен и на него ничего нельзя приобрести[.] побочного заработка нет[,] хотя летом 1923 года и ходили работать в Суздальский Комбинат всежтаки труд рабочих не о блачивался[,] платили только на 2 ф. хлеба чтобы не мор ли с голоду[.] чтоже приходится делать[?] если взяться за выращивание скота, то

*The Impact of the Revolution* 53

пожалуй опять дело не выдет[,] если будешь иметь с выше двух голов рогатого скота продналог стебя возмут на котегорию выше[.] или задумашь производить кирпич или пойдешь на побочный заработок хотя бы в плотники, пильщики, шерстобои и т. д. [,] необходимо выправить патент и т.д. [ . . . ]

Пока достаточно этого, а если одобрите мою статейку пришлю еще и возможно буду вашим корреспондентом. Просьба переработать ее и поместит в к-ой газете остаюсь с почтением к вам крестьянин с молодыми чувствами и сочувствующий Сов. власти [адрес, имя].

*Translation*

I ask the editors of the p[easan]t newspaper to publish my article below about the life of a peasant in general, and what depends on the Soviet government in the first place in order to make the peasant's situation better.

It is not unknown both to everybody and to the Soviet government that the peasant of Soviet Russia is in the most critical condition and ekes out a pitiful existence of his life. [ . . . ]

Produced by peasant product is depreciated, and you can't purchase anything for it. There's no income on the side. Although in the summer of 1923 we went to work at the Suzdal' Factory,[15] all the same, workers' labor was not remunerated, they paid only enough for two pounds of bread, so we don't die from hunger. What can we do? If you take up growing cattle, this will again most likely not work out: if you have more than two heads of cattle, they will raise your produce-tax to the next category. Or if you go to an outside work, as a carpenter, or to cut wood, or to process wool, etc., you have to obtain a license, etc. [ . . . ]

That would be enough for now, but if you approve my article I'll send you more and perhaps become your correspondent. Please rework and publish in the p-t newspaper I remain a respecting you peasant with youthful feelings and sympathizing with the Sov. government [address, name].

*Comment*

The linguistic polyphony of this text goes beyond anything one could find in pre-1917 letters, as it reflects the twists and turns of the new regime: the initial promise, followed by the violence of the civil war, followed by attempts at reconciliation, frequently inept and self-contradictory. The letter is in a corresponding conflict with itself: a respectful opening is followed by sharp criticism that flows into the closing that professes sympathy and a desire to cooperate.

In genre, this letter is not a petition but an offer of advice. Its first sentence after the opening paragraph uses two sophisticated phrases: one a western borrowing ("в самом критическом положении" (Meromskii would be pleased), the other a Church Slavonic phrase ("жалкое существование") that, incongruously, comes with a redundant Genitive, as in Example 2.5 ("влачит жалкое существование жизни"). The middle passage is extremely illiterate—clearly not written by a scribe. The elided text talks about families where children cannot go to school because a family of seven has only two pairs of boots, "и то не совсем хорошие" (and even those not very good). The closing comes as something of a surprise.

## 2.8 DIRECTIONS OF CHANGE

The rest of this chapter builds on accumulated examples to catalog in more precise terms several specific directions of influence from the new language of state. They are listed below, grouped into Lexicon, Syntax, and Phraseology features. The lexicon features have been much discussed since Maison (1920) and Kartsevskii (1923), and will be of secondary interest. Syntax and phraseology will be central in the rest of this chapter as they are in the rest of the book. For lack of space, no more complete letters are presented; the exposition consists of small selections annotated by features they illustrate.

1. Lexicon
   a. new nomenclature of organizations, government agencies, positions of authority
   b. neologisms, including many abbreviations for #1a
   c. borrowings, including many abstract nouns
   d. elements of SovYaz: slogans; common clichés.
2. Word formation: many deverbal, abstract, collective nouns
3. Syntax
   a. fewer verbs; more nouns and adjectives
   b. phrases with abstract and deverbal nouns
   c. non-standard use of cases, especially the Genitive and the Instrumental
   d. cumbersome syntactic constructions
4. Phraseology
   a. new formulaic expressions
   b. contaminated and blended formulaic expressions
   c. wrong Lexical Functions
   d. expressions with redundant components, especially nouns in the Genitive
5. General: verbosity, in sharp contrast with the usual conciseness and economy.

These are common features of post-revolutionary language that were much discussed at the time in urban contexts. (See especially Selishchev 1928, Vinokur 1929, and Uspenskii 1930 with a comprehensive bibliography.) They are deployed, with a variety of artistic intentions, in the prose of Zoshchenko, Pil'niak, Platonov, Bablel', Seifullina. Contaminations in syntax and phraseology have been found in all large corpora of spoken language, including much later recordings of Russian urban speech. (See examples and references in Lapteva 1976:106.) However, peasant material has remained largely unexplored, which is, in effect, the reason for this book.

## 2.9 CATEGORIES AND EXAMPLES

### Deverbal Nouns and Their Syntax

In Chapter 1 it was noted that deverbal nouns in -ание/-ение are extremely rare in peasant speech records. The very first example of this chapter showed such a noun and the awkward syntax it may impose: "с самого начала приобретения им у нас в селе нашем господской земли" (from the very beginning of his acquiring of land in our village). Such examples proliferated after the revolution. Several of them are collected in 2.12. If an example has two glosses the first one is more literal, to indicate the irregularity of the original.

### Example 2.12 Examples with deverbal nouns

a. кулаки наши ивановские начали делать брожение (GN:25)
   *Translation*: our Ivanovo kulaks started to do unresting / started an unrest
   *Comment*: "делать брожение" is the first of many examples of incorrect Lexical Functions, as in "делать забастовку," Example 2.2.
b. я его получил в Москве, во время излечения моих ран (GN:30)
   *Translation:* I received it in Moscow, during the healing of my wounds.
   *Comment:* "during the healing" is quite similar to "the beginning of acquiring." As often, some precision of the verb is lost: was it when "his wounds were healing," or when "the doctor was healing his wounds"?
c. председатель совета из предыдущего поселка узнал, что неподалеку остановился отряд красных и спешил сообщить о выбытии и держащего направления шайки бандитов (GN:38)

*Translation:* The chairman of the Soviet from the preceding settlement learned that a Red detachment was nearby and hurried to inform about the departing and the holding direction of a gang of bandits/about the departure of a gang of bandits and the direction they were keeping.

*Comment:*
1) выбытие is a deverbal noun that one would not expect in peasant texts. It is formed from a verb common in bureaucratic language.
2) "сообщить о выбытии и держащего направления шайки бандитов:" This phrase is badly mangled in multiple ways. Untangling them all is relegated to a footnote.[16] In summary, the speaker wanted to put together a lot of content but this would require fairly complex syntax, as the gloss indicates. Instead the last four words are held together by two very simple syntactic constructions, adjective (participle) + noun, and head-noun + noun in the Genitive. Both are overused in peasant letters of the 1920s.

## Vague Genitives

Example 2.13 illustrates the use of Genitive as a default when the correct syntax is unknown. This usage can be termed "vague Genitive" on analogy with "vague adjectives" of Example 2.1. Both are found in 2.13.

## Example 2.13 Vague Genitives and adjectives

a. Мы взяли на себя всю **обязанность социалистического строя**. (GN:25)
   *Translation:* We took upon ourselves the entire obligation of the socialist order.
   *Comment*: The intended meaning was "ответственность за социалистичекий строй" (responsibility for the socialist order). There are two problems: two abstract nouns, обязанность and ответственность, are confused; and their precise syntactic frames are unknown to the author, so the Genitive has to do.

b. главным **препятствием неосуществления** такого закона является финансовый кризис (PVV 19)
   *Translation:* The main obstacle of non-implementing of such a law is financial crisis
   *Comment*: What is meant is, of course, "главным препятствием к осуществлению" (the main obstacle **to** implementing) but one would need to have a better knowledge of the syntax of препятствие (requires a preposition) and its semantics (contains negation). In the absence of such knowledge, Genitive is a simple syntactic solution, and the erroneous negation can be attached to the deverbal noun.

c. если я пойду купить 1 ф железа надо 10 к за фунт, до войны 5 к. А нам крестьянам болия негде денег взять как только за свои **мозольныи продукты** (KI #39, p.64)
   *Translation:* If I go out to buy 1 pound of iron I'll need 10 kopeks per pound, before the war 5 kopeks. But we peasants don't have any other

source of money other than our callused products [i.e., products of our labor from which we have calluses on our hands].

*Comment:* One could think of phrases of this sort as compressions of more explicit but verbose phrases into simple ones that are easier for the writer but require more inferential work from the reader: "спорный сад--сад, о котором идет спор" (controversial garden—garden, about which there is a controversy) (GN 85); "видная зажиточность--зажиточность у всех на виду " (visible prosperity-prosperity that everyone can see) (KI 100); "Красная советская рука--рука красной советской власти" (The red Soviet hand—the hand of red Soviet power) (GN 18) Such compressions can be intentionally used by a writer who wants to slow down the reader. This may be why "мозольныи продукты" sounds like something Platonov could write. (See a later section on Platonov.)

## Recollection Letters

A number of peasant letters of the 1920s were requests for help that would start with the personal history of the author's exploits in the civil war, and base the request on that history. I will call them "recollection letters." Their language typically shows a great number of new influences, as in 2.14, the opening of one such letter.

## Example 2.14 Opening of a request letter: the author introduces himself. GN:24

Редакции газеты "Правда" от гражданина Кубанской области, [ . . . ] рожденный в селе Ивановке 1888 г. июня 20 дня Глинский Михаил Антонович, ярый большевик по идее Владимира Ильича Ленина. Я опишу свою историю первоначального моего политического учения, как поступило это дело к нам на Кубань.

*Translation*

To the editorial board of "Pravda" from a citizen of the Kuban' province [ . . . ] born in the village of Ivanovka 1888 y. on the 20th of June, Glinskii Mikhail Antonovich, fervent bolshevik on the idea of Vladimir Il'ich Lenin. I will describe my story of my initial political teaching / learning, as this whole thing arrived to us at Kuban'.

*Comment*

Unlike most peasant letters of the time, this one has a solemn opening. It does not have a title, like 2.10, but it does have sections with titles. The first one starts right after the opening, titled "История" (The Story, or The History).

In the opening itself, there are multiple distortions. The phrase "по идее [ . . . ] Ленина" is intended to mean something like "a follower of," as indicated by a later sentence: "Я прошел в совет и еще со мной *по такой же политической идее* товарищ Ковшик" (I was elected to the Soviet and with me, on the same political idea, comrade Kovshik). The phrase "как поступило это дело" is an attempt to provide a time frame. The reference of "это дело" is unclear.

The main point of interest is the deverbal "учение," which with a possessive usually means "teaching," as in Ленинское учение (Lenin's teaching), or учение Маркса (the teaching of Marx). Here it most likely means "learning." This is a common problem with deverbal nouns, especially when used with the Genitive case: is this a Genitive of subject or object? The problem, as it presented itself in the language of that period, is extensively discussed in Vinokur (1929:56–84).

The letter concludes with a request.

## Example 2.15 Request and offer of service

я инвалид третьей группы, у меня телесных недостатков: 1) правого глаза нет, и слух испорчен, и у ногах ревматизм от простуды на фронте. Я доброволец Красной Армии и инвалид гражданской войны, не могу быть механиком и на крестьянскую работу не способен, и меня собес о тталкивает, не дает мне инвалидность по словам у нас на Кубани. Если бы я мог доехать до Москвы, много доклада мог бы сделать в пользу нашей власти, что творится между казачеством, да не за что ехать.

*Translation*

I'm an invalid of the third group; of physical disabilities I have: 1) no right eye, and hearing is damaged, a rheumatism in my legs from a cold at the front. I'm a volunteer of the Red Army and an invalid of the civil war, cannot be a mechanic and incapable of doing peasant work, the social support office pushes me away, does not give me invalid status on my words here at the Kuban region. If I could get to Moscow I could make much report to the benefit of our government, what is going on among the cossacks, but there's no money for travel.

*Comment*

"собес" is a syllabic abbreviation for "социальное обеспечение" (social support programs). This abbreviation survived throughout the entire Soviet period. Apparently it required some documents that Glinskii could not provide. The noun доклад (report) is treated as a mass noun.

## Why Deverbal Nouns?

Peasant letters use deverbal nouns because they proliferated in the language of power and authority. Why they proliferated there is something of a mystery, but they were certainly used with abandon. Example 2.16 illustrates. It is a circular from Glavlit, which is short for "Главное управление по делам литературы и издательств" (the Main Directorate for the Affairs of Literature and Publishing Houses). This was the central censorship office, charged with preventing anti-Soviet propaganda, religious propaganda, disclosure of military secrets, fake news, and pornography. Its staff counted 86 in 1927, 192 in 1934, and 6,453 in 1947. The circular in Example 2.16 shows its broad understanding of what is secret and anti-Soviet. The message is addressed to the network of subordinate offices around the country: every guberniia (province) had a *gub-lit*, every krai (region) a *krai-lit*, and so on. The "lit" in all these titles stands for "literature."

### Example 2.16 Glavlit circular. Danilov et al. 1999, vol.1:71

Deverbal nouns (9 words out of 50) are in italics.

16 апреля 1927 г. Сов. секретно.

Всем гублитам, облитам, крайлитам, окрлитам, главлитам автономных республик и уполномоченным при издательствах (главлитам союзных республик для сведения).

Главлит предлагает Вам принять все меры к полному *недопущению появления* в печати каких-либо *сообщений* (статей, заметок, и т.п.), говорящих о *затруднениях* или сбоях в деле *снабжения* страны хлебом, как могущих, без достаточных *оснований*, вызвать панику и сорвать проводимые правительством мероприятия по *преодолению* временных *затруднений* в деле хлебозаготовок и *снабжения* страны.

Начальник Главлита Лебедев-Полянский

*Translation*

16 April 1927. Top secret.

To all gublits, obllits, krailits, okrlits, glavlits of autonomous republics and deputies at publishing houses (to glavlits of union republics for information).

Glavlit instructs you to take all measures toward the complete prevention of appearance in print of any communications (articles, notes, etc.) talking about difficulties or interruptions in the task of providing the country with bread, as capable, without sufficient foundation, of provoking panic and disrupting the measures that are being taken by the government aimed to overcoming temporary difficulties in the task of bread procurement and supplying the country.

Head of Glavlit Lebedev-Polianskii

*Comment*

This message was simultaneously distributed by the GPU to their own network, with a cover letter that had an equal measure of deverbal nouns. It is a single long bureaucratic sentence with phrases like "при сем препровождается для сведения и строгого руководства" (herewith forwarded for your information and strict guidance). The last two words of this phrase are as vague as any Genitive in the preceding section, meaning either "you are to be strictly guided by this message" or "you must strictly guide the locals to adhere to this message."

## Quasi-deverbals

The Genitive of subject-object also appears in peasant letters as a complement of nouns that are not strictly speaking deverbal. Consider "бремя жестокой, но славной борьбы [ . . . ] за свое достояние страны" (the burden of brutal but glorious battle [ . . . ] for our property of the country) GN:78. I deliberately do not gloss достояние as "possession" because that would make the English smoother than the original: "possession" is a deverbal noun, but "достояние" is not, even though it has the -ание suffix, which is what probably influenced the author's syntax.

Sometimes the Genitive of subject-object is used even in the absence of any such suffix. In the phrase, "большие и малые пиявки трудового крестьянства" (the big and small leeches of the laboring peasantry" (GN 24), the Genitive does not indicate possession, as it normally would, but rather the object of the blood-sucking action. In the phrase "the leeches of world capital" it would indicate the subject.

An interesting case is the phrase "кучка самозахватчиков власти" (a bunch of self-grabbers of-power), in Glinskii's letter, GN:21. "Захватчик" is not a deverbal noun but the Agent of the verb захватывать "occupy, grab." The phrase "захватчики власти" was used in the period after 1917 and in later memoirs of that period, almost exclusively by the defeated party in reference to Bolsheviks. The earliest example in RNC is from senior priest (протоиерей) V. P. Sventitskii (1919): "Захватчики власти, превратившие русскую жизнь в дикий кошмар" (The power grabbers who transformed Russian life into savage nightmare). Glinskii adopted the phrase but with a neologism самозахватчики, probably an abbreviation, in the spirit of the time, of "самовольные захватчики" (unauthorized grabbers).

## Other Abstract and Collective Nouns

In addition to deverbals there is an abundance of abstract and collective nouns formed from nouns and adjectives. In most cases, a simpler alternative is easily available. Consider 2.17.

## Example 2.17 Abstract and collective nouns

В 1921 г. в Поволжье [ . . . ] размножились шайки бандитизма, часто делали налеты на крестьянские населения, грабили крестьян скотиной и тем, что попадет под руку (GN 37).

*Translation*

In 1921 in the Volga region gangs of banditism multiplied, they made frequent raids on peasant populations, robbed peasants of animals and whatever they could grab.

*Comment*

It would be very easy to say "шайки бандитов" (gangs of bandits) and "крестьянские деревни" (peasant villages). Note however that "грабить скотиной" is a traditional peasant usage of the Instrumental noted in Chapter 1.

In 2.18 a collective noun is similarly misused. The letter is remarkably illiterate and uses elements of old orthography, but claims to be from somebody in Moscow, probably a ruse.

## Example 2.18 A denunciation with a collective noun

В редакцию Крестьянской Газеты
Писмо
Унасъ в селенье ест кулачество Александра Николаевна Цветкова и съ сыномъ Гордеемъ Петровичемъ делаютъ крестьянской бедноте полное издевательство во всехъ отношенияхъ руководятъ етой беднотой как имъ вздумается выражаютъ свое хамское отношение к бедноте а тагже и средняку [ . . . ]
[Подпись] И.Вологотский Москва

*Translation*

In our village there is kulakism Aleksandra Nikolaevna Tsvetkova and with son Gordei Petrovich make total bullying to our peasant poor in all respects[,] order those poor around as they feel like[,] express their boorish attitude to the poor and also to middle peasantry [ . . . ]
[Signed] I.Vologotskii, Moscow

*Comment*

The word "kulakism" is an admittedly awkward attempt to render the Russian collective noun. As in the preceding example, it would be very easy to say simply кулаки (kulaks).

The inserted commas are guesses: the first one could equally well go before "in all respects," the second before "as they wish."

The phrase "perform mockery" is meant to convey how unnatural the Russian original is. It would be easy to use the verb "издеваться" (bully, jeer, torment), except one would need to know that it is used with the preposition "над." Instead an abstract noun is used, with a generic verb "делать" for the Lexical Function that combines with it to form a verb phrase. (Recall "делать забастовку" in Example 2.2.) As noted, irregular Lexical Functions are very common in the letters of the period, usually in phrases with abstract nouns.

## Wrong Lexical Functions: Contaminations of Metaphors and Syntax

This section shows a collection of improvised Lexical Functions illustrating the common strategies of improvisation: use a very common word (большой big; делать do); use a Conceptual Metaphor (упадшее настроение); or use an analogy: "обнажить саблю - обнажить револьвер; понести потери - понести ошибку."

## Example 2.19 Artisanal Lexical Functions

a. Я вам *несу большую благодарность*. (Мер 54.); I carry big gratitude to you. (The related standard phrase is выносить благодарность "express gratitude.")

b. В этом случае автор *понес ошибку*. (Мер 55); the author suffered a mistake. (The related standard phrase is понес потери "suffer losses.")

c. я *хорошо уверен* (GN 74); I am well confident. (The related standard phrase is Я совершенно уверен "I'm perfectly confident;" or я хорошо помню "I remember well.")

d. когда *разгорелась Окт. Революция* (GN 75); when revolution flared up. (The related standard phrase is разгорелась борьба "struggle flared up.")

e. Кто-то *провокацию строит*, чтобы рабочие волновались. (GN 317); Somebody is constructing a provocation. (The related standard phrase is строить планы "make plans.")

f. Вот начали мы *занимать себе широкую агитацию* по всему нашему отделу (GN 26); We started occupying broad agitation for ourselves over our entire sector. (The related standard phrase is занимать позицию "take a position.")

g. Сухов послал меня *собрать* и *сделать агитацию* (GN 28); Sukhov sent me to gather and make agitation. (The related standard phrase is развернуть агитацию "organize agitation.")
h. зажиточные *пользуются всеми инициативами* в Советской республике и плюс к этому *делая насмешки* против тех лиц, которые служили в Кр. армии (KI 77). the well-to-do are using all the initiatives in the Soviet republic, and plus to that making derision against those persons who served in the Red Army. (The related standard phrase is пользоваться привилегиями "enjoy the privileges.")
i. Такие условия крестьянскую сельскую хозяйственность *поставили в ненормальность* (KI 101); Such conditions put our peasant agricultural activity into an abnormality. (The related standard phrase is поставить в ненормальное положение "put in an abnormal position.")
j. в нашей местности *проводится много неправильности и негодности* согласно инструкций и газет (KI 72). In our area much incorrectness and uselessness is conducted in accordance with instructions and newspapers.

This last example also illustrates the *contamination* of formulaic expressions: the phenomenon of bringing together two formulaic expressions in such a way that their connection has to be established by a long sequence of idiosyncratic steps. The intended meaning of 2.19j is that if you consult instructions and newspapers much of what is done is incorrect and results in waste (негодность). This is difficult to extract from the lexical and syntactic jumble of two clichés brought together in an arbitrary order. Example 2.20 collects several more instances.

**Example 2.20 Contamination of formulaic expressions**

a. В Кольчугиной пошли в полном смысле аресты (GN 29); In the village of Kol'chugina arrests started in the full sense [of the word].
b. он нам испортил весь аппетит военного настроения (GN 31); He spoiled for us the entire appetite of warrior mood.
c. Но крестьяне, бодрые духом, скрепя свое сердце, перенесли яростный гнев белогвардейцев на своих плечах (GN 32) But the peasants, buoyant in spirit, fortified their hearts and endured the violent wrath of the Whites on their shoulders.
d. мне пришлось все время быть на фронтах, а мои соседи набивали карман, а тепер у меня образовалос разбитое карыто (KI 99). I had to be on the frontlines all the time while my neighbors were stuffing their pockets, and now for me just a broken washtub emerged. (The correct folk saying is остаться у разбитого корыта "to be left with the broken washtub," i.e., with nothing.)

## On Platonov

The reader may have noticed some similarities between examples of this section and the prose of Andrei Platonov. It seems clear that he carefully observed peasant speech and used its features in his writings. This was not, of course, the only source of his style, which absorbed many voices of the time, but the peasant voice is clearly heard. Example 2.21 lists a few examples, classified by the same categories as 2.12–2.20. They are quoted from Platonov (1983) abbreviated as PP and Platonov (1987)—PGG.

## Example 2.21 Quotes from Platonov

a. Невдалеке от станции строился поселок жилищ. PP 28.
   Near the station a settlement of dwellings was being built.
   (Redundant Genitive, Cf. *влачит жалкое существование жизни* Example 2.11, KI 61; *нет сырья производства* Известия. 16 мая 1926 г., с.1; *в обратном пути возвращения* GN 39; *о будущем нашего состояния* 2.5.)
b. уже использованный сельской общественностью лес. PP 28.
   lumber already appropriated by the general public of the village
   (an abstract noun—cf. У нас есть кулачество)
c. Это затмение основной директивы по линии партии, данной всерьез и надолго. (Platonov 1987:Gorod Gradov)
   This is an eclipsing of the main directive in accordance with the party line, given in seriousness and for permanence.
   (Contamination. Cf. ярый большевик по идее Владимира Ильича Ленина, 2.14)
d. его туда втолкнули задние спешные люди PP 41.
   he was pushed in the by behind-him urgent people
   (Compressed adjective, cf. спорный сад, мозольные продукты)

An analysis of how Platonov appropriates and transforms peasant language could be the subject of a separate study. Nakhimovsky (2017:132) offers "as an exercise" a paragraph put together out of quotes from Platonov and from peasant letters, inviting the reader to distinguish which is which.

## CONCLUSIONS

The confusion and occasional flamboyance of peasant letters of the 1920s was short-lived. By 1933 most peasants had become kolkhozniks, and it was fairly obvious that complaining or begging was useless. Literacy spread, especially among young men who migrated to cities or were drafted in the army. However, as the personal letters of the next chapter show, peasant language still lived among many, it just disappeared from letters to power. The two collections of such letters from the 1930s (Sokolov 1998; Orlov and Livshin 2002) present a bleak picture: while requests, complaints, and advice are all but gone, denunciations persist and multiply.

## NOTES

1. As a word of caution, Kotkin's (1997:198–237) term "speaking Bolshevik," is about workers in the 1930s, which is very different from peasants in the 1920s. Moreover, Kotkin discusses letters that were actually published in newspapers, heavily edited or simply composed by the editor/censor, as opposed to letters composed by peasants and never published. It is well-known that if a letter was published, all kinds of deformations had occurred.

2. A pood (пуд) is about 16 kilograms or 40 pounds.

3. http://ruscorpora.ru/instruction-syntax.html#Лексические.

4. Сделать забастовку is found in a play by the Odessa writer Semen Iushkevich (see RNC), but it is unlikely that peasants from central Russia could have been influenced by Odessa dialect.

5. After the start of WWI, the Germanic name Петербург (Peterburg) was changed to the Slavic Petro-grad, renamed in 1924 as Lenin-grad; in 1991 it went back to Petersburg.

6. For contrast, the price ratio of flour to salt on Amazon (Feb. 14, 2018) was 1.46. For unprocessed grain the ratio would be higher but not 3 to 1; and the Bolshevik salt of 1923 would not be the same quality.

7. Phone conversation with M. K. Vladimirov, Aug. 6, 1921. Babel's story "Salt" should be read in this context.

8. The numbers are from Zubov (2011), vol. 1, pp. 486, 561.

9. One is reminded here of the first conversation between Ostap Bender and Vorob'ianiov in the popular Soviet novel *The 12 Chairs*.

10. Today's members of the Russian security service, FSB, still proudly and nostalgically refer to themselves as Chekists.

11. The use of the word мандат shows a sharp spike around 1920, and it was mostly used to refer to a document. Glossing it as "mandate" would be misleading; I use the transliteration in italics.

12. Mokienko and Nikitina (1998).

13. Shafir, Ia. 1923:50; also Selishchev 1928:211. As explained shortly, Selishchev summarized much of Shafir's slim volume. When a quote from Shafir is also in Selishchev (1928) I cite the latter because it is much easier to access: there is a PDF on the Web, and the book was reprinted in 2003 as part of Selishchev's collected works. My quotes from Selishchev give pages of the original edition.

14. In a curious quirk of history, every person in this paragraph (except for Fenomenov, the son of a Russian Orthodox priest) came from a bourgeois or rabbinical Jewish family.

15. Суздальский Комбинат, now Суздальский молочный завод (Suzdal' Dairy Factory) still exists, incorporated 1993, part of the Russian company Вимм-Билль-Данн, owned by PepsiCo.

16. The errors are all in the phrase "держащего направления шайки бандитов" It is in the wrong case, Genitive instead of Prepositional. Internally, the constituent "шайка бандитов" should have been the subject of "держать направление," a formulaic expression in which the noun is the direct object of the verb. It is used instead as the Genitive of possession attached to one component of the formula, so the last three words mean: "the direction of a gang of bandits." This would make sense on its own, but the writer wanted to use the fancy formula "держать направление," so he attached the participle of "держать" before "направление." As a result, "направление" becomes the subject of the semantically empty verb of the formula. An analogous confusion in English would be the phrase "the giving speech of the director" in reference to the director giving a speech.

*Chapter 3*

# Personal Letters, 1939–1940

## 3.1 THE SOURCE AND THE BACKGROUND

The main source for Chapter 3 is a collection of personal letters from 1939–40, henceforth referred to as "the Corpus." Compared to Chapter 2, this represents a change of genre and a historical gap of twelve momentous years that included collectivization, a famine, the Great Terror, and the beginning of WWII. These were also the years of LikBez, an abbreviation for Likvidatsiia Bezgramotnosti (liquidation of illiteracy), the Soviet program to teach reading and writing to adults. For children, universal elementary schooling was introduced in 1930. By 1940 the Soviet government claimed ninety-percent literacy in the country. The material of the Corpus presents an opportunity to evaluate that claim.[1]

As a background, the chapter begins with a brief overview of earlier materials and earlier history from the first half of the 1930s.

### 1930s: Letters to Power

The 1930s really started with the upheavals of 1928–29, the two simultaneous campaigns of total (сплошная) collectivization and the "liquidation of kulaks as a class." Recall from Chapter 2 that kulaks—rich peasants—were declared class enemies that had to be liquidated. In practice, this meant the immediate confiscation of all property followed by one of three gradations of punishment: execution; remote exile to harsh places in the Russian North or Siberia; or local exile. Since in any event the confiscated property remained in the village, there was an incentive to stretch the definition of the rich to include those who were simply better off, meaning the середняки (middle peasants).

The most common transitive verb for violent action against kulaks and their families was "раскулачить," literally to "de-kulak" somebody. As pointed out in Chapter 1, the Imperfective of раскулачить in the standard language is раскулачивать; in peasant texts it is more commonly кулачить. In some parts of the country there were local names for this action. Some of them appear in the peasant narratives recorded in the 1990s, in which dekulakization is often the most painful part of historical memory.

In parallel to dekulakization, there was strong pressure on the remaining peasants to form a collective farm, best known by the syllabic abbreviation kolkhoz, for *kollektivnoe khoziaistvo* "collective enterprise." Those who joined became *kolkhozniks*—kolkhoz members. In many specific and painful ways, illustrated by the materials of this chapter, kolkhozniks were second-class citizens of the Soviet Union. Those few who persisted in remaining outside the kolkhoz were called единоличники, which the dictionary translates as "individual farmers"—but of course they did not really have farms, only small plots and perhaps a cow or two and a few chickens. *Edinolichniks* were oppressed even more than kolkhozniks: smaller plots, higher taxes. For more on *edinolichniks,* see Chapter 4.

The campaigns of 1929–1933 were poorly conceived, explained, and executed. Many peasants saw them as a return to the policy of war communism. A typical 1930 letter to Pravda says: "Жизнь, можно сказать, крестьянам плоха до невозможности. Берут у крестьянина все без исключения и хлеб и картошку." (Life for peasants, you can say, is bad to impossibility. Everything is taken away from the peasant, both bread and potatoes) (Sokolov 1998b:27). Letters to power continued but changed in tone, if not in language. If in the 1920s the range of attitude was from acceptance and friendly advice to complaint, sometimes quite bitter, in the 1930s the range was from effusive praise to complete despair. 3.1 and 3.2 show samples of both.

### Example 3.1 Forward to Socialism! (1930) (Orlov and Livshin 2002:136)

Письмо колхозника А.М.Жернакова в "Рабочую газету"

Деревня--вперед, к Социализму! По данным сведениям перерабатывая съезд ВКП(б), деревенские коммунисты и беспартийные колхозники подошли к заключению, в своем докладе тов Сталин выяснил достижения партии в деле индустриализации страны, тов Сталин выяснил все темпы, взятые нашей коммун партией, выяснил заграничное положение С А Ш Америки. [ . . . ] Крестьянин взял прямую линию к колхозу и говорит, разобравши статью тов Сталина: "Нам без колхоза не обойтись."

*Translation*

A letter by the peasant Zhernakov to *Workers newspaper*
 Countryside, forward to Socialism! Based on given information processing the XVI congress of the All-union Communist Party (bolshevik), the village communists and non-party kolkhozniks approached a [this] conclusion, [:] in his report comrade Stalin figured out the achievements of the party in the task of industrialization of the country, comrade Stalin figured out all the tempos taken by our party, figured out the foreign situation of the UAS of America. [ . . . ] The peasant took the direct line to kolkhoz, and he says, after working through the paper by comrade Stalin: "Without kolkhoz—there is no way."

*Comment*

This borderline gibberish had to be tweaked in translation (as shown in brackets) so it could make more sense. The text shows some of the same confusions that were presented in Chapter 2. In particular, the phrase "пришли к заключению" (arrived at the conclusion) is given as "подошли к заключению," literally "walked up to the conclusion." The name of the USA is a blend: initially, the Russian name for the new state was Северо-Американские Соединенные Штаты (САСШ) before becoming США; the writer seems to imply Северо-Американские Штаты Америки.

## Example 3.2 From peasants who want to leave. Sokolov 1998b:42 (1932)

Кто успел во-время удрать на производство, ему хорошо, живет и хлебушка ест, а остальные кинулись, да поздно, справку сельсовет не дает, говорит: "Все уйдете, некому будет работать." Сейчас остались голые, босые, 200 г. ячменного хлеба в день и капусту без масла кушаем. Жутко смотреть, когда здоровенный мужчина плачет, а он плачет оттого, что обманули колхозом, что остался без хозяйства, без хлеба, без одежды, и свободу потерял.

 Нам ничего не надо, оставим свои хаты и родные места, только бы дали справку, чтобы на производство поступить [ . . . ]

*Translation*

Those who managed to run away in time, to get a factory job, those are in good shape, they can live and have bread to eat; the rest rushed out, but it was too late, the village office does not give the release document, says: "If you all leave, there will be no one to do the work." Now we are stuck here naked, barefoot, 200 g. of barley bread a day, and cabbage without oil to eat.

It's terrible to see a big strong man crying, and he is crying because he was deceived with the kolkhoz, left without any peasant things, without bread, without clothes, and he lost his freedom.

We are not asking for anything, we'll leave our homes and our native land, if only we could get the document to go work in the industry.

## Comment

Russian has a category of suffixes called the "affectionate diminutive." They can be attached to nicknames (as explained in the section on personal letters as a genre) as well as a great number of other words, including хлеб (bread). This letter says, wistfully, хлебушек.

This passage highlights one of the many ways in which peasants were second-class citizens. In 1932 all Soviet citizens except kolkhozniks received internal passports that were necessary for residency registration and travel. In order to leave their kolkhoz residence, kolkhozniks needed a release from the chairman, which was sometimes readily available, sometimes required a bribe, and sometimes was refused. The Soviet policy was schizophrenic: kolkhozes needed labor because productivity was low, but cities also needed labor in construction and industry because the country was undergoing crash industrialization. So it was possible to make your way to the city, find a job, get a place in the dorm, and eventually obtain the passport. There were also recruiters in the countryside looking for workers and helping with the release document. The time between arriving in the city and obtaining the passport was for many migrants the time of exploitation, misery, poor pay, poor living conditions.

The phrase "его обманули колхозом" (he was deceived with respect to kolkhoz) shows the familiar bare Instrumental that is found in peasant speech.

The word "хозяйство," refers to everything in the household that is needed for life and work, from tools and cattle to kitchen utensils and furniture. All of this could indeed be confiscated if you were deemed to be a kulak or failed to pay your taxes. (See 3.3.)

## 1930s: A Personal Letter to City

The sudden and extreme changes of 1929–33 were incomprehensible to many. The natural response was to write to somebody you knew who could explain and perhaps even do something to stop those changes. One possibility was to write to a relative who had left for the city. Migration to the cities was already in the millions and accelerating, and it was a natural assumption that city dwellers had better information about what was going on. Example 3.3 is a letter from parents to their son in "the center," which could be a local district capital or a big city. The letter shows some typical features of peasant personal letters, such as the use of the second-person pronouns, that will be discussed in detail with the multiple examples in the Corpus. Apart from the Corpus, 3.3 is *the only example of a peasant personal letter* for the entire decade. It is cited will only minor omissions.

**Example 3.3 Parents to son. Danilov 1999 vol1:663**

Письмо крестьянина дер. Дементьевки Самарской губ. М.Д.Михайлина сыну о хлебозаготовках
    Letter from peasant M.D. Mikhailin of village of Dement'evka, Samara Province to his son about grain duty.

*Part 1*

Письмо от Ваших родителей.
    Добрый день, дорогой сын, шлем тебе от всей семьи привет, и от родных, и знакомых. Получили мы от тебя письмо и деньги 15 р., за которые очень благодарны.
    Вы спрашивали об урожае, с весны до Троицы была засуха, с Троицы пошли дожди. Так что теперь хлеба немного отдохнули, хлеба для семьи наберем, хотя хлеба-то наберем, но дать-то нам едва дадут, у нас идет хлебозаготовка. На нас наложили 20 пуд., а мы сами покупаем с зимы. У [нас] описали жеребенка и четыре овцы, отбирают все в кредит у каждого в деревне, у кого есть две лошади и две коровы, то одну берут лошадь и одну корову и оставляют на каждый дом одну лошадь и корову. Оставшееся все отбирают. Овец всех до одной берут. И у кого не хватает скотины, забирают, у кого что есть хорошее: одежду, мебель и посуду. В Королевке у дяди Васи Бадинова взяли лошадь, корову, телку, полуторника, семь голов овец, взяли машину швейную, самовар, суконный тулуп, перину, куделю и даже шерсть [ . . . ]. Ходят по дворам и ищут у всех хлеб, [ . . . ], оставляют только один пуд на едока. Хлеба купить негде, не найдешь, и нельзя продать. [ . . . ] Вот, Митюня, пропиши, как на это к чему это дело клонить, у нас есть слухи, будет скоро сильная война, если не война, хотят всех сгонять в колхозы, и будем работать все вместе.

*Translation*

Letter from your parents. Good afternoon, dear son, we send you welcome from the whole family and from relatives and friends. We received a letter from you and money 15 r., for which we are very grateful.
    You asked about the harvest, from spring to Pentecost we had drought, after Pentecost it started raining. So the fields have rested, we'll collect bread

for the family, but even though we will collect, it doesn't look like they give it to us, there's bread-procurement going on, they levy 20 poods, even though we have been buying bread for ourselves since winter. From us they assigned to the government a colt and four sheep[;] they take away everything on credit from everyone in the village, if you have two horses and two cows they take away a horse and a cow, leaving for each household one horse and one cow. The rest they take away. The sheep are all taken to the last sheep. Who doesn't have enough cattle, from them whatever they have of value is taken: clothes, furniture, dishes. In Korolevka, from uncle Vasia they took a horse, a cow, a heifer, a young calf, seven sheep; they took their sewing machine, samovar, his felt coat, their featherbed, even their wool [ . . . ]. They are going from house to house looking for grain [ . . . ], and leave only one pood per mouth. There's no bread to buy anywhere, and you can't sell. [ . . . ] So, Mitiunia, write to us where all this is going, we have rumors that there will be a big war soon, and if not war, they want us all corral into kolkhozes, and we will all work together.

*Comment*

In the Russian Orthodox calendar, the holiday of Trinity (Троица) is on the same day as the Pentecost, 50th day after Easter.

Митюня is a nickname for Dmitrii (Митя) with an extra suffix of emotional value. This is explained with multiple examples in discussing the Corpus.

Bread-procurement (хлебозаготовка) was a cover term for the government's procedure to procure enough bread from the peasants to feed everybody else. Under war communism of 1917–1921, the procedure was to simply confiscate everything according to government-dictated quotas, which were frequently exceeded. From 1921–1928, the government used relatively predictable taxation. After 1928, several procedures were tried, one of them leading to the famine of 1932–1933. Relative stability was reached only in the mid-1930s, but materials in the Corpus show how difficult the situation remained.

*Part 2*

Пропиши, что у Вас в центре делается, народ сильно расстроился, даже не хотят хлеб сеять. Пропиши нам вот на все это и пропиши нам, что этот декрет из центра выслан или здешняя власть так распоряжается, мы этого ничего не знаем. Еще вот что было: наняли срубы рубить, хотели мы срубить на 12 аршин длиною и 7 аршин шириною, теперь мы отложили, что у нас скотину описали в казну, и мы хотим погодить до осени, может быть, будет какая-нибудь перемена, если сгонят нас в один колхоз, то нам это не надо. Получишь это, пиши, какие у Вас есть слухи. Хотя у нас хлеба и нет, все-таки мы не скитались из хлеба, запаслись с весны, так что до новины хватит, скоро пожнем новый. Затем до свиданья. Пиши ответ, все мы живы и здоровы, того же и тебе желаем, [ . . . ]. Как можно пиши поскорее, что у Вас там творится.

*Translation*

Write how things are in the center, here people are very upset, don't even want to plant the fields. Write to us about everything, and write whether that decree was sent from the center, or it's our local authorities give such orders, we don't know anything about this. Here's another thing: we started building some storage, wanted to do 12 by 7 arshin [about 8.5 by 5 meters], now stopped because our cattle was assigned for the government, and we want to wait till fall, there may be some kind of a change, if they herd us into a kolkhoz, we don't need it. When you receive this, write what rumors you have there. Although we don't have bread, but still we didn't wander around for bread, saved up some from spring, so we have enough till the new crop, we'll start harvesting soon. With this, good bye. Write back, we're all alive and well, wishing you the same [ . . . ]. Write as soon as you can what's happening where you are.

*Comment*

There are beautiful examples of peasant syntax in this passage but nothing that has not been noted in earlier examples. Some details will be revisited when discussing similar features in the Corpus.

## 3.2 LETTERS TO THE ARMY AND PEASANT "MOODS"

The other large group of sons and brothers was in the army. In December 1926, the entire army counted 580,625 (mostly) men, of whom 77.4% were of peasant background (Tarkhova 2006:82–85).[2] The letters that they started to receive from home in 1928 are similar to 3.2 and 3.3 but with an additional nuance: soldiers were asked not only for information and advice, but also for protection. In the eyes of the village soldiers had guns, and therefore power. Unsurprisingly, this was immediately registered as a dangerous development. Already in January 1928 there was a high-level meeting of chief political officers of all military districts. One of their directives to the subordinate hierarchy of political officers down to the company level was to "carefully study all the moods of red army soldiers related to the carrying out of the party policy in the village, especially the latest measures, and describe those moods in your regular informational reports" (Tarkhova 2006:93). The reports followed this directive by liberally quoting from letters soldiers received from home, and, to a lesser extent, from conversations soldiers had among themselves. These letters thus form "a source of precious epistolary information emerging from the village" (Tarkhova 2006:94), and a reflection of peasant moods.

Like the word "элемент," the word "настроение" (mood, sentiment) had a special meaning in SovYaz. Although it was possible to have good, legitimate moods, e.g., a festive mood on May 1, most of the time the word was used with "bad" adjectives like "anti-soviet" or "nationalistic."[3] The unspoken connotation was that Bolsheviks did not have moods, they had convictions that contained structured propositional content. Enemies of Bolsheviks had shapeless, nebulous, sometimes smelly moods. ("He smelled of nationalism,"—says one of the witnesses at the 1952 trial of the Jewish Anti-Fascist Committee [Naumov 1994:205]). The term would certainly apply to peasant soldiers influenced by letters from home. Very quickly the phrase крестьянские настроения (peasant moods) was so common that it was abbreviated to its initials, KH. The abbreviation seems to have appeared first in the reports within OGPU, which started monitoring "peasant moods" even before the army.

There are no general estimates of numbers, but the metaphor "поток писем" (flood of letters) was common. In one piece of anecdotal evidence, the garrison of Novocherkassk (a city in the North Caucuses) consisting of 5,000 men received up to 6,000 letters in the early 1928. (Tarkhova 2006:95) Multiplying by days and garrisons, the order of magnitude has to be in the hundreds of thousands of letters. There must have also been also a return flow of letters back to the village (Tarkhova 2006:98). The remarkable fact, and a symptom of the chaos in peasant life throughout the century, is that none of those letters, to or from the army, has been preserved. With the exception of Example 3.3, not a single one "sank to the bottom of the archives" (отложились в архивах), to use Tarkhova's phrase (p.94). All we know about them is from descriptions and quotes in secret police reports. The quotes listed by Tarkhova (pp.95–96) sound very similar to Examples 3.2 and 3.3: "to everyone they come at night and take away the grain," "all the mills are closed," "in stores, they sell only for grain," "you can't buy anything for money," "who doesn't have grain, they take away the horse and the cow, whatever the man has," "in paying a peasant for grain, they force state bonds on him," "they force you to sell bread to state coops, when a private trader is offering more," "they forbid to sell bread in the markets, and the poor have no place to buy bread, it will be difficult to live until the new harvest," "they buy bread for 1 r. 15 kopeks, but to buy seed grain from them it's 1 r. 35 kopeks."

Such quotes are important documents for historians, but both as human documents and as linguistic material they are much less valuable than complete letters. It is all the more remarkable that the Corpus of about 300 letters, half of them from peasants/kolkhozniks, has remained largely unexplored. The reasons will become clear in a later section that describes its provenance and publication history.

## 3.3 PERSONAL LETTERS AS A GENRE: TRADITION, STRUCTURE, AND FORMAL ELEMENTS

The letters of the Corpus were written primarily by people from the lower classes of Soviet society, including peasants. Just as peasants formed a sharply defined social group, economically and legally, in the Soviet Union of the 1930s, peasant letters form a sharply defined group of texts within the Corpus. They stand apart both because of the social conditions of their writers as second-class citizens, and because they are informed by the textual tradition of peasant letters that goes back centuries, in parallel to the tradition of letters to power. Pankratova (1969:137) notes that even in the seventeenth century, peasant letters formed a distinctive group of texts that contained common formulaic elements specific to the group. Yokoyama (2008), a meticulous investigation of a peasant family archive from the late nineteenth century, provides more immediate perspective. Some repeating formulaic elements of 1939–1940 have obvious antecedents in Yokoyama (2008) and thus go back to even earlier traditions. Others seem equally old but are not found in Yokoyama (2008); their origins proved difficult to establish. In effect, the personal letter traditions of the nineteenth to twentieth centuries are not known much better than those of the seventeenth. Almost nothing in the shared formulas of the peasant letters in the Corpus shows any influence from Bolshevik linguistic innovations.

The structure of a personal letter minimally includes an opening and a closing. Even in the seventeenth century, both were fairly elaborate and clearly influenced by tradition; the same is true of 1939–1940. Moreover, no-peasant letter openings also fall into several patterns associated with recognizable social groups. Just studying letter openings reveals a good deal about the structure of Soviet society at the time, bringing more diverse and authentic data (unpublished, unedited, uncensored) to historical arguments about the relationship between the Soviet state and the Soviet people at that time.

The common formal elements of any personal letter include forms of self-identification, forms of address, and the second person pronouns. In Russian, as in French, there are two such pronouns: the more familiar *ty*, grammatically singular, and the more formal or remote or respectful *vy*, grammatically plural. We will often refer to them by their first letters (same as in French): the T and the V pronoun. Among the educated the pronoun is determined by the relationship between the speakers; transition from V to T is a meaningful step in a relationship, reversed only as a result of falling out. One of Pushkin's poems, often cited in language textbooks, begins: "She accidentally replaced the empty Vy with warm Ty, and thus awoke happy dreams in my loving soul." Peasant usage was different; see below.

Russian forms of address also include several levels of formality. Excluding the honorific *tovarishch* followed by the last name, the most formal in personal conversation or correspondence is full-name+patronymic (NP). If a man's name is Oleg and his father's name is Igor, then he would be addressed or referred to as Oleg Igorevich, the patronymic formed from the father's name with two suffixes -ev/-ov and -ich. Oleg's sister Anna would be Anna Igorevna, with suffixes -ev/-ov and -n- followed by the feminine ending -a.

The ultimate in formality are official documents in which the address or reference starts with the last name followed by NP: Ivanov, Oleg Igorevich. The NP in this context would often be reduced to initials: Ivanov, O. I. This is a common form on envelopes when indicating the addressee or the sender.

The next level down the formality ladder is full first name: Anna, Varvara, Ivan, Mikhail. Since the collapse of the Soviet Union and the demise of name+patronymic (too many words), this has become a common form of address between those who are not close enough to use the nickname (NN). For almost every Russian name there is a corresponding nickname or two, such as Petia (Pete) or Misha (Mike) for men; Ania (Annie) or Varia (Barb) for women. This is not very different from the situation in English but Russian adds another level of informality by its assortment of affectionate diminutive suffixes. (Imagine the sequence *Robert-Bob-Bobby*, but generalized to all names, with a couple of possible suffixes for each.) Most of those suffixes indicate closeness and endearment but some add a touch of coarseness. Starting with Misha one could produce Mish-en'k-a or Mish-ul'-a or Mish-unchik, all meaning something like Misha-my-dear; or alternatively Mish-k-a (Mike, with a touch of familiar rudeness). The same kinds of suffixes can be added to names of family relations. Thus брат (brother) can become брат-ик, брат-ок, брат-ишк-а, брат-ель-ник.

In translations and commentaries of this chapter, when talking about pronouns and forms of address, the following abbreviations are used: the capital T and V indicate the pronoun; NP = Name+Patronymic; LN and FN are Last Name and (full) First Name; NN = nickname; NN+ = nickname with added suffixes; Rel+ = name of relation with added suffixes.

The combination of the two pronouns and multiple levels of formality in addressing creates a fairly nuanced system that has changed over time but at any time also varied across the social class of the speakers.[4] Common to the educated classes was the principle that the choice of pronoun and form of address depended on the relationship and remained largely stable across contexts and situations. The only variability was between NN and NN+: the suffixed form could be used to indicate emotion. Peasant usage was different, as illustrated by this example from a nineteenth century letter from father to son (Yokoyama 2008, vol. 1:27–28). The translation of the example is mine. It is more awkward than Yokoyama's (2008, vol. 2) in that it reflects the word order of the original more closely. It does not try to render irregularities in spelling, capitalization, word division, punctuation, and syntax. The point of the example is to show the traditional letter opening and the use of pronouns and forms of address.

**Example 3.4 Yokoyama. Father to son, beginning. Yokoyama 2008, vol. 1:418–421**

Сѣло Паздеры,
    Любезный Сын Алѣксей Лаврович!
    Письмо Ваше получилъ и деньги 25р. Благодарю Васъ. Исписьма вашего видно что Вася приехалъ въ тюмень. Я думаю Чтобы онъ Тебе непомешалъ окоторомъ вы думайте делѣ - Снимъ Много Неговорите. Я Постараюсь дедушка Свозить Городъ Сарапулъ а Метрическое Свидетельство пошлемъ.
    Алешинька денегъ намъ нужно лесничий унасъ былъ и говоритъ Кромѣ васъ не одамъ некому луга. [ . . . ]

*Translation*

The Village of Pazdery,
    Dear Son Aleksei Lavrovich [NP]!
    I have received Your [V] letter and the money, 25 rubles. Thank You [V]. From your [V] letter I can see that Vasia [NN] joined you in Tyumen'. I'm concerned lest he hinder you [T]; about the business you [V] have in mind don't talk [V] to him. I will do my best to take grandpa to the city of Sarapul, and we will send the Registry Certificate.
    Aleshin'ka [NN+] we need money. The ranger stopped by and said Other than you [V, or possibly plural] I won't give the meadow to anybody. [ . . . ]

*Comment*

In the opening, the father addresses the son by NP and the V pronoun. In line 2, when giving advice, he momentarily switches to T, then back to V in discussing the son's business. A sentence later, when asking for money, he switches not one but two steps down the formality ladder using NN+. In other words, the pronoun and the formality of address vary with context, and both are at their most formal in the formulaic opening.[5]

Fast forward almost sixty years to 1939, through three revolutions, two major wars, two famines, systematic state violence against the peasants, and a major educational effort. Here, the wife is writing to her husband. This letter is considerably more literate than 3.1: the spelling is mostly correct and almost all punctuation and capitalization are in place. All the more striking, then, is the traditional opening and the evolving use of pronouns and forms of address, reflecting the emotional evolution of the letter. The example is divided into annotated sections but only the last division before Section 4 corresponds to a paragraph break in the original.

All examples from Zenzinov are cited with the letter number and the page number in the book. This is further explained in Section 3.3.

## Example 3.5 #2, p.284. Wife to husband

### 3.5.1 Formal Opening, Report on Correspondence

Во первых строках моего письма посылаю привет дорогому супругу Алексею Алексеевичу еще кланяется вам сын Ким Ал. Милый Леня, я ваше письмо получила, за которое очень благодарю. Леня, я уже вам посылала 2 письма и от вас тоже 2 получила и 100 р. денег получила.

### Translation

In the first lines of my letter I am sending greetings to my dear spouse Aleksei Alekseevich [NP], your son Kim Al[ekseevich] [NP] also sends regards to you [V]. Dearest Lenia, I have received your [V] letter for which I am grateful. Lenia, I already sent you [V] 2 letters and from you [V] also received 2 and also received 100 rubles.

### Comment

A very formal beginning with traditional formulas ("In the first lines of my letter [ . . . ]). Even the little boy is referred to by name and patronymic. Ironically, the boy's name is a new-fangled Soviet one, an acronym for "Communist Youth International." After the opening, both the address and the reference to the boy change to NN.

The opening contains a formulaic grateful acknowledgement of a recent letter. In Russian the relative pronoun is separated from the noun it refers to (the letter); the word order is "Your letter I received, for which [ . . . ]." This is a very common formula that occurs also in Yokoyama and in many letters of our corpus. Sometimes there is more material between the noun and the relative pronoun, e.g., письмо я от тебя получил 21-го ноября, за которую очень[6] тебя благодарю. (literally: "letter I from you received 21st November, for which I am very grateful," #47). In the rest of the paper, to indicate the presence of this old-fashioned formula, I translate it as "I received your letter, *for which letter* I am very grateful."

### 3.5.2 Report on Circumstances

Леня, Кима [NN] учится ничего, но только сильно балует ничего меня не слушается. Леня, я на работу только еще поступила С 1 числа пойду работать. Леня дровами плохо. Дров я не купила, бьюся коекак. Милый Леня, я очень скучаю, и все мне сны снятся плохие. Кима тоже скучает нет, нет да и заревет.

*Translation*

Lenia, Kima is OK at school, but very naughty, disobeys me all the time. Lenia, I've just found work, will start on the first. Lenia, with firewood it's very bad. I didn't buy firewood, getting by somehow. Dearest Lenia, I'm very sad, and have bad dreams all the time. Kima is also sad, every now and then bursts out crying.

*Comment*

Typically for a letter, the opening is followed by a report on circumstances at home. Typically for a *peasant woman* letter, almost every sentence starts with a nickname address, which make is sound like a lamentation, but also serves as a connecting paratactic device that propels the narrative forward. This particular writer, with unconscious skill, moves the narrative from external to internal condition: the naughty boy turns out to have complex inner life; the woman who had just found work has bad dreams. At this point of breakdown, in the next subsection, she switches to T. She also starts the pattern, common in peasant letters, of quoting the husband's questions and answering them.

The Russian verb скучать, translated as "be sad" in this passage requires a comment. In literary Russian it means "to be bored," and the matching noun скука is "boredom," but they are never used in that meaning in the peasant language. (Obviously little Kim does not burst into tears because he is bored.) In literary Russian, if there is a prepositional complement, as in Она скучает по мужу (She misses her husband), the verb means "to miss somebody," but this is a secondary meaning. It is the only one in peasant letters. A letter that says: "Я работаю и никуда не хожу кроме работы, в общем скука страшная." (I work and don't go anywhere except to work--in a word, terrible boredom. #189) immediately identifies itself as a non-peasant letter.

Also in this section is a sentence quoted early in Chapter 1 that shows the exclusively peasant use of the Instrumental case without a preposition: "Леня, дровами плохо" (with firewood it's bad).

### 3.5.3 Answers to Questions

Леня, ты пишешь, какие имеются у нас продукты. Продуктов у нас нет никаких. Леня твой год брали, и все уже пришли обратно. Леня, ты пишешь, как мы правим домом. домом правим плохо, хоть уходи на квартиру. Леня, где твои вещи? Почему ты мне не напишешь? Леня, я посылаю тебе 2 карточки. Смотри на свою жену и не забывай. Милый Леня, неужели мы с вами не увидимся.

*Translation*

Lenya, you [T] write what food do we have. We don't have any food. Lenia, those of your [T] year who were drafted all came home already. Lenia, you [T] write, how do we manage the house, the house we manage very poorly, I'm thinking of moving to a rental room. Lenia, where are your [T] things? Why don't you [T] write to me? Lenia, I'm sending you [T] two photos. Look [T] at your wife and don't forget [T]. Dearest Lenia, is it possible that you [V] and I will never see each other again.

*Comment*

This section uses the T pronoun until the last sentence, which is a common trope, and probably for that reason uses V. It is structured as a sequence of quoted questions and answers to them, a common device. The sequence is interrupted in the middle by a sudden outburst: your year's draftees are all back! The syntax of this sentence stands out as very colloquial; it will reappear in the discussion of grammar.

### 3.5.4 Closing and Final Request

Леня больше писать нечего. До свидания. Целую вас [V] 1 000 раз вместе с Кимой. Леня, пришли [T] мне справку на получение денег на Киму.

*Translation*

Lenia, there's nothing more to write. Good bye. I kiss You (V) 1000 times and Kima also. Lenia, send (T) me a document for receiving money for Kima.

*Comment*

There is a formulaic "1000 kisses" sentence that uses V, and a brief matter-of-fact request to send a document for child support that uses T.

There are several unexplained details in this letter: Where is the husband? Why is she asking about his things? What is the document she needs? Why would they never see each other again? Most importantly for our purposes, how do we know that she is a peasant woman and this is a "peasant letter"? In order to answer these questions, we need historical background and a better understanding of what it meant to be a peasant in the Soviet Union in the late 1930s.

## 3.4 THE SOURCE AND THE HISTORICAL BACKGROUND

The letter in 3.5 comes from a book published in New York in 1944 by Vladimir Mikhailovich Zenzinov. Zenzinov sent the book to his friends, including the writer Vladimir Nabokov. Nabokov wrote back:

> I read [your book] from cover to cover and appreciated the enormous labor and the enormous love you put into it. Gloomy and poor and intolerably happy is the Russia reflected in these pathetic scrawlings, and as you quite rightly remark, nothing, nothing has changed--the same soldiers going mad from the same hunger and grief as five hundred years ago, and the same oppression and the same bare-bellied children in the mud, in the dark. For their sake alone all these vile "leaders of the people" [ . . . ] should be destroyed forever. I consider this the most valuable book about Russia of all those that have appeared during these twenty-five despicable years. (Quoted from Boyd 1991:84 and fn. 22)

Zenzinov's life story deserves a brief digression. He was born in 1880 to a wealthy Old-Believer merchant family in Moscow. After graduating from a classical gymnasium he spent four and a half years in elite German universities, (Berlin, Heidelberg) studying law and economics. With all this education, he could not think of anything better to do than join the SR party in 1903, rapidly rising through the ranks. In the course of just one year, 1905, he organized a terrorist act, was arrested, got exiled to Arkhangelsk, immediately escaped to Europe, and then secretly returned to Russia, where, at the age of 25, he became a member of the SR central committee. In 1906, arrested again, he was exiled to Yakutsk, deep in Siberia, and escaped again. Pretending to be a gold-digger, he traveled 1000 miles to the Pacific port of Okhotsk, from where, via Japan, Singapore, and the Suez Canal, he returned to Europe. His next exile, in 1910, was even deeper into Siberia: Russkoye Ustye (the Russian Delta), 50 miles from where the river Indigirka empties into the Arctic Ocean. There was no escape from Russkoye Ustye, and Zenzinov stayed there long enough to write two ethnographic books, Zenzinov 1914, 1916. The books received good reviews; he was still in his early 30s.

In 1914 he returned to European Russia. After the February 1917 Revolution he was again elected to the SR central committee, as well as to the

Petrograd Soviet and the Constituent Assembly, whose purpose was to write a constitution for the new democratic Russia. It was disbanded by the Bolsheviks after they came to power. In 1918, after a year of fighting Bolsheviks, Zenzinov left Russia for his final exile. History did not leave his alone: he lived in Berlin until 1933, in Paris until 1939, and on the Upper West Side of Manhattan until his death in 1953. But he did not come to the US directly from Paris. In 1939, still in Europe, he went to Finland as a newspaper correspondent to report on the Soviet-Finnish war. He came back with about 500 pieces of mail that had been found on the frozen corpses of Soviet soldiers.[7] Very few of them had envelopes; most were just pieces of paper ingeniously folded or sewn together to serve as their own envelopes. Some of them contained letters or brief notes from more than one family member. Zenzinov's book contains a detailed description and perceptive analysis of the content as well as a meticulous transcription of 276 pieces of mail, an "enormous labor" indeed. In the book they are numbered 1 through 277, with number 149 inexplicably missing. In what follows I refer to letters by their numbers in the book. If a piece of mail has more than one letter or note in it, I add a subscript to differentiate the writers. Example 3.5 examined letter #2. Example 3.7 examines letter #83a.

Zenzinov had a hard time publishing his book. No emigre publisher wanted to touch it because it could offend "Uncle Joe," by then an indispensable ally in WWII. Zenzinov published it on his own modest means, with a copyright page declaring: "Copying and translating permitted." The originals of some of the letters are preserved in Columbia University's Bakhmeteff archive. I compared several of them with Zenzinov's transcriptions and did not find a single mistake.

The book did not have a happy fate. There were several reviews in the 1940s, including one from Karpovich (1946). It was mentioned in some historical studies: Holquist (1997) describes it as "[a] source that has not received the attention it deserves," and Kelly (2002) has two pages of perceptive remarks but no sociological or linguistic analysis. Koznova (2016:148–53) reviewed a number of letters in her analysis of peasant memory, noting very low expectations, complaints, and a mixed tradition of holidays combining "the October" and St. Michael's day. (See Example 3.7.) About 20 letters from the book are included in Ushakin and Golubev (2016), with spelling and punctuation significantly normalized and no linguistic analysis. The book has thus remained unnoticed in linguistic literature, even though it constitutes an outstanding sociolinguistic resource. Usually, surviving war letters are from soldiers writing home. In this case, the disastrous Soviet campaign and the unusually severe winter combined to preserve a great number of letters *from* home, from a diverse group of writers, most of them women. Several other features make them particularly valuable:

- The letters are practically simultaneous, all written between November 1939 and February 1940. They are a snapshot of Soviet society from an unusual group of people, many of whom never wrote letters before or after.
- About half of the letters are from peasants, reflecting the social composition of the troops.
- Virtually all letters are dated, and the return address is provided.
- The recipients are all roughly the same age: young men (and a few women) conscripted into the army.
- Correspondingly, the senders fall into three clearly delineated generations:
  - parents, godparents, uncles and aunts
  - wives, siblings, siblings-in-law, friends, girlfriends
  - children, godchildren, nieces and nephews, much younger siblings
- The educational level of the authors varies greatly, from barely literate to fairly advanced. There are only ten completely literate letters, again reflecting the social composition of the troops.
- With very few exceptions, it can be easily established from the level of literacy and the content of the letter whether it is from a peasant or not. The return address is less helpful because of the massive migration out of the countryside that had recently taken place.
- During the 1930s tens of millions of peasants moved from the countryside to cities and towns to escape the hardship and low social status of peasant life. Some of them received additional education and on-the-job training. Others retained their language unchanged but gradually absorbed some city vocabulary and phraseology. We refer to the authors of such letters as "recent peasants." Recent peasants are well represented in the Corpus.
- The degree of political awareness is as diverse as the level of literacy. While some letters, if one ignores their kolkhoz references, could have been written during WWI, others, especially from schoolchildren, the better educated, and Komsomol members, contain signs of the twentieth century, including a dose of SovYaz.

## Historical Background 1: The Winter War

In order to place the dates of the letters in their precise historical context, here is a quick summary of the events leading up to the Winter War:

- August 23: the Molotov-Ribbentrop (Stalin-Hitler) pact divides the territory between Germany and the Soviet Union into "spheres of interest." The secret addendum included a map.
- September 1: Germany attacks Poland; start of WWII.
- September 17: Soviets enter Poland, start Sovietization (arrests, exiles deep into Russia, new power structures including secret police).

- October: Soviets station troops in the Baltic states of Estonia, Latvia, Lithuania and start Sovietization there. Formal annexation followed in 1940.
- October: Soviets demand pieces of territory from Finland; Finland declines.
- November 26: Soviets stage an artillery barrage directed at Soviet troops, ostensibly from inside Finland. There are casualties: four dead and nine wounded. The episode is repeatedly broadcast on Soviet radio for internal consumption.
- November 30: Soviets invade Finland.

These dates are important to keep in mind: if a soldier wrote a letter on Nov. 20 and it arrived on Dec. 7, the recipient had no way of knowing whether the soldier was involved in the fighting.

The Soviets expected a quick victory and did not even provide adequate winter clothes for the troops. Soviet generalship was very poor. The Finns were well trained, well equipped, and highly motivated. The "Mannerheim line"[8] of defense proved very effective, much more so than the French "Maginot Line" five months later. The war lasted 105 days; in the end, Finns were overwhelmed by superior numbers, but the Soviets lost 150,000 dead, more than the entire Union Army in the entire four years of the American Civil War.

As the letters show, these events were reported selectively by the Soviet media. In the entire corpus, there is not a single mention of the German attack on Poland that started WWII, as if it never happened. There are several letters from fellow soldiers about how they liberated the Ukrainian and Belorussian masses from their Polish oppressors. The "Finnish artillery attack" and the resulting casualties are frequently brought up as a cause of deep concern and, for some, righteous indignation. In #137, a Soviet woman functionary writes: "сволочь финляндия--такая козявка и тоже рыпается куда-то" (that stinker Finland, such a little insect, and trying to resist). This kind of sentiment never shows in peasant letters where the mood is the same mixture of fatalism with a glimmer of hope as in everyday life.

After the start of the war, reports in the media were upbeat but sparse. Letters from the Finnish front traveled slowly, with added time for censors, so the war was already on when the last pre-war letters were reaching their destinations. The wife in #159 is responding to a letter written a week before the war, on Nov. 23; she received it on Dec. 12, by which time thousands of men had been killed--and she lived in Leningrad, less than 50 miles from the frontline. The families thus did not know whether or not their loved ones were involved in the fighting. This is why the woman in 3.5 says: "[ . . . ] is it possible that you and I will never see each other again." The wife in #260 tried to find out:

**Example 3.6 #260, p.540. я ездила узнавать в военкомат**

я Петя ездила узнавать воинкомат что ты жив или нет а мне начальник сказал если будит убит то тебе известят через месяц а сейчас ты небеспокойся

*Translation*

Petia (NN), I traveled [to] the Army office to find out that are you alive or not, and the commander said if he is killed you will be notified in a month, and in the meantime you (T) don't worry.

*Comment*

This short quote pretty much classifies the writer as a peasant by her spelling, her missing preposition, by how she renders the direct speech of the military officer and uses the complementizer что ("that") to introduce a yes-no question ("are you alive or not"). From the rest of the letter we learn that the woman is a "recent peasant" who had just moved to the city and is not sure that the kolkhoz will pay her for the last year of her work there.

The casual cruelty of the military officer is quite typical of interactions between authorities and peasant women.

## Historical Background 2: Social Classes and Peasants among Them

An important feature of the Corpus is that it mostly represents lower classes of the Soviet society of its time, completely out of proportion to their cultural significance and epistolary archives. It is useful to place them in the context of an influential model of social stratification in the USSR of the mid-1960s from Inkeles 1968:151–52. Inkeles starts from the official Soviet model of two classes—workers and peasants—and one "stratum" (intelligentsia), but realistically divides each of the three groups into subgroups, listed below in the same order as in Inkeles (1968) but in a single numbered list rather than three separate sublists.

1. The ruling elite, a small group of high party, government, economic, and military officials, prominent scientists, and selected artists and writers.
2. The superior intelligentsia, composed of the intermediary ranks of the categories mentioned above, plus certain important technical specialists.
3. The general intelligentsia, incorporating most of the professional groups [ . . . ].

4. The white-collar group, largely synonymous with the Soviet term for employees [служащие] which ranges from petty bureaucrats [ ... ] down to the level of ordinary clerks and office workers.
5. The working class "aristocracy," the most highly productive and skilled workers.
6. Rank and file workers, those in one of the lesser skill grades.
7. Disadvantaged workers [ ... ] close to minimum wage level.
8. Well-to-do peasants [ ... ] advantaged by virtue of the location, fertility, or crop raised by their collective farms [ ... ] or those whose trade, skill, or productivity pushes them into the higher income brackets on the less prosperous farms.
9. The average peasant, shading off into the least productive or poor peasant groups.

Levels 1 and 2 are not represented in our corpus at all, and levels 3, 5, and 8 are in single digits.

Level 3, the intelligentsia, is represented by people whose addressees are a military doctor or the conductor of a marching band. Of all the categories, the highly skilled workers of Level 5 are the happy people of the Soviet Union. They write about how they make very good money, buy consumer goods, and are chased by recruiters because their skills are in high demand and short supply. Level 8, the well-to-do peasants, would be tractor drivers or low-level kolkhoz functionaries, like the director of the kolkhoz dairy farm, or a work-team leader (бригадир) as in letter #29, Example 3.14.

The remaining, more numerous groups are white collar (4), workers (6, 7) and peasants (9). They are well-represented in examples, but a few preliminary observations will be useful.

- In the context of the late 1930s, levels 6 and 7 can be grouped together. They are mostly recent migrants from the village, the lower ranks of the working class. Letter #141, Example 3.15, presents a young man operating a mechanical saw, who calls that work "simple but dangerous."
- The gap in literacy between the intelligentsia and white-collar workers is significant. So are the gaps between workers and peasants, and within peasants between men and women.
- Schoolchildren also show a significant gap between those from intelligentsia and peasant families.
- Red Army soldiers writing to their friends on the Finnish front from other parts of the county show a higher level of literacy than writers from other groups, along with clear traces of political education.

The sociolinguistic classification of letters uses some of the same class labels that are used for social classes, with an understanding that a "peasant letter" is not necessarily written by somebody who is currently a peasant. Later in this section I describe the procedure that is used to classify a letter as "peasant."

## The Peasant-Kolkhoznik Condition ca. 1939

The first section of this chapter showed peasants reacting with shock and disbelief to the onslaught of the Bolshevik state. By the mid-1930s, "the self-identification of village dwellers had changed," writes Koznova (2016:146). She quotes from Chugunov (1968): "What kind of a peasant am I? I'm a kolkhoznik, a serf farm-hand." (ibid) Indeed, kolkhozniks were different from peasants. They did not own land. They did not work the same piece of land through the growing season. They did not work with their families but in arbitrary бригады (work teams) that received work assignments every day. They did not own the product of their labor, but instead were paid for it. Worse yet, they were paid in abstract units called labordays, whose relationship to actual days of labor was indirect: work that required more qualifications would receive more labordays per day; members of the administration received a fixed number of labordays per month, higher than for kolkhozniks who did actual work in the field. Furthermore, the remuneration for a laborday (e.g., how much grain) was determined only after all the government quotas were fulfilled and all taxes paid. In other words, government quotas were fixed in absolute terms but the value of a laborday depended on the harvest: whatever was left was divided by the total number of labordays. If there was little or nothing left, then kolkhozniks had to provide for themselves from their little personal plots, which were also taxed. Kolkhozniks were the only Soviet citizens who paid real taxes. Everybody working for state enterprises received monetary wages from which, theoretically, some taxes were deducted, but since these taxes went back to the same state that paid the wages, this was just an abstraction: the state could just as well have reduced the wages and collected no taxes at all. Peasants, by contrast, had to pay the state out of the meager sums they received from the kolkhoz. They also had to pay taxes in kind (meat, eggs, etc.), and contribute a required number of days of free labor each year. (It was not lost on them that these obligations were quite similar to some practices of serfdom.) Unlike state-employed workers, kolkhozniks did not have a trade union--and for all their subservience to the state, Soviet trade unions did serve as a conduit of some social benefits and as a place where one could complain about the local boss.

Example 3.2 mentioned that in 1932 all Soviet citizens except kolkhozniks received internal passports that were required for residency registration and travel. Apart from restrictions on travel, the absence of a passport resulted in multiple other conundrums when dealing with the state. In particular, peasant wives back home often needed a confirmation from the army that their husbands were indeed in the army, in order to receive child support or tax relief. One can imagine how easy it would be for a private to obtain such a document in the middle of intense fighting. The letters showcase the casual cruelty of local authorities who refused to help soldiers' wives who did not have documents, even when they knew perfectly well that the husband had been drafted. These were kolkhoz chairmen, and it was their budgets, which, within flexible limits, they could spend the way they wanted, so there was a clear motivation to withhold subsidies.

## Letters from Basic Peasants, Derived Peasants, and Recent Peasants

We can say that example 3.7, letter #83a, is definitely from a peasant woman because she mentions both the kolkhoz and taxes. I refer to such letters as "basic peasant." There are 71 such letters in the Corpus, about 25%.

Basic peasant letters have many linguistic features in common, some of them also shared with their nineteenth-century antecedents in Yokoyama (2008). This cluster of features forms a "peasant letter profile" that makes it possible to classify some letters as "peasant" even though they do not directly mention the realia of the kolkhoz. I call such letters "derived peasant."[9] The essential empirical fact that justifies this classification is that such "possibly-peasant" letters include a fairly complete cluster of peasant features, and the entire cluster is mostly absent from non-peasant letters. Peasant letter features are summarized in Section 3.8, after most of them are encountered in the examples.

Clusters of peasant features also appear in letters whose return address is in a city, and whose content shows that the sender lives and, if not very old, works there. (There are a few letters from young urban housewives, but they are not peasant women.) This city-based peasant group consists of recent migrants to the city, i.e., "recent peasants." Their presence testifies to the astonishing rate of peasant migration to Soviet cities beginning in 1928. Fitzpatrick (1994:80–81) provides some numbers: "More than two and a half million peasants moved from village to town in 1930, compared with about a million a year in the late 1920s. Four million moved in 1931. [ . . . ] Over the period 1928–1932, the total transfer of population from village to town was in the range of 12 million"; "the number of peasant households in the Soviet Union dropped from 26 million in 1929 to 19 million in 1937." Even at three persons per household, a low estimate, this is over twenty million people.

By the end of the decade, when the Corpus came into existence, the number of migrants was clearly in the tens of millions. Many of them became industrial or construction workers and received some further education, which resulted in improved letter-writing skills. But a great number ended up in low-level menial jobs that had no impact on their literacy or writing habits. The same recursive procedure we used earlier can be applied to their writing as well: if a letter shows a preponderance of peasant-letter features, with perhaps a small admixture of city vocabulary and everyday detail, then it is a "recent-peasant" letter, rather than simply a "derived peasant" letter or a "worker letter." The linguistic practices of recent peasants show the penetration of new vocabulary and phraseology into peasant language and the formation of the *prostorechie* (SimpleTalk), briefly introduced in Chapter 1 and discussed in greater depth in Chapter 4. If a recent peasant is a Red Army soldier, then the influence of Soviet clichés is common. The Corpus contains several examples of partial urbanization and Sovietization of peasant language.[10] Chapter 4 has an extended discussion of how basic peasants and by-then-not-very-recent peasants would diverge in their language by the 1990s.

A peasant could become a recent peasant without even leaving the kolkhoz by "getting a job" there, like accountant or librarian. This is probably the destination of the literate woman of 3.5. A job implies regular hours and monetary wages or a fixed number of labordays per month. Kolkhozniks did not have "jobs," they just worked every day doing what the foreman would tell them to do, and receiving the number of labordays determined by the foreman.

## 3.5 EXAMPLES OF LETTERS 1: THREE GENERATIONS

The characters in this section are: a soldier's wife (3.7); her much younger sister, a schoolgirl (3.8); and an old but still vigorous father (3.9). They represent three different levels of literacy. I have graded the letters for literacy on the levels from 0 to 4. On that scale, 3.5 is level 3, near the top, while 3.7 is level 0. After the opening sentence and the capitalized first word of the second, it consists of an undifferentiated flow of words, with no punctuation, capitalization, or paragraph breaks. Word divisions are erratic, and most words show illiterate phonetic spelling. There are many dialectal words. The letter has to be spoken in order to reconstruct its syntax. However, as a discourse it does divide into recognizable parts similar to those in 3.5. They are presented as annotated sections below. The translation makes no attempt to convey the orthography of the original but for illustrative purposes all orthographic errors are noted in the Russian original of Section 3.7.3.

### Example 3.7 #83a, pp.366–67. "basic peasant"

*3.7.1 Opening*

Письмо от известной вашей супруги Колесниковай А. Н. Пишу свому дорогому коли впервых страках моево письма я стараюс передат свой ниский сирдечный привет дорогому свому коли коля ище тебе ниско кланиза сынок виктор Николаивич свому дорогому папи

*Translation*

This letter from your (V) known spouse, Kolesnikova A. N. I'm writing to my dear Kolia. In the first lines of my letter I am trying to convey my humble warm-hearted regards to my dear Kolia. Kolia, also a humble bow to you (T) from your little son Viktor Nikolaevich (NP) to his dear papa.

*Comment*

The opening is formulaic: the (V) pronoun in the first sentence, very formal reference to herself, old-fashioned adjectives modifying the "bow," the NP reference to the little boy. The word "spouse" is very formal in Russian; the phrase "your known spouse" (or "parent," or "sister") is a frequent formula in traditional openings. All these stand in contrast to extremely poor orthography: almost every word is misspelled.

The woman's name is Aleksandra, the nickname is Shura, mentioned later in the letter.

*3.7.2 Report of Circumstances*

дорогой мой коля теперя я тебя прописвою свою жизнь коля моя жизня ниважная и сказат савсем плохая коля живеш так от горя некуда деца и вопче унас жизня очен плохая и хужай быт некуда коля а твоя жизня ище хужай моей коля писмо я твою получила и кричу кажный день и так об табе думаю дорогой мой коля дажно я тебя болшай нюсвижу коля ты ба мне хут ба прислал карточку я ба на тебя поглядела ато дабре скучилас потабе и дюжа дюжа скучилас

*Translation*

My dear Kolia, now I am describing my life. Kolia, my life is not so good, and, to tell you, very bad. Kolia, the way life goes you can't find a place to hide from grief, and in general our life is very bad, can't be worse, Kolia, but your life is even worse than mine. Kolia, I received your letter, and I'm crying every day, and that's what I'm thinking about you, my dear Kolia, that I will probably never see you again. Kolia, I wish you would at least send me a photo, so I could look at you, for I very miss you, and very very miss you.

*Comment*

As in 3.5 but even more so in this letter, almost every sentence starts with the nickname, Kolia. In the 276 words of the letter it repeats 27 times. Otherwise, this section says: our life is bad and can't be worse, but your life is even worse, and I miss you very much. As in 3.5, the verb for "miss somebody" is a form of the verb denoting boredom in literary Russian.

### 3.7.3 About the Kolkhoz and Economic Conditions

*To indicate the quality of writing, in this section I annotate all errors: Sp - Spelling; WD - Word Division; Pn - Missing punctuation; Cap - Missing capitalization; Gr - Grammar*

коля [Cap, Pn] налоги накладают [Sp] очен [Sp] болшыя [Sp] коля [Cap, Pn] но смине [Sp, WD] ниспрашивают [Sp, WD] ничаво [Sp] коля [Cap] вколхози [Sp, WD] унас ничаво [Sp] нидали [Sp, WD] коля [Cap, Pn] я тебя прошу [Pn] как нимога [Sp, WD] пришли ты мне свои пинжак [Sp] ато [WD] мне насит [Sp] нечева [Sp] палто [Sp] моя [Gr] стала вся худая коля [Cap] свалинки я себе подшыла [Sp] отдала 10 рублей

### Translation

Kolia, the taxes were imposed very heavy, Kolia, but from me they are not asking anything. Kolia, in the kolkhoz they did not give us anything. Kolia, I'm asking you, any way you can, send me your jacket, for I have nothing to wear, my coat is full of holes. Kolia, I had felt boots made for me, paid 10 rubles.

### Comment

Shura specifically mentions taxes. Peasants learned late in the fall what the taxes would be. In the fall of 1939 taxes were raised sharply, but Shura was spared because her husband was in the military. She also says that the income from labordays has so far been zero, and it is not clear whether anything would materialize later. She then asks to send back home the civilian jacket that Kolia was wearing when he was drafted. For the family back home, a jacket (пинжак) or a pair of shoes would be a source of invaluable protection from wet and cold. Cf. in 3.5: "where are your things? Why don't you write to me?" It's not that he did not write, but he had not yet told her where his things were. Sometimes the wife and the husband's family would fight over those clothes.

### 3.7.4 Family News

коля папа работает в горочевки мама отдохнула дорогой мой коля была я сынком унаших у празника умихалова дня начавала уних три ночи ани мине привичают коля почему ты мне так ретка шлеш письмы коля жду я жду и никак я от вас нидаждуся писмо

*Translation*

Kolia, papa works in Gorochevka. Mama rested. My dear Kolia, I went with our little son to family on the holiday on St. Michael's day, spent three nights with them, they are welcoming to me. Kolia, why do you (T) send letters so rarely, I am waiting and waiting and still are not getting a letter from you (V).

*Comment*

It was possible for a member of a kolkhoz household to have an outside job that would bring in some reliable wages. The next example, # 83b from Shura's younger sister, provides more detail about the parents and explains the somewhat cryptic "mama rested"—rested from what?

The "family" in the next sentence must mean "the husband's family." In a number of letters, wives complain about their in-laws, so the welcoming was very much worth noting.

St. Michael's day is celebrated in the Russian Orthodox church on Nov. 8 in the Julian calendar (November 21 in the Gregorian). Since many letters were written in late November-early December, St. Michael's is often mentioned, sometimes together with Revolution Day, also in November.

*3.7.5 Q&A and Closing*

коля ты мне пишыш шура что народу многа увас взяли коля народу унас взяли пока мала коля ванка взяли тожа вармию коля ты мне пишыш шура низабут миня коля тогда я тебя забуду когда мои гласки закроюца коля ты мне пишыш пришли мне митрошкин адрес коля яба табе прислала он уже 3 месеца ниприсылал писмы. коля болшай писат пока нечева остоюс жыва здорова и тово тебя жалаю.

*Translation*

Kolia, you're writing to me so Shura, have many been taken (drafted)? Kolia, so far few have been taken. Kolia, Vanek also has been taken to the army. Kolia you're writing to me Shura don't forget me. Kolia, I will then forget you when my eyes close. Kolia, you're writing to me send me Mitroshka's address. Kolia, I would send it to you [but] he for three months has not been sending letters. Kolia there's nothing more to write for now, I remain alive and well and wish you same.

*Comment*

This section exhibits the very common peasant-letter feature of switching between narrative and direct speech without any orthographic devices (not a single peasant letter uses quotation marks). Recall Shpil'rein's quote in the Introduction about "unspoiled peasant language that is characterized by short sentences, liveliness, and abrupt transitions from reported to direct speech and back." Yokoyama (2008, vol. 1:415) notes that narrative-direct speech switching happens even in the presence of the conjunction что ("that") that would normally introduce reported speech. Her examples are very similar to this one from #17 in the Corpus, written by a woman: "Я получила от брата николая письмо 29го октя он пишет что меня взяли в армию 6го нояб. отправка" (I received a letter from my brother nikolai 29 octo he writes that I was drafted in the army 6th nov departure). It was, of course, the brother who was drafted.

The letter from Shura is followed on the same piece of paper by a brief note from Shura's younger sister Lidiia. Zenzinov's comment says that she has a schoolgirl's handwriting.

**Example 3.8 #83b**

Пущина письмо 25 ноября 139 го [sic!] Коля как твоя Служба. Пропишу я вам сапчаю Витюшка стаит адин зовет няня и дядя. я сижу с витий хорошо. Коля учусь я хорошо. Мама радила девучку мертваю сама асталась жива Витёк балел насил оддахнул. Папака работает Враяно палучая 250 рубль. Коля Пришлы мне овет. писала Прокошина лидия Порфиривна.

*Translation*

Letter sent 25 November 1[9]39. Kolia, how is your service. I'm writing to you (V) informing [that] Vitiushka (NN+) stands by himself, calls nanny and uncle. I stay with vitia (NN) well. Kolia, I do well at school. Mama gave birth to a dead girl but herself survived Vitiok (NN+) was ill barely recovered [literally "rested"—AN]. Papa works in the district education office receiving 250 ruble [Sic!-Singular]. Kolia, send me a response. Written by Prokoshina Lidiia Porfir'evna.

*Comment*

Lidiia is more literate than her older sister but is still very far from real literacy, even though she "does well at school." Like most peasants, she uses the noun письмо (letter) as a Feminine. Her note is all about the family. The little boy Vitia (Vitiushka, Vitiok) is making progress: he can stand up and call his nanny. He was seriously ill and barely recovered. In literary language the verb she uses for "recover" means "to rest," and this explains the cryptic sentence in Shura's letter: "Mama rested," which refers to the stillbirth that Lidiia describes. It seems that in this family there are no words either for boredom or actual rest.

The examples so far have been from the younger generations: a school girl (3.8) and two young women, one a basic peasant (3.7), the other a derived/recent peasant (3.5). For generation and gender balance, the last example of this section is from the father, with many greetings and a detailed discussion of his family's economic condition. The letter is to the son whose wife Fima lives in the town of Umba and sends help to the peasant branch of the family.

The letter forms one uninterrupted paragraph. It is broken into sections for ease of annotating. Its orthography is better than in 3.7—there are capital letters mostly in the right places—but spelling, word division, and punctuation are weak. The spelling of the phrase "departure from Umba" could be rendered as "de parture Fromumba."

One significant difference between 3.9 and women's letters is in the use of the nickname, Misha. The father uses it structurally, to indicate what in a literate letter would be paragraph breaks.

## Example 3.9 #36, pp.318–19. From father and family, village of Turchasovo, Arkhangelsk province

3.9.1

Добрый день Здравствуй Дорогой сын Михаил Дмитриев Отец ваш Дмитрей Андреевич и сестрицы Маруся и Валя Шлем вам свой сердечный Привет и Жаем вам всего хорошаго службе вашеи главное здоровья первои строкои сего письма спешим сообщит что посланое вами Письмо имели удовольствие получит и Письма видим что находитес нафинской границе [ . . . ]

*Translation*

Good afternoon, greetings dear son Mikhail Dmitriev (NP). Your (V) father Dmitrei Andreevich (NP) and sisters Marusia and Valia send you our warm regards and wish you (V) all the best in your service, health the main thing. With the first line of this letter we hasten to inform the letter sent by you we had the pleasure of receiving, and from the letter we see that you are located on the Finnish border. [ . . . ]

*Comment*

Although the orthography is weak, the wording is full of old-fashioned, imperial-time letter writing clichés: "hasten to inform," "had the pleasure of receiving." The pronoun is the formal V throughout.

### 3.9.2

Миша После вашего от езду Сумбы Мы получили денег от Фимы (100 руб) и посылку 70 руб. Она послала мне нарубашку сатину Мани материе Нажакетку Вали наплатье и двой чулки и 2е осминки чаю и Сахару килограму два. Заето Миша вам болшое спасибо, что незабывайте Нас

Миша Вы Пишите Ходательству насчет натогов унас уплачены страховые все и сельско хозяйственные все только неуплочено 14т килограмов Мяса 39 год. [ . . . ] Сечас налог сельско хозяйственый поновому закону скот облагаице весь и земля усадебная чем засеено беретче. всего я вам неупоминаю унас скота нету налог 50 руб. Страховыя 46 р. мясного 27 килограм и картофеля 154 килограмм самообложение 20 руб.

*Translation*

Misha, after your departure from Umba we received money from Fima (100 rub) and a parcel 70 rub. She sent me sateen for a shirt, cloth to Mania for a jacket, and to Valia for a dress, two stockings; a quarter pound of tea and about 2 kilos of sugar. For this, Misha, many thanks to you that you don't forget us.

Misha, write a petition about taxes. We have paid all insurance and all agricultural taxes except 14 kilos of meat for 1939. [ . . . ] Now the agricultural tax—there is a new law all cattle is taxed, and all that is planted on the personal plot some part is taken. I'm not listing everything, we have no cattle, the tax is 50 rub., insurance 46 r., meat 27 kilos and potatoes 154 kilos; self-taxation 20 rub.

*Comment*

The parcel contains the typical items unobtainable in the village: tea and sugar; fabrics; stockings. Other letters mention soap, nails, and tobacco. These are the same items that are listed as unobtainable or very expensive (the "price scissors" of Chapter 2).

Taxes were both in money and in kind (meat and potatoes in this letter). Self-taxation was a kind of local tax that the kolkhoz itself imposed on its members, to support the school, or road and bridge repair. The state, of course, interfered heavily, setting quotas and regulations.

In terms of discourse organization, the father uses the NN address Misha more sparingly than the women authors of 3.5 and 3.7, inserting it precisely at the logical paragraph breaks. Within the "paragraphs" the text flows in the same linear paratactic fashion as in the earlier examples.

### 3.9.3

Миша я скажу вам что нужно ходательствават от вашего начальства месное начальство неповерит что взяты красную армию хотя поверит нужно справка которое время вы поступили Красную Армию как ето вышлите и на пособие тоже я тогда могу ходатойствоват сейчас без нечего ходатойстват безполезно это надо делать неупуская времени Обяснит начальству вашему какое семейство хозяйства оно Больше знает законы [ . . . ]

*Translation*

Misha I would say to you (V) that you should petition your superiors; our superiors will not believe that you were drafted in the Red Army; and even if they do, we need a document about when you entered the Red Army. When you send this, and with respect to subsidies also, I can then petition; now, without anything, it's useless to petition. This must be done without delay. Explain to your superiors what is the family of the household, they know the laws better.

3.9.4

Миша мы живем постарому хотя неочень хорошо несовсем плохо Валя ходит школу учеце пока хороша первую четверет отметки поведение отлично впридметам хорошо плохо и посредственно нету аперет незнаю что будет сней маня коцила работу напочте 1 ноября уже был вербовщик гнал в лес назначена сельсоветом я ответил что незаконо назначат напроизвоство нету 18 лет напроизвоство принимаю от 18 лет погода стоит теплая снег выпагает и сходит [ . . . ] Миша бут осторожне Вином неупивайсе Это время нужно пережить наеам кончаю писать новостей особеных нету если возможно письма пишите чаще ждем ответа. Сприветом семейство Глебовых. 19/XI 39

*Translation*

Misha, we live as before, although not very good but not completely bad. Valia goes to school, studies well so far, in the first quarter her grades are: behavior excellent, in subjects good, no poors or fairs, and in the future I don't know what will be with her. Mania finished her work at the post office on Nov. 1, the recruiter already stopped by, tried to send her to the forest as appointed by the village Soviet. I said that against the law appoint her to duties like this, not 18 yet. The weather keeps warm, snow falls and melts away. [ . . . ]

Misha, be (T) careful, don't overdrink (T) vodka. We have to get through this time. With this I finish my letter, there aren't any special news. If possible write (V) more often, we're waiting for a reply. With greetings, the Glebov family. 11/19/39.

## Comment

The attitude of "not very good but not completely bad" is very common in peasant letters. "Life is good" can be found only in young men who are out of the village—industrial workers or Red Army soldiers.

Mania of this paragraph is the same sister that was referred to as Marusia in the very beginning, both NNs for Mariia. It seems that Mania is 17, finished high school, and worked at the post office. The kolkhoz is trying to send her to do logging in the forest, the most dangerous of kolkhozniks' responsibilities.

In the last paragraph of the letter, when dispensing parental advice, the father briefly switches to the T pronoun. The advice is not to drink too much. He uses the word вино that means "wine" in the literary language but "vodka" among the peasants.

This father of three is strong enough to stand up to the village Soviet and protect his daughter. In the next section, two very old people come to terms with the approaching end of their lives.

## 3.6 EXAMPLES OF LETTERS 2: OLD PEOPLE

### The Old Man

The author of #227 is a truly old man. His letter is marginally more literate than Example 3.7 but not nearly as literate as 3.5. He does use some fairly sophisticated vocabulary, even if misspelled: в настоящое время (at the present time); визически (physically, manually); существать (exist). The last verb drops the -ова- suffix of the literary form, conforming to item 4 in the peasant profile of Chapter 1.

The man lives alone in a small village. His two daughters, Nastia and Liuba, are both schoolteachers who moved away to larger villages that have schools. His wife lives with one of them, Liuba. The letter starts and ends with an explanation of how difficult it is for him to go see them.

The letter forms a single paragraph of text with only the last concluding line separated from it. I present the original as is but divide the translation and comments into two parts.

### Example 3.10 #227, p.511

Здорово мой дорогой сынок Коля сопщаю о себе живу пока благополучно. от мами и люби и насти писма получаю часто меня просят чтобы я кним приехал хотя наодну неделю после перевыборов. Надо уних побывать.

придеца нанять лошать А немене нужно платить денег 50 руб взат
иперот Аденьги я уже потратил которые вы мне посылали. я тебе
писал 2 писма поетому Адресу где находитись в настоящое время. Коля
я скучаю овас непришлось тебе побывать дома т/е вотпуск. Мне силно
хотелось повидать тебя. но что поделаш. нужно все переживать А я
уже силно постарел волоси стали совсем белые. И плохо вижу. только
могу видеть усебя под носом. А наволе рядом не могу узнать человека.
конечно дело неважно ночто поделаш надо доживать какнибут досм
Коля тебе в тех писмах все описывал как живут в колхозах живут
неважно хлебы были плохие гот бил сырои. я сам себя обработать
невсилах А существать надо маме тоже хочеца жить в своем доме А
работать визически тоже неможет время бы ей наодых. дети у нас
теперь выучены работают учительницами могут обеспечит отца имать
я справил двой валенки себе и любе. насте послал свинини 7 килограм
маме и любе тоже нужно послать. или может побываю сам хотя
ненадолго тока незнаю как попаст силно далеко 80 киломтров нужно
ехать налошаде ивсе требуюци деньги пока досвиданья дорагои сынок
коля спривет к тебе твой папа 30 ноября
        пиши ответ буду ждат

*Translation Part 1*

Hello my dear son (Rel+) Kolia I inform about myself I live so far OK. From mama and Liuba and Nastia I receive letters often They ask me that I come visit at least for a week after the reelection.[11] I should visit them. I'll have to rent a horse. But this will cost money at least 50 rubles there and back. But I already spent the money that you (V) sent me. I wrote to you (T) 2 letters to that address where you are located at the present time. Kolia I miss you (V). It didn't work out for you (T) to visit home, i.e., on leave. I very much wanted to see you (T) but what can you do. One has to carry on through everything. But I got quite old, my hair became completely white. I see poorly, I can only see what's under my nose. And when outside I cannot recognize people. Of course, things are not good but what can you do I have to somehow make it through till death.

*Comment*

The old man lives alone. His wife and two daughters live in a bigger village, but the only way to get there is to hire a horse-drawn cart. He is trapped. (It may not be an accidental word choice when to express the meaning "outside the house" he says на воле, which usually means "out of prison or labor camp.") The sentence что поделаешь (what can you do) repeats twice. The last sentence says: I have to somehow get through the remaining living till death. The Russian text is more paradoxical, it literally says: I have to somehow live long enough to get to death. The last phrase is not spelled out completely, he wrote the equivalent of "till dth."

In practical terms, the old man's problem is: how do you live the last years a long life in a world without pensions or health care? If this problem persists over many generations, and is shared by many people at any given time, a cultural attitude of fatalistic endurance is likely to develop. A hint at this attitude is in one of the most striking sayings by the peasant Platon Karataev in *War and Peace* (vol. 4, ch. 14): На болезнь плакаться--Бог смерти не даст (Complain too much about illness—God will not give you death.) Outside literature, Bogoraz (1924a:11) reports a complaint from an old village witch: "худо мне--умереть не могу. Никто моей силы не принимает." (On p.16 Bogoraz notes that sorcerers and witches were common in Russian villages, even though they were persecuted by both religious and secular authorities.)

In the case of Russian peasants, the problem and the attitude clearly persisted into the late 1930s. In #257, pp.537–38, it is expressed with a touch of bitter irony by an overworked middle-aged woman: "очень устаю хожу почти каждодневно в город, туда молоко, а оттуда хлеб, зато помирать будешь жалеть не будеш жизни" (I get very tired, go to the city almost every day, take milk, bring bread, the good thing is you won't feel sorry when it comes to dying.)[12]

*Translation Part 2*

Kolia in those letters I described to you (T) how life is in kolkhozes. Life is not very good. The grain harvest was bad, the year had been wet. I don't have the strength to provide for myself. But we have to exist, mama also would like to live in her own house. But she cannot do physical work either, it's time for her to retire. Our children are now educated, work as schoolteachers, can provide for father and mother. I made two pairs of felt boots, for myself and Liuba. To Nastia I sent 7 kilogram of pork. I should send some to mama and Liuba, or perhaps I'll visit them even if briefly but I don't know how to get there, 80 kilometers to go by horse cart, and everything takes money. So long, good by my dear son (Rel+) Kolia, with regards to you (T) your (T) papa. 30 November.

Write back I will wait.

*Comment*

Throughout the letter, the use of pronouns clearly follows the content and emotional context. When he says "I miss you" it is, of course, T; when he says "the money you sent me," it is V. When he says "my dear son," he uses the endearing Rel+ form сынок that is common in addressing children.

## The Old Woman

The next letter is from an old mother. It is one of the shortest letters in the Corpus but carries a lot of content in its few words. The old mother lives in a big city, probably with one of her children. The letter forms a single paragraph of text with almost no punctuation or capitalization, but, as in 3.7, the text is divided at logical paragraph breaks by a NN address, Pavlusha or Pasha (for Pavel). The original is presented as is, the translation is divided into sections by paragraph breaks. The sections are familiar: greetings and acknowledgement of the last letter; discussion of correspondence; about myself; good bye.

### Example 3.11 #12a, p.295

Добрый ден дарагой Павлуша мы твое получили письмо 29 ноября все может быт все будит все хорошо мы знаем что у вас делается порадиво паша мы получили твой карточки закатораи очен даволны мы много получили письмы и мы много посылали тебе письмы и денеги посылали а ты ничево нам ни пишеш что получил или нет. ни ужели ни доходют до тебе наше письма паша осебе я пишу я жыву ты знаеш как ты видил и так и сечас может тебе дождся тебе и моя жызн будит другая ничево буду тебе ждат если тебе нибудет то и мене нибудит до свидание тебе целую остаеся твоя мат

*Translation*

Good afternoon, dear Pavlusha. We received your letter 29 November. All maybe will be all right. We know what is happening where you are from radio.

Pasha, we received your photos for which we're very pleased. We received much letters, and we sent you much letters, and money too, but you don't write us anything that did they came or not. Don't our letters reach you?

Pasha, I write about myself. I live you know how, you saw, and it's still the same. Perhaps I will live to see you, and my life will be different. Anyway, I will be waiting for you. If you are no more, I am no more. Good by, I kiss you, and remain, your mother.

*Comment*

There are two linguistic features in this letter that have already been noted: the formulaic confirmation of the receipt of photographs, with a delayed relative clause; and a yes-no question after the complementizer что (that).

This last paragraph is unique. In writing about herself, she does not recount everyday events but rather talks about the overall shape of her life: "There are no events, everything is the same as you saw it. If you come back, then my entire life will be different, it will have an event: my son came back home. And if you are no more, then I am no more." It is difficult to convey in English the impact of the last sentence because it has only one content word in it, the verb "to be." The rest are pronouns, conjunctions, and the negative particle that she spells together with the verb: "If you not-will-be then me too not-will-be."

The radical simplicity of how this is expressed seems crafted by a talented writer but it is simply what happens when people use very simple vocabulary and syntax to express their depth. A similar example was in Ex-3.3 when the young woman writes to her husband: "I will then forget you when my eyes close." The combination of radical simplicity and depth is, in effect, another occasional feature of a peasant letter.

## 3.7 EXAMPLES OF LETTERS 3: RECENT PEASANTS AND SOME SUCCESS STORIES

Technically, the old woman of 3.10 is a *recent peasant* living with a radio in a big city, but linguistically her letter is entirely in line with other peasant letters. This is not surprising: she is old, not working, and probably isolated from city life. The next example, a letter from Leningrad, is from a younger woman in very different circumstances: she works, her son is in daycare, she lives in a big apartment building. The ways in which her letter is similar to those by peasant women will help to describe the definitive profile of a peasant letter.

### Example 3.12 #107, p.389. Recent peasant in Leningrad

*3.12.1 Opening and News about Herself and the Boy*

Добрый день Ваня шлем мы тебе с вавой понискому поклону и желаем всего хорошего в твоей жизни Ваня писмо твое получили 5 числа за которые очень благодарим Ваня я очень беспокоюсь овас внастоящие время а тем боле после того как прочитала твое писмо и узнала что ты находился в городе где первых стали воевать Ваня мы живем пока несовсем плохо но очень скучаю в такой неприятной обстановке даже несплю ночь Ваня о вовки небеспокойся он сечас вочегеры нескучает ведет себя очень хорошо пает песни пляшит общем живет вова хорошо но о тебе очень скучает Ваня вова одет тепло и чистенько я ему купила коечто помелочи Ваня я сечас работаю на санитарных вагонах работаем 12 часов каждый день

*Translation*

Good afternoon, Vania (NN), I and vava (NN) are sending you (T) a low bow each and wish all good in your (T) life. Vania, we received your letter on the 5th for which letter we are very grateful. Vania, I am very worried about you (V) at the present time, and especially after I read your (T) letter and learned that you (T) are in the town where the fighting first started. Vania, we live so far not completely bad but I am very upset ["bored"] in such unpleasant circumstances, don't even sleep at night. Vania, don't worry about Vovka (NN+), he is now in daycare is not unhappy ["bored"], behaves very well, sings songs, dances, in general Vova (NN) lives well but misses you very much. He is dressed warmly in clean clothes, I bought him a few little things. Vania, I now work in the cars of a hospital train, we work 12 hours every day.

*Comment*

The opening of this letter is much simplified but includes "low bows" for greetings and a formulaic acknowledgement of a received letter that is a typical peasant feature. To preserve the word order of the Russian formula, it could be rendered as "Your letter we received on the 5th for which (letter) we're very grateful." In Russian, the relative pronoun "which" agrees with the head noun "letter" in number, gender and case. The gender is Feminine: recall that in standard Russian "letter" is a Neuter noun, but in most of our letters it is Feminine. (Neuter had been losing its position in the dialects for a long time.) And in this particular letter the pronoun is, inexplicably, in the Accusative Plural.

There are also unmistakable signs of urban life: she works and collects regular wages (it is unclear whether she is a custodian or a paramedic); she has enough money to buy warm clothes for the boy, and there is a store where she can buy such clothes; most strikingly, there is no concern about food. (Apart from food in the stores, the boy is fed in daycare, and she is fed at the hospital and can probably bring some food home.) The letter has two somewhat fancy phrases--*at the present time*; *in such unpleasant circumstances*--but otherwise it has the feel and flow of a peasant letter: no punctuation; the only capital letter is for the husband's nickname that repeats in almost every sentence; there is a T-V pronoun change; the verb скучать ("be bored") is again used for various kinds of anguish.

### 3.12.2 *Family and Neighbors' News*

Ваня сашка опять также пьет и дажа дерется сомной и с мамои он унас непрописан а начует унас потому что нам с Ним нечево делать Ваня

Аркадия я давно невидила спросила у иры она говорит что он уже с 8 ноября и непишет писмы. Ваня Сашка Зинькин еще с 30 числа писмы тоже не присылал общем сознакомых некто писмы непишит как начали ваевать Ваня в 6 номере [ . . . ] дядя Яша работает на кировским заводи заработок 500 р. Анатолия учится все тамже где и работал Ваня в 7 номере умерла тонька ванькина умерла после родов теперь Ванька остался вдовец а Яшка тоже служит вофлоте как уехал ниспишет писмы досвидание пиши писмы чаще Ваня желаем тебе всего наелутшего втвоей жизни Ваня бут осторожен чтобы вернутся домой Ваня досвидание целуем тебя свовой несколько раз

*Translation*

Vania, Sashka (NN+) is again drinking as before, and even has fistfights with me and mama. He does not have a residence permit with us but spends the night with us because we can't do anything with him. Vania, I have not seen Arkadii for a long time, asked Ira, she says he has not been writing letters either since 8 November. Vania, Zinka's (NN+) Sashka (NN+) has also not sent any letters ever since 30 November. In general, of all I know nobody writes letters after fighting started. Vania, in number 6 [ . . . ] uncle Yasha (NN) works at the Kirov plant, makes 500 rubles a month. Anatolii studies at the same place where he worked. Vania, in number 7 Van'ka's Ton'ka died, she died after childbirth, so now Van'ka is a widower; and Yashka is also serving, in the navy, no letters from him since he left. Good by, write letters more often. Vania, we wish you all the best in our life. Vania, be careful so he can return home. Vania, good bye, we kiss you several times, Vova and I.

*Comment*

The similarities with peasant letters continue, except that village news is replaced with news from apartments in the same building. It is worthy of note that the wages of the industrial worker uncle Yasha are much higher than anything a kolkhoznik would make.

All the examples so far are filled with anguish and, except the ones from big cities, harsh poverty. Most peasant letters are like this, but there are also success stories. There were successful kolkhozes where food and drink were in relative abundance. Or a recent peasant, out of kolkhoz, could do well as an industrial worker. The examples of this section illustrate the options. In the first (#162}, a soldier's sister from the Murmansk province writes to her brother:

**Example 3.13 Excerpts from #162,**
**pp.446–47, sister from the village of Kuzreka**

[ . . . ] Ваня женка у тибя живет на заводи с юркой я уних была ездила с тони из серьки мы уловили песца везли [ . . . ] на завод рудакову но денек ни получили не было рудакова дома но писец голубой самый дорогой [ . . . ] Ваня мы живем пока что ничев все здоровы яловила всерьки хорошо с весны на 1,200 Руб. и на сенокоси заработала рублей 300 но еще все ниначислено за ето [ . . . ] Ваня меня в стахановки выделили будут примировать 5-го ноебря. ни знаю чем мы годовой план перевыполнили и Батаманская а другие тони ни могли [ . . . ]

Ваня ни знаю как зиму жить опять наверно влесозаготовку прогонят Ваня я от гераски получила письмо опять думат соитись сомнои я ни знаю как ствоей стороны можно сойтись или нет [ . . . ] Пока Досвиданья с Приветом к вам сестра Ульяна пишы [ . . . ] Иван елисеевичь низабывай нас. но мы тибя ни забудем пока живы Писаля Уля 23.11.39 г. была брашка октябрская провели весело

*Translation*

Vania your wife lives at the plant with Iurka (NN+), I visited them, traveled from our fishing ground in Ser'ka, we caught a sable, took it [ . . . ] to Rudakov (LN) at the plant but didn't get the money, Rudakov wasn't home—but it's a blue sable, the most expensive [ . . . ] Vania we live so far OK, everybody's in good health, I fished well in Ser'ki from spring 1,200 rubles worth, and at the hay harvest I made about 300 rubles but it's not all added up yet for this. [ . . . ] Vania, I was promoted to be a Stakhanovite, will get an award on 5th November, I don't know what kind. We exceeded the annual quota, and the Batmanskaia team also, but the other fishing grounds couldn't. [ . . . ]

Vania I don't know how I will live in winter, they will probably send me off again to do logging. Vania I received a letter from Geraska (NN+), he's thinking of getting again together with me, I don't know, what would you say, could I get together with him? [ . . . ] So long, good bye Ivan Eliseevich (NP), don't forget us but we will not forget you (T) as long as we live. Written by Ulia (NN) 23.11.39. We had an October get-together, had a good time

*Comment*

The young woman Ul'iana (FN) or Ulia (NN) writes to her brother Ivan (Vania) and mentions his wife and son Iurka (FN Iurii, NN Iura, NN+ Iurka) who live at some "plant," probably processing local fish and buying furs. Ulia's letter has a simple opening (elided) followed by multiple greetings from relatives and friends. She then recounts her successes in fishing, mowing and trapping. She is promoted to be a Stakhanovite and receive a bonus. But then it turns out that, for all her successes, she has no idea what she will be assigned to do during the winter and expects to be sent to do logging. (The verb she uses, прогонят, implies coercion: they will chase me off to do logging.) She then touchingly asks her brother for advice about getting together again with a young man she used to be with--perhaps even asking his permission to do so. The final piece of news is that she had a good time at the October revolution party.

The letter has a simpler opening and some new vocabulary items for new things in life (promote, Stakhanovite, quota) but no Soviet cliché. In its orthography, syntax and mode of exposition the letter is entirely peasant.

The next example is from an optimistic upbeat letter by a бригадир (work team leader). This was an administrative position: those leaders did not themselves work in the field, but rather assigned work to their team in the morning and supervised during the day. This particular letter seems to be from a prosperous kolkhoz on good lands in central Russia, adjacent to Ukraine. (There are Ukrainianisms in his language.) The excerpt is the "Now I tell you about myself" section of the letter. It is distinctive for its higher literacy and concentrated use of SovYaz.

## Example 3.14 #29, p.310. From brother-in-law (sister's husband)

Дарагой мой шурин Ф. Н. я сичас тибе опишу сваю жизн моя жизня сичас на бальшой. Жина моя это умница как и вы [ . . . ] усе здаровы хлеб есть одежа есть я выпиваю каждой день, работа в мине на сто, читаем всегда газеты пра самураев финах как оне нас сулят 10 штук за однаго фина. Это им одурманит англицкая буржуазия быть битом усем и на ихней територии дарагой мой шурин помню я ваши слова и помню я все досвидания жилаю я тибя свой бригардирский привет навсегда

*Translation*

My dear brother-in-law F.N., now I will describe to you (T) my life. My life is now thumbs-up. My wife is a bright-mind like yourself (V) [ . . . ], we're all healthy, have bread, have clothes, I take a few drinks every day. My job is 100%, we always read newspapers about samurai Finns, they promise us 10 ours for one Finn. This is English bourgeoisie befuddles them to be beaten up and on their territory. My dear brother-in-law, I remember your (V) words, I remember everything, and I wish you (T) my brigade-leaders greeting forever

*Comment*

This man is more literate than most other kolkhozniks, but his language has distortions, partly because of Ukrainian influences, but also because of his pretensions that are in the same line as many examples of Chapter 2. The sentence about English bourgeoisie does not handle the verb одурманит very well: wrong case of the pronoun, syntactically incorrect infinitive. "I wish you my [ . . . ] greeting" is a mismatch between the verb and its direct object. The continuity between the material of Chapter 2 and examples from the Corpus will be systematically explored in the end of this chapter. The curious reference to "samurai Finns" is addressed in the section on mythological geography and the image of the enemy.

The final example of this section is from a recent peasant who lives and works in the city but keeps close ties to his village. Linguistically, it has many features of peasant letters; socio-economically, it shows a huge gap between the conditions of the urban working class and the peasants: they almost lived in two different countries.

## Example 3.15 #141, p. 426. Brother in Briansk, a loving son

### 3.15.1 Greetings. A Coat

Здравствуй многоуважаемый брат Архип Иванович с приветом к вам ваш брат Василий Иванович Архип Ив. во первых строках своего письма о том, что я от вас получил письмо 23.11.39 за которое очень большое спасибо. Дарогой брат Ар. Ив. в котором я узнал, что тебя перегнали в другое место и ты пишешь чтобы я узял в свахи польто разреши узнать, что ты прислал-ли польто или вовсе оставил еще когда ты взежал и почему ты ниписал раньше что польто в свахи ну лано это будем говорить дальше

### Translation

Hello my highly respected brother Arkhip Ivanovich (NP) with greetings to you (V) your (V) brother Vassilii Ivanovich. Arkhip Iv. in the first lines of my letter [verb missing] about that I received from you (V) a letter 23.11.39, for which letter many thanks. Dear brother Ar.Iv. from which I learned that you were shipped to a different place and you are telling me to take your jacket from your mother-in-law[13] please let me know that whether you sent her that coat or simply left it when you were going away and why didn't you write before that your mother-in-law has the coat. OK we'll talk about this some more later.

### Comment

The opening is somewhat simplified but still has the NP and the V pronoun, and the formulaic acknowledgement of a received letter. To show how tenuous the young man's grammar is, the next sentence, capitalized after a period, contains a relative clause with the antecedent in the preceding sentence. The subject matter is a coat left with or sent to a relative, and the pronoun appropriately shifts to T. In that last sentence there is again the complementizer что, followed by a yes-no question, as in Letter 12a and others.

### 3.15.2 Village News

тепер Дорогой браток я тебя на пишу новости женится унас ребята которые приехали с армии [ ... ] теперь опишу про Мотю мотя в'ехала в Москву кажется по ворб. наверно захотела[ ... ] тут нету ребят дак она в'ехала туда теперь опишу насчет своей жизни моя жизнь пока ничего купил себя валики с галошам за 150 руб. купил кастюм за 130 руб домой езжу с почти каждый выходной вожу хлеба по 5-6 буханок и привез гвоздей кг. [ ... ] матери туфли и двое чулок и думаю купит тут у одного гармошку за 170 р с этой получки

*Translation*

Now my dear brother I will write news to you (T). There are marriages here by the boys who came back from the army. [ ... ] Now I will describe about Motia (NN) Motia went to Moscow, I think she was recruited, probably she wanted to [ ... ] there are no boys here so she went there. Now I will write about my life, so far so good, I bought myself felt boots with galoshes for 150 rub., bought a suit for 130 rub., go home almost every week, take 5–6 loaves of bread and brought a kilo of nails, shoes for mother and two pairs of stockings, and I'm thinking of buying from a guy here an accordion for 170 rub. from my next pay.

*Comment*

The paratactic structure of this passage is held together by variations on "now my dear brother I will describe to you," rather than by the repetition of the nickname, as in women's letters. (The word "brother" is modified by the same affectionate suffix as the word "son" in the old father's letter of 3.10.)

The list of purchases is impressive, he clearly has disposable income. He also takes good care for his mother. The workweek at the time was six days with a single day off, and he frequently spends that day "home," as he puts it. It seems that the city is not yet home `for him. He brings loaves of bread, door nails, and other things for the house.

### 3.15.3 Plans and Farewell

Дорогой браток сегодняшни год хочу пустить 5ку гусей и будет тельная корова и зарежу одного порасенка пусть мать есть отпуза а сам пора ботаюсь в Брянск я работаю сейчас на станке на пиле работа легкая но опасная [ ... ] досвидание остаюсь жив и здоров чего и вам желаю присылай ответ к сему ваш брат В. Никущенков

## Translation

Dear brother, this year I want to start five geese and there will be a cow for mating and I will slaughter a piglet so mother could eat all she wants, and I will keep working in Briansk, I'm working now on a machine that is a saw, the work is easy but dangerous [ . . . ] good bye, remaining alive and well which I also wish to you (V) also, send (T) me an answer, to which your (V) brother V. Nikushchenkov.

## Comment

The young man clearly remains a peasant in his heart and his plans, even though his stable income and fixed-hour work day put him in a very different world. As in the preceding letter there is a note of danger: the machine must have been very unsafe for a young Russian man of the time to notice.

Just as in the preceding examples, there are new lexical items for new realities, but in its orthography, syntax and mode of exposition the letter is entirely peasant.

## 3.8 THE DEFINING FEATURES OF PEASANT LETTERS

This section brings together the definitive features of peasant letters scattered in the comments on the examples. Occasionally, an additional piece of data may be needed to provide a missing detail, especially when showing contrasts with letters from other social groups: industrial workers, Red Army soldiers, managerial types, semi-educated white-collar urban youth, and intelligentsia. To a surprising degree, social divisions postulated by political scientists find clear correlations in our linguistic data.

Peasant-letter features fall into four groups: those resulting from the shared realities of peasant/kolkhoz life; orthographic features indicating the level of literacy; discourse and pragmatic features specific to the genre of personal letter; and the syntax, lexicon, and phraseology features of the peasant language as presented in Chapter 1. They are discussed in this order. The features are all listed in a table, a row for each letter, 49 columns for features and feature combinations. Their values add up to the "peasant index" of a letter.

### Shared Realities

The set of common references to the realities of peasant life is linguistically rather uninteresting: a list of lexical items and semantic categories that appear frequently in peasant letters and occasionally in letters about peasant life (such as a young man writing to his brother about their parents' life in the village). Most of those words and categories have already come up in the examples and will reappear in the rest of the chapter. Apart from *kolkhoz* and *laborday* they include references to:

- food, especially bread and potatoes, the two main staples of peasant diet. Concern about food: will there be enough for the winter? Even those who had money to spend complain about lack of food in the local store; loaves of bread have to be brought from the city. Sugar is frequently lacking for weeks and months.
- grain harvest, including wheat and rye for people, oats for animals and chickens. Chaff is also an important staple.
- animals and domestic birds: cows, heifers, calves, goats, pigs; chickens, geese.
- clothes and shoes, both for grownups and children, who sometimes lack shoes to go to school. The soldier's clothes, either left behind or languishing somewhere in the army are a frequent and exclusively peasant subject of discussion.
- налоги (taxes), as mentioned before, are an exclusively peasant concern.
- справка (a document or certificate), usually a request to the soldier to send such a document home, so the family could receive a subsidy, or a relief from taxes, or some other benefit from the kolkhoz, such as a horse to bring home firewood for the winter.
- дрова (firewood), although a concern for some urban dwellers was an essential for peasants living in wooden houses heated by one big stove.
- essential industrial goods: soap, doornails, cotton cloth (ситец), kerosene.

Eleven lines in the letter-table refer to these shared realities. Their values together add-up to the "peasant index" of a letter. A letter with the peasant index of 0 can still be qualified as a peasant letter, derived or recent, on the basis of orthography and discourse features.

## Orthography and Literacy

Orthographic errors fall into these categories: spelling, word divisions, punctuation, and capitalization. Textbooks also include hyphenation as an orthographic feature but it is practically non-existent in peasant letters. Yokoyama (2008:370–76) has a detailed discussion of spelling in her collection. Some of her observations apply to the peasant letters in the Corpus as well, although generally Yokoyama's subjects are more literate.

### Spelling

Most errors are phonetic in nature: words are spelled the way they are pronounced. This provides extremely valuable data for dialectologists interested in local dialects. The subject is outside the scope of this book, and could easily fill a book of its own because the Corpus contains a wide range of dialects, from Murmansk and Vologda in the North to Eastern Ukraine, Rostov and Stalingrad in the South; and from Smolensk and Belorussia in the West to Volga regions in the East. One can only hope that this aspect of the data will attract the attention it deserves.

A striking feature of peasant spelling is that the characters ь, ъ ("soft" and "hard" signs) are very rare. The hard sign is used 25 times in the Corpus, of which only two are "correct" uses to indicate the sound [j], the rest are at the word-end, as in the pre-revolutionary orthography.

*Word Division*

Most errors here are from confusing prefixes and prepositions: writing prefixes separately or prepositions together with the following noun. The negative particle не (not) is often attached to the following verb. The particles не and ни are frequently confused, a tricky point of Russian spelling.

*Punctuation and Capitalization*

Many letters have very little punctuation, and if they do it would be a period or a comma. A question mark, an exclamation point, or a quotation mark would immediately indicate that the letter is not from a peasant. Capitalization is sparse and somewhat erratic. Some of it may be the result of erroneous transcribing. In the absence of orthographic indications, syntactic analysis of the text depends on articulation, and syntactic ambiguities are not uncommon. There are also "errors" when the same syntactic component is shared by two structures. This is discussed and illustrated in the section on Syntax.

## 3.9 ON LITERACY AND LETTERS FROM SCHOOLCHILDREN

To associate letters with levels of literacy I have graded them, elementary school fashion, on a scale from 0 (fail) to 4 (excellent). Ten letters get a 4, eight of them from urban professionals, one from a student in Moscow, and one from a precocious schoolgirl in Leningrad. Grade 3 letters are mostly from urban dwellers, #2 (Ex.3.5) being the only exception. Grades 1 and 2 are mostly from young men but also from somewhat educated young women, like the village schoolteacher. The most common groups in this category are Red Army soldiers, blue collar workers, kolkhoz personnel who are not peasants, and low-level functionaries of various kinds. Grade 0 letters are all from peasant women young and old, and peasant men of the parents' generation.

To put this data in perspective, the 1897 census put the overall literacy in the empire at 21.1%, including 29.3% for men and 13.1% for women, with higher literacy among urban populations than in the countryside. In 1939–1940, these proportions remained unchanged. For many peasants, literacy simply meant learning the alphabet, i.e., the correspondences between sounds and character shapes. The process of writing consisted of using those character shapes to render the intended content the way it would be spoken, simply pouring out speech on paper. Fifty-seven grade 0 letters in our corpus fit this description, forty-nine of them from peasants.[14]

## Letters from Village Schoolchildren and a Schoolteacher

Important for evaluating the Soviet literacy effort are letters from schoolchildren. In Example 3.8, #83b, the schoolgirl reports that she does well at school, but her grade is at best a 2 on our scale. Example 3.16 is another such letter. Its grade is 1; the two sentences with village news are badly garbled.

## Example 3.16 #164b, p.448. From a Schoolboy

Дядя валодя если есть мыло пришли кусочка 2. с посылкам. Мы остались об однои городе. один у нас отрезали весь. Дядя Валодя ты спашиваеш про витю как он Тибя позабыл или нет он тибя реско помнить Дядя Валодя ты спрашиваеш где товарищи Санёк Зотов на нашей машини работает санька. И взяли в красную Армию. Ваську П. тоже палу Армию дядя валодя не обижайси что я так плохо написа.
Дядя Валодя я учуч на хор. и отл.

*Translation*

Uncle Valodia [NN for Vladimir] if you have soap send us a couple of little pieces in a parcel. We are left with one kitchen garden, one was all cut off. Uncle Valodia you're asking about Vitia whether he forgot you or not, he rarely remembers you. Uncle Volodia you're asking where your friends are. Sanek [NN+ for Alexander] Zotov works on our truck, san'ka [another NN+ for the same person]. And they drafted into the red Army Vas'ka [NN+ for Vasilii] P. also Pal [probably Pavel] to the Army. Uncle Volodia don't be offended that I wrote so poorly.
Uncle Valodia I get As and Bs at school.

*Comment*

Children were of course aware of shared realities of peasant life, like lack of soap.

Small private plots, usually with a vegetable garden, were essential for kolkhozniks' survival. The policy during the 1930s was to gradually reduce their allowed size, giving more land to the kolkhoz. There was another such effort in 1939, mentioned in several letters.

The boy repeats "Uncle Valodia" the way the women in #2 and #83a repeat the nickname. "Uncle NN" could be addressed by children to any adult man--in a recent Russian song young adolescents refer to Vladimir Putin as "Uncle Vova"[15]—but in this case the boy is really the soldier's nephew, and the first cousin of little Vitia, the soldier's son.

Assuming the boy is telling his uncle the truth about his grades, this note is a severe indictment of Soviet elementary education as practiced in village schools. It is further confirmed by letter #48, written by a village schoolteacher but with a literacy level below 3. There are errors in her spelling, punctuation, and word division, and her treatment of reported speech is no different from what her peasant neighbors would write:

### Example 3.17 #48, p.333. From a village schoolteacher

ваня, ты просишь адрес Преснякова Гриши, я ходили они мне сказами что уже 3 месяца мы от него не получали, а ему послали то наше письмо вернулос назад и они сами не знают где он.

*Translation, with Italics Added*

Vania, you're asking for Grisha Presniakov's address, I went, they told me that *for three months already we have not heard from him, and [when] [we] wrote to him then our letter came back* and they don't know themselves where he is.

*Comment*

The italicized sentence is, of course, direct speech. It contains the same syntactic feature as earlier examples in this chapter and in Chapter 2: lack of a conjunction in the subordinate clause followed by a conjunction in the main clause: ему послали то наше писмо вернулос назад. The Russian literally says: "and to him [we] sent then our letter then came back."

The next example, a quote from a village schoolgirl, gives additional reasons for poor performance.

### Example 3.18 #3, p.285. Books, notebooks

Моя учеба проходит не плохо у четверти небыло ниодного плохо. Посредственно и хорошо. Книг много у меня нет и чрез это посредственные отметки, тетрадей тоже нет, для того чтобы конспектировать.

*Translation*

My schoolwork is going not bad, in this quarter not a single F. Cs and Bs. I don't have many books and because of that C grades; no notebooks, either, in order to write summaries.

*Comment*

Summaries were the most common form of written homework in Soviet schools: they ensured that the students had done the assigned reading without asking for any ideas of their own.

The situation with paper was generally catastrophic. Many letters are written on blank documents of various kinds. Those who had paper (typically pages from a school notebook) would often include a blank sheet so the addressee had paper to write back.

The letter from a Leningrad schoolgirl, who received our top grade of 4, shows a better-supplied school:

### Example 3.19 #259, p.540. A schoolgirl from Leningrad

В школе у нас сейчас большое оживление сегодня 60-ти летие со дня рождения нашего вождя И. В. Сталина. сейчас выпустили фотогазету на тему 'жизнь и революционная деятельность тов. Сталина'. Там поместили вырезки из газет и журналов.

*Translation*

There is a lot of excitement at school now, today is the 60th birthday of our leader I. V. Stalin. We produced a photo-newsletter on the topic "The life and revolutionary activity of comrade Stalin." We included clippings from newspapers and magazines.

## 3.10 DISCOURSE AND PRAGMATIC FEATURES

This section summarizes the prominent features of how peasant letters in the Corpus are organized as a discourse. It should be kept in mind that these are not letters "on occasion," or to initiate a conversation about some family affairs. The purpose of the letters is to be in touch, to express feelings, to unburden yourself. This is why many of them include the formulaic phrase "there's nothing much to write about," because the letters are really not "about" something.

As indicated in many examples, a prominent feature of most peasant letters is the traditional opening, itself a structured entity that includes some or all of the following.

- use of NP in addressing the recipient and/or in reference to a child.
- use of the V pronoun within the close family or friends, later usually switching to T.
- the word "spouse," especially in the phrase "from your known spouse."
- other uses of "known" (известный), usually spelled phonetically as извесный, without the unpronounced letter "т." This feature is not in Yokoyama's letters, and its origin is unknown.
- a formula acknowledging the receipt of a letter, frequently included in the opening or immediately following it, using a specific formulaic word order, with the fronted word letter: "Your letter we received on such-and-such a date, for which (letter) we are very grateful."[16]
- multiple greetings from family members. These may also migrate, or be repeated, at the end of the letter.

Beyond the opening, the most prominent organizational feature is the repetition of a form of address, usually a nickname or the name of a family relation. In some letters, this seems to serve simply as a paratactic connector, the way the conjunction "and" is used in the Bible. More skillful writers deploy the form of address to indicate a change of topic. Here too orthography is usually of no help because paragraph breaks are sparse and sometimes random.

Other discourse patterns in the body of peasant letters include: alternating V-T pronouns that follow the mood and the content; the question-answer pattern that is present in 3.5 and 3.7; and a few repeating elements of content that arise in the section on village and family news. Together with shared socio-economic circumstances and bottom-level orthography, these discourse features create the unmistakable look and feel of a peasant letter.

To see how sharply their look and feel separate them from the rest of the Corpus, the next section shows samples of decidedly non-peasant letters.

## 3.11 OVERLAP AND INTERPENETRATION WITH OTHER SOCIAL GROUPS

Non-peasants, unsurprisingly, form a diverse group. There are letters from educated urbanites; people in positions of some responsibility, doing serious work; careerists, climbing the Soviet or Party hierarchy; and housewives living in Leningrad and going to concerts in the evening. There is no systematic overlap between these letters and letters written by peasants, except for spelling errors (often the same ones, but peasants have many more of them). Such overlap as there is occurs among younger people who comprise the generation of wives and siblings; they listened to the same radio and consumed the same propaganda and popular culture. In this case, the non-peasant letters show in more concentrated form some elements that are occasionally also found in peasant letters. Non-peasant letters fall into two groups that I label "Soviet" and (anachronistically) "pop-culture." The ways in which they differ from peasant letters can often be detected in the letter's opening lines.

## "Soviet" Letters

This group features generous use of official Soviet clichés. Many letters from Red Army soldiers belong in this group. This example is from a brother serving in the army in Ukraine:

### Example 3.20 #24, p.305. From a brother who is also in the Red Army

Здравствуй брат Борис. Шлю пламенный красноармейский боевой привет и массу наилучших пожеланий и желаю финских басурманов бить покрепче.

*Translation*

Hello brother Boris. I am sending you my fiery red-army-soldier's fighting greeting and a big load of best wishes, and I wish you great success in beating up Finnish infidels.

*Comment*

All the adjectives modifying the "greeting" are Soviet newspaper clichés. The "fiery (flaming) greeting" makes an appearance in a few peasant letters. What is never found in peasant letters are insults to Finns. The "infidel" insult is amusing because it is usually addressed to people of non-Christian faith, specifically Muslims. (The Russian word is a garbled derivative from the word for Muslim, and can be used as a generic invective.) This is not the only generalized word for "enemy" applied to Finns: 3.14 (#29, from the brigade leader) and two other letters speak of "Finnish samurai," because in 1938 the Soviet army fought a brief and victorious battle with the Japanese in Manchuria.[17]

Some "Soviet" letters expand on the subject of Finnish aggression at great length:

### Example 3.21 #130, p.414. From sister working in a factory

Здравствуйте много уважаемый брат Костя шлю вам самый наилучший привет и желаю Вашей молодой жизни хорошего Костя среди наглого обстрел финляндской военщины советских войск вызвал огромное возмущение коликтив рабочих и интелгенции нашего завода. В обеденные перерывы и некоторых цехах прошли митинги протеста против наглого действия финдлянского правительства и фендлянской военщины, отвергающей мирное предложение Советского Правительства и провоцирующих войну с СССР.

*Translation*

Greetings, my highly respected brother Kostia [NN for Konstantin], I send you my very best regards and wish all the best to Your young life. Kostia, in the midst of insolent bombardment of the Finliandskii military of the Soviet troops elicited great indignation from the collective of worker and intelligentsia of our factory. During the lunch break some shops had meetings of protest against the insolent action of the Findlianskii government and the Fendlianskii military, who rejected the peaceful proposals of the Soviet government and are provoking war with the USSR.

*Comment*

Much of this letter seems copied from a newspaper, with grammatical and orthographic errors in copying. Some orthographic errors are the familiar ones of missing punctuation and capitalization. The "difficult" words for "collective" and "intelligentsia" are misspelled.

The syntax of the second sentence is badly garbled, in ways that are reminiscent of the 1920s. There is a deverbal noun обстрел (bombardment) and two noun phrases, one for the subject, the other for the object, that should have been in the Genitive, but they are not. The noun itself is both the object of the preposition среди (among, in the midst of), which would require Genitive, and the subject of the verb phrase that follows, that requires Nominative. The phrase "среди наглого" is left hanging.

The adjective "Finliandskii" is of particular interest. It is spelled three different ways, the first time correctly. The misspellings are instructive and, in other letters, reveal interesting conceptual confusions.

## The Name of the Country and Its People

The Russian name for Finland is "Finliandiia," where -iia is the noun ending. To make it into an adjective, the noun ending is dropped and replaced with the adjectival one, -skii. But the result, "Finliandskii," is hard to pronounce and therefore hard to spell. Three problems present themselves:

- The vowel letter "i" in the first, unstressed syllable is reduced, and the syllable would be pronounced the same if that letter were "e," which is the spelling adopted in many letters, including the last spelling in 3.21, #130.

- In the consonant cluster in the end, -dsk- the sound [d] is dropped, which is reflected in the last two spellings of 3.21, #130.
- The opposite happens in the middle of the word: the consonant cluster [nl] is difficult for Russian articulation, and in the last two spellings of 3.21 it is broken by inserting a [d]: Findliandiia. More often, the cluster is simplified by dropping the [n] sound: Filiandiia. However, the sound is preserved in the name of the people, Finns. This may result is confusion, as in the next example:

### Example 3.22 #239, p.525. From Poland to Finland

стринацатого синтебря пошол ослобождать польский народ, и да 8го Декабря этого года а на стоящий момент нахожусь Филяндии ослобождать филенский народ от финских бело бандитов, Филяндии нахожусь с 13 Декабря этого года.

*Translation*

From 13 September I went to liberate Polish people and up until 8 December of this year, and at the present moment I am located in Filiandiia to liberate the filenskii people from Finnish white bandits; in Filiandiia since 13 December of this year.

*Comment*

In the mythological world of this letter, the county is Filiandiia, populated by the "filenskii" people who are oppressed by Finnish bandits of unknown origin. The adjective "white" attached to Finns was a master stroke of Soviet propaganda, aligning the Finnish conflict with the Civil War struggle between Reds and Whites. The ploy worked even on the educated: a female student from Moscow, with impeccable grade 4 grammar and spelling, writes (#263): "Я очень рада, что вы так быстро и победоносно двигаетесь по Финляндии, освобождая ее от белогвардейцев." (I am very happy that you are so quickly and victoriously moving across Finland liberating it from the white-guard [the Civil War moniker]."

In general, the entire corpus of letters presents a certain view of the geography of Eastern Europe that can only be described as mythological. Finland is populated by Moslems (басурманы), samurai, and the white guard. Germany and Germans do not exist (there is one mention of "the German" in #47), and WWII has not started. Poland is populated by Ukrainians and Byelorussians oppressed by a handful of Polish landlords and officers.

### A Letter from Western Ukraine

The next example clearly shows the link between the informal opening and the Soviet ideology. It is one of the longest letters in the Corpus, and a success story: the young writer is a happy man. He is a soldier serving in Poland, writing to his friend on the Finnish border. The letter is quite literate but interesting for the psychological type it presents and its unfiltered reflection of Soviet ideology. The example presents three excerpts from the letter separated by long stretches of text.

**Example 3.23 #47, p.330. From Western Ukraine / Eastern Poland**

*3.23.1*

Привет с Западной Украины!! Вязовому Александру Алексеевичу, от друга Евтеева И.М. Добрый день уважаемый Саша! Саша! мы не будем друг друга величать по отечеству, я считаю это лишним, а лучше здорово Сашка или Ванька. И вот я посылаю тебе свой кр-кий товарищеский привет! и желаю тебе больших успехов в красноармейской жизни и учебе.

*Translation*

Greetings from Western Ukraine!! To Viazovoi Aleksandr Alekseevich (LN NP), from his friend Evteev I. M. Good afternoon, dear Sasha! (NN for Aleksandr) Sasha! we're not going to use patronymics, I consider this unnecessary; a better way is just Hi there, Sashka or Van'ka. (NN+ for Aleksandr and Ivan) And here I am sending you my R-A (Red Army) comradely greeting! and I wish you great successes in the Red-Army life and study.

*Comment*

The letter starts with a very formal address and self-reference, but it is the formality of an official document. It immediately proceeds to an explicit rejection of formality, going all the way down to the familiar-rude NN+ Sashka, followed by a Soviet-style greeting. Army is, again, a place of study: the recruits are not only trained but also educated and indoctrinated.

*3.23.2*

По приказу партии и правительства мы отправились на запад. Правда в дороге мы ехали очень весело, время проводили шумно ребята все были веселые и дружные и все ехали с охотой [ . . . ] Нашей красной армии было поручено задание, чтобы освободить Украинский и Белорусский народ от панского гнета под которым народ находился 20 лет. И взять его под защиту, так как Польское Правительство при первом столкновении с немцем не смогло защищать свое государство. Польское правительство абонкротилось и разбежалось оставив людей на произвол судьбы. На нашу долю выпало счастье, дать помощь этому народу, и взять его под защиту освободить от гнета польских панов и офицеров. [ . . . ] Присоединили западную Украину к советской Украине, и установили Власть рабочих и крестьян власть советов.

*Translation*

On the orders of the party and the government we started moving West. Frankly, along the way we had a great time and great fun, all the guys were fun and friendly, and we traveled with enthusiasm [ . . . ] Our Red Army was given the mission to liberate the Ukrainian and Belorussian people from the yoke of Polish landlords that had been on them for 20 years. Also to take them under our protection because the Polish Government in the very first clash with the German could not protect their state. The Polish government went bankrupt and ran away, leaving people to their fate. It was our happy destiny to give help to those people, take them under our protection, and liberate from the yoke of Polish landlords and military officers. [ . . . ] We joined Western Ukraine to Soviet Ukraine and established the rule of workers and peasants, the Soviet rule.

*Comment*

"Party and government" as the seat of authority was a very common phrase, always in this order. This passage shows both the rationale the Soviet people were given for invading Poland, and the expectations they had for the incursion into Finland.

3.23.3

Саша! девочи здесь хорошенькие. Здесь есть Полячки, Украинки, Еврейки на лицо очень красивенькие но плохо, что они очень богомольные они так сильно уверены в бога, что не поддаются ни каким доказательствам. Ей предлагаеш слушай пане? пойдем в кино, а она тянет в костел по нашему в церковь.

*Translation*

Sasha! The girls are very pretty here. There are Polish girls, Ukrainian girls, Jewish girls, all with pretty faces, but the bad thing is they are very religious, and so convinced in god (Sic!) that don't yield to any arguments. You tell her: "Listen, miss, let's go see a movie," and she drags you to her "kostel," like our church.

## Comment

This young man would, of course, follow orders and execute Polish officers or load cattle cars with Polish intellectuals to be exiled deep into the Soviet Union, but his attitude to local girls seems sweet and respectful. He is so atheistic that he even forgot how to say "believe in God" correctly.

The Polish word for "church" is ultimately from the Latin *castellum* because, as Vasmer's dictionary explains, "medieval churches were fortified like castles."

In some sense, this and other "Soviet" letters are not surprising and do not say anything that is not yet known. However, they have a freshness and authenticity that add new detail to the familiar picture. How their inner world of non-peasants from the Corpus manifests itself in their personal letters could be the subject of a separate study.

### Semi-Educated "Popular Culture" Letters

Many letters of this group can again be identified by their opening. About 25 of them start with a little ditty or two, clearly a fashion at the time. The most common one is a variation on the opening lines of #146: "Добрый день веселый час пишу письма не вижу вас" (Good day, merry hour, I'm writing a letter and I don't see you).[18] Another favorite is "Беру перо в руки, пишу письмо от скуки" (I'm taking a pen in my hand and writing a letter from boredom), where скука does mean "boredom." There is a version of this in (somewhat misspelled) Ukrainian, #62: "Сидаю за стол ад скуки беру перо в руки пишу крупными словами поливаю дрибными слезами." (I'm sitting down to my desk from boredom, take my pen in my hand, and write in big words that I'm watering with small tears.) How those things emerged and spread seems a total mystery.

The writer is sometimes an unmarried young woman who had a romantic relationship with the addressee. The very first letter in the Corpus is a fine example:

### Example 3.24 #1, p.283. From Leningrad, the initial fragment with some rhymes

Привет из Ленинграда
 Добрый день веселый час что ты делаеш сейчас брось дело все свое прочитай письмо мае
  Может быть оно утешит
  Может быть развеселит

может быть больное сердце кое чем разговорит.

Здравствуй Тима письмо я твое получлиа закоторрое большое спасибо, письмо получила 29 а пишу сразу же вечером.

Тима ты пишеш что мои письма неполучаеш я низнаю почему квам нидоходят письма я тибе пишу накаждое письмо ответ последнее письмо послала числа 16-го этого месяца.

Тима ты пишеш что я тибя хочу забыть, нет Тима я тибя никогда низабуду. Тима паверь есьтьлибы я нихотела с табой письмами пиреписаватся то давнобы кончила всю эту волокиту [ ... ]

*Translation*

Greeting from Leningrad
 Good day and happy hour what are you doing right now drop what you're doing and read my letter
 Perhaps it will console
 Perhaps it will cheer up
 Perhaps it will engage your wounded heart in a conversation
 Hello Tima. A letter from you came for which letter many thanks. The letter came on the 29th, and I am writing the same evening
 Tima you are writing that you are not receiving my letters. I don't know why my letter don't reach you. I write to you an answer on every letter, the last letter I sent on the 16th of this month
 Tima you are writing that I want to forget you, no Tima I will never forget you. Tima believe me that if I didn't want to write letters with you I would have finished all this hassle a long time ago

*Comment*

Judging by her writing, the author is a recent peasant. We see the repetition of the nickname; the formula acknowledging the receipt of a letter; phonetic spelling and missing word boundaries; and very sparse punctuation. Later in the letter she mentions that she has a job ("I remember you everywhere, even when I'm at work"), but she also asks Tima whether he has any news from the village, clearly indicating that they grew up together. She also mentions that her parents still live there. All the more curious, then, is the extensive piece of poetry that opens the letter. Its spelling is not perfect but much better than that of the letter itself, which probably means that it was copied from a source that she had in her possession.

Some letters from wives also start in this playful fashion, among them, remarkably, letters from peasant wives. Unlike the Soviet openings of the previous section, the ditty openings penetrated into peasant letters. There are about a dozen such, including the example below, in which the opening is completely desemanticized. It is just a sequence of words you can plunk in the beginning of a letter, in this case in jarring contrast to what follows:

**Example 3.25 #203, p.488. From a village in Leningrad oblast**

Добрый день веселый час пиши [intended *пишу*] письмо и жду от Вас. Витя у нас нового нет ничего, а худого много. Витя кланиемся вам все [a list of names] а Васиньки у нас нет он лежит в больнице. С нашей деревни лежать 15 человек. [a list of names] Дядя Петя. приежал домой 22 числа ему подали 3 тилиграмы и его насилу отпустили и Павла Петровича тоже на 3 тилиграмы. Но дядя Петя приехал и не застал жену Дуня умерла. [ . . . ] Витя твоя кресна умерла. И наш Вася будет жив или нет. Мы едим через день а другой раз каждыи день у нас строго сеичас очень [ . . . ] Досвидание кланиемся тебе и желаем тебе хорошего. Пиши ответ жив или нет Пиши ответ будем жит Температура у Васи [letter stops here]

*Translation*

Good day, merry hour, I'm writing a letter and expecting from you. Vitia (NN) we have nothing that's new and a lot that's bad. Vitia, bows to you from all [a list of names] but Vasin'ka [NN+ from Vasia, NN for Vasilii—Basil] is not with us, he is in the hospital. From our village 15 are in the hospital. [a list of names] Uncle Petia came home on the 22nd, they had sent him 3 telegrams and he barely got permission to leave, and Pavel Petrovich [NP] also after 3 telegrams. But uncle Petia didn't catch his wife, Dunya [NN] was already dead. [ . . . ] Vitia, your godmother died. And our Vasia maybe will live and maybe he won't. We go there every other day and sometimes every day. The rules are very strict now. [ . . . ] Good bye, bows to you, and wishing you well. Let us know, alive or no. Write back, let us live. Vasia has temperature

*Comment*

The presence of the playful formula in a letter about epidemic and death shows the importance of formulaic openings and their detachment from the content of the letter. This is true even if the formula did not come from an old tradition but from contemporary lowbrow city culture.

*Repeating Nicknames or Other Forms of Address*

In the body of the letter, a clear contrast is found between the use of nicknames. Repeating nicknames are, as we saw, a fixture of peasant letters. They are also found in a few non-peasant letters but with a difference: the nicknames are variously embellished with suffixes. Example 3.17 from the not-very-literate village schoolteacher presents a striking example: she repeats variations on the nickname Vania twenty-four times. The letter opens with the jolly exclamation "Vaniushonok!!!," which is Vania with two suffixes: imagine something like "JonnieSweetiePie." In total she uses five variations: plain Vania, Vaniushonok, Vaniusha, Vanek, and Vaniushok. Similarly, in #25, a better-educated woman who lives in a big city and holds a job, addresses her husband twelve times in a 300-word letter using these forms: Толюсенок, Толюся, Толюсеночик. All of them are modifications of the simple NN Толя (for Anatolii) which is never used. This particular innovation did not infiltrate peasants: if a peasant letter included a suffixed form, it would be a meaningful move to greater closeness, as in the father's letter from Yokoyama (2008), Example 3.4.

## 3.12 VOCABULARY, SYNTAX, PHRASEOLOGY

In this final section of the chapter, I strip off all the details of the medium (writing) and the genre (personal letter) and try to treat the rest as a record of peasant speech, similar to ethnographic records in Chapter 1. (This is also how the texts of letters are treated in Yokoyama's [2008] essay on "Linguistic features of the text.) The goal is to see whether the peasant language profile presented in Figure 1.1 is still present in the text of the peasant letters of the Corpus. The presentation is organized by the 10 points of Figure 1.1, reproduced here (in italics) in an abridged form. There are also features that were not present in the pre-revolutionary data but seem of similar historical age. They are presented after the ten points of the profile.

Some profile points receive only a brief comment, others call for a more extended treatment, beginning with the first one.

### 3.12.1 Review of Profile

1. *There are many dialectal words with very narrow specific meanings, designating specific details of peasant life.*

The Corpus does not have enough data to establish whether this remained true in the 1930s. There are, of course, dialectal words in peasant letters, especially those from the Murmansk oblast' having to do with fishing and reindeer herding. Most of them are found in dictionaries and thus can be assumed to be not very local.[19] Here is a representative passage.

## Example 3.26 #185, p.469. Dialectal words for reindeer

олени вышли две важенки слопанками один моя а втора была из старого вонделка дак та вышла слопанкой да вышол бык большорогой [ . . . ] видели встади но все еще непойман шардуй вышол

*Translation*

The deer came out, two *females* with *little ones*, one mine and the other [ . . . ] a *younger female*, that one came out with *a little one* and a bull with big horns came out, he was seen in the herd but not yet caught, a *male* came out

*Comment*

The italicized words are dialectal in the original: важенка, лопанок, шардуй, вонделка. The first two are found in the Dal' dictionary and in the writings of Prishvin, a well-known nature writer of the twentieth century. Шардуй is a variant of шардун, also found in Dal' and used in the more literate letter #186. Вонделка was found in one 1933 document on the Internet.[20] However, metaphoric uses of concrete dialectal vocabulary have not been found in the Corpus.

Outside the Corpus, this aspect of peasant language was addressed in the linguistic literature of the time under the rubric of "progress in language as peasants become kolkhozniks."

The *locus classicus* for this line of work is the often-quoted Filin (1936).[21] Filin's main thesis is articulated in the opening sentence: "The collectivization of agriculture began to move peasant speech toward the literary language, in a way unprecedented in any other country in the depth, scope, and speed of this development." (p.135) The article also contains a vicious attack on Selishchev (1928) which, according to Filin, "views the terminological neologisms of the contemporary village through the prism of the kulak worldview" (p.148, fn.9). However, Filin was of peasant stock himself, and his article contains a great deal of interesting material collected in the village of Selino, Tula oblast', where he was born and grew up. He is thus describing the passing away of the language of his childhood, and one can hear nostalgia in his otherwise turgid Soviet-academic writing. In discussing toponymics he writes: "There has been a rapid extinction of local names for landscape features, first of all of those that designate small openings in the forest, little valleys and hills, and so on. Young people do not even have any memories of them" (p.138). Filin cites a great number of imaginative, sometimes poetic, sometimes sharply descriptive older names, such as портки (pants) for a meadow that juts out into the neighboring field in two "sleeves," and observes that they all "lose their individuality" (p.138), getting new purely functional names, such as "field one, field two, field three [ . . . ] according to the order of planting," or "team 1 cell, team 2 cell, [ . . . ]" according to the team working on those plots (p.139).

One can assume that this process applied to the entire country, splitting generations. The older generation seems to have preserved the old toponymics: in the next chapter, a peasant character born before 1917 could even in 1992 describe in great detail all the little nooks and lanes in his village, what their names used to be, and why (Kovalev 1996:229).

2. *There are few adjectives; appositive (i.e., purely decorative) adjectives are absent.*[22]

This observation certainly holds: peasant letters do not contain descriptive prose. Adjectives appear mostly in formulaic expressions.

3. *Word formation is concise: in most cases when there are different forms in the standard language and peasant language, the peasant form is shorter.*

There are a number of examples of this in the Corpus. A few are given below, together with the literary form and the nearest big city, to indicate the spread:

испыток (#54) испытание, Voronezh
   своячина (#64) свояченица; Udmurtiia
   распута (#185) распутица; Murmansk
   кланится кланятся (3d person Sg and Pl forms, mostly in greetings) found in #54 Voronezh, #70 unknown, #155 Voronezh, #164 Tambov, 169 Пенза; 236 Voronezh) кланяться кланяются. This form is well represented in folklore but absent in current dictionaries.

4. *The suffix ова-ива is uncommon in peasant speech, especially in forming the imperfective counterpart to prefixed perfective verbs.*

Examples are presented in the same way as in point 3 above. The spelling of the examples is preserved.

ходатойствать (#36) ходатойствовать
наклодать (#83а) наклодывать
существать (#227) существовать

The point is not so much that the forms with the simpler suffix are found but that the literary suffix is uncommon.

5. *The verb ratio is high, and transitive verbs are frequent.*

There are no new examples of transitive verbs that would be intransitive (e.g., with prepositional phrase complements) in the literary language. However, the verb ratio remains very high.

6. *There are few deverbal nouns; nouns with the Church-Slavonic suffixes –ени(е)/–ани(е)/- ити(е) are extremely rare.*

This remains true.

7. *There are few abstract nouns like участие 'participation,' and no phrases with semantically empty verbs like принять участие 'take part.'*

This remains true.

8. *There are no present active participles or other Church Slavonic forms, which contributes to the stylistic profile and shortens the average word length.*

This remains true.

9. *Conjunction-less complex sentences are common.*

This is a common feature of spoken language of the educated as well.[23] However, there are variants that are specific to peasant spoken syntax. A conjunction introducing *the main clause* after a conjunction-less subordinate clause was illustrated in 3.17, from the village schoolteacher. Here are more examples; the conjunction is то or дак.

## Example 3.27 Conjunctions *то* and *дак*

3.27.1

как поехали говорили что будем помогать но придеш **дак** все нетак, в вдругу сторону

When they left they said that we will help, but [when] I come everything's wrong, in the opposite way. #42a, p.324. Kandalaksha

3.27.2

денег у меня уже не много без работы жить **дак** к весне не останется нечево

I am already low on money, [if] I live without work, by spring there will be nothing left. #51, p.336. Murmansk

3.27.3

скока ни работали вколхози **то** нет ни чево
However much we worked in the kolkhoz, there is nothing (or: we have nothing) #14, p.296. Gomel', Belarus

3.27.4

миша ты писал и насчот своих делов **то** я ездил ивану и он хотел все устроит
Misha you wrote about your business also so I traveled to Ivan and he wanted to arrange everything. #191, p.476. Arkhangelsk

Some of these sentences can be described in non-syntactic terms: the initial conjunction-less clause sets up the topic, and the conjunction signals the comment, the new information pertaining to that topic.

While то is common in the literary language, the conjunction **дак** is one of the best predictors of "peasantness." The Corpus provides material for an interesting analysis of its uses.

10. *Formulaic expressions of various kinds are very common. Many are formally structured by a rhyme or a syntactic parallelism.*

Creative uses of language are not frequent in the peasant letters of the Corpus. Neither the genre nor the circumstances were conducive for linguistic creativity. Those with energy and optimism were not peasants, and their innovations were more in the style of letters to power of Chapter 2, see the next section.

Structured poetic language mostly appears in the descriptions of grief:

коля тогда я тебя забуда когда мои гласки закроюца #83а
Kolia, I will then forget you when my eyes close.
я тебя тогда забуду когда закрою свои глаза и зароют меня взѣмлю #222
I will then forget you when I close my eyes and they put me in the ground.

## Losses and Echoes of the 1920s

By the 1930s, some features of earlier peasant language were already lost. Earlier, with respect to pre-revolutionary material, we noted that while the language had a lot of proverbs, these were never used decoratively; and also that the distancing phrase 'как говорится' was never employed to introduce them. This is no longer true in 1939. In #191, the father writes: "миша бут немного осторожнее пословица говорится что бережоново и бох берегот так и тут" (Misha be a bit more careful, the saying goes that he who stays protected him God also protects, so it is here too).

In imitations of SovYaz there are instances of baroque syntax and jumbled vocabulary reminiscent of the 1920s. One such was noted in 3.21:

### Example 3.28 An excerpt from 3.21, #130, p.414

Костя среди наглого обстрела финляндской военщины советских войск вызвал огромное возмущение коликтив рабочих и интельгенции нашего завода.

*Translation*

Kostia (NN) amid the insolent shelling of Finliand military of Soviet troops evoked huge indignation the community of the workers and intelligentsia of our factory.

There are examples of redistribution of meaning to adjectives and of extra Genitives with vague semantic connection to the head of the noun phrase:

### Example 3.29 Extra Genitives, vague connections

*3.29.1*

желаю я тебе главного здоровия твоей службы
  I wish you main health of your service [i.e., My main wish is for your health in your service.] #125, p.408.

*3.29.2*

я говорила это в порыве нервного состояния
  I was saying this in an outburst of my nervous condition #188, p.473.

There are echoes of Platonov and Babel':

### Example 3.30

*3.30.1*

ибудь честным и преданным красноармейцем за дело рабочего класса.

and be an honest and dedicated Red Army solider for the cause of the working class #207, p.492.

3.30.2

желаю тебя хорошего здоровья и счастливой жизни вашей молодости
    I wish you (T) good health and the happy life of your (V) youth #252, p.534.

3.30.3

Писмо таварищу Половинкину Зоту Михаловичу пишить таварищь Жупиков Димитрий Анисимович собщет тибе таварыщ Жупиков Димитрий втом что я нахажусь врядах Красной Армии и молодым патриотом Красноармии
    This letter to comrade Polovinkin Zot Mikhailovich is writing comrade Zhulikov Dimitrii Anisimovich informing you comrade Zhulikov Dimitrii in that I am located in the ranks of the Red Army and as a young patriot of the Redarmy. #161, p.445.

These were probably the last gasps of that kind of flamboyance. The Great Patriotic War, coming up just eighteen months later, was too enormous for it.

## CONCLUSIONS

The main conclusion of this chapter is that the number of peasants was dwindling, but those who remained preserved their language habits and their separateness reasonably well. Preservation was helped by the ongoing tradition of the genre of personal letter, although the mechanisms by which it happened are completely unknown. It was also helped by government policies that kept peasants as separate second-class citizens and restricted their access to many economic and social benefits available to urbanites, including access to quality education.

    There were also losses, especially in the kinds of creativity exhibited in pre-revolutionary materials. It should be remembered that tens of millions of peasants, the best and the brightest among them, had been lost to civil war, famine, government violence, and migration to cities. The approaching Great Patriotic War and another famine (1946) would add many more millions to those losses. The war also resulted in a lack of materials that persisted until the late 1950s. What emerged after the silence is the subject of the next chapter.

## NOTES

1. Platonov's novel *Котлован* (The Foundation Pit), written in the late 1920s, shows LikBez in action, in its distilled essence. The "activist" teacher, the only male in the room, asks a student what words she knows that begin with the letter "a." She lists avant-garde, activist, advance (payment), arch-leftie, antifascist. Upon approval by the teacher, the women, all of them lying on the floor for lack of chairs, write the words on the floor with pieces of plaster (no chalk).

2. Most of this section is based on Tarkhova's very informative book. Like Graziosi (1996), she stops her exposition in 1933, "before the great famine," because it was a watershed event not only in the village and the army, but in the entire country. (11–12) As argued in Chapter 4, it was a linguistic watershed as well.

3. Detailed analysis of moods (настроения) in SovYaz is found in Nakhimovsky (2015), based on an internal NKVD report, and Nakhimovsky (2018), based on the transcripts of the trial of Jewish Anti-Fascist Committee.

4. For the late Soviet usage see Nakhimovsky, "Social distribution of forms of address in contemporary Russian." 1977.

5. An analogy with this variable use of pronouns can be found in Shakespeare's *Richard III*, in a dialog between Richard and Anna in which they switch from *you* to *thou*, in opposite directions, following the dynamic of their conversation.

6. Those familiar with Russian grammar will notice that письмо (letter) which is a Neuter noun in standard Russian is treated as Feminine in this letter and, in fact, in most letters of the Corpus. As noted in Avanesov (1964) the Neuter gender had been losing its position in Russian dialects and in some of them was lost altogether.

7. Boyd 1991 fn. 22 incorrectly states that the letters were collected from prisoners of war.

8. Carl Gustaf Emil Mannerheim (1867–1951) was born in Finland, then part of the Russian Empire. He had a distinguished military career in Russia, reaching the rank of lieutenant general during WWI. In 1918, after Finland declared independence, he led the war effort that defeated the Finnish "Reds" and their Bolshevik allies. He was Commander-in-chief again in 1939 and led Finland through two wars, unavoidable difficult cohabitation with the Nazis, an even more difficult armistice with the Soviets, and the post-war reconstruction. He was admired by both Hitler, who flew to Finland for his 75th birthday, and Stalin, who personally crossed off his name from the list of Finnish war criminals. He remains the greatest national hero in his country, "the Greatest Finn Who Ever Lived."

9. The terminology is from recursive definitions in math and computer science, e.g., the recursive definition of an integer: 1 is an integer (base); any integer plus 1 is also an integer (derivation). These two rules together "derive" the entire infinite set of integers. Our set is not infinite but an explicit procedure that identifies it seems useful.

10. This is a good example of how synchronic variation indicates future diachronic change, the subject matter of "variational sociolinguistics."

11. There were reelections of local Soviets on 24 December 1939.

12. Peasant attitudes to death as found in the Corpus in comparison with Tolstoy's novella "Master and Man" form the subject of my paper "20th century peasant letters as background to 19th century Russian literature," 2019.

13. The text says сваха, which ordinarily would refer to a son's, not brother's mother-in-law, but the usage might have been fluid.

14. Litovskaia (2016:637) writes: "Universal literacy of the Soviet population had been reached by 1940, so women write their letters themselves." This fails to distinguish gradations of literacy and the social divisions they reflect.

15. https://www.youtube.com/watch?v=7kpd74vcmUo.

16. Yokoyama (2008:414) call these "long-distance" relative clauses and provides some striking examples. Although she does not associate them with a specific formula serving a specific discourse purpose, her examples do fall into this formulaic category.

17. This brief battle had two momentous consequences: it established the reputation of Zhukov, who became the main Soviet commander in WWII, and it convinced the Japanese to make peace with the USSR. This allowed the Soviets to move Siberian divisions west and defend Moscow in the decisive battle of the war.

18. Outside the Corpus, I have found this opening in a newspaper piece of 1935, but clearly it is much older, probably from the time of early NEP, when popular culture was full of energy.

19. One exception is the word шитник (#141) which sounds like a recent English borrowing but is, in fact, recorded in the dictionary as a special kind of boat. However, in the letter it is clearly used in a different meaning: an item that the son brings to his mother in the village, along with nails and stockings.

20. http://kolanord.ru/html_public/col_periodicals/Karelo-Murm_kray/KMK_1933_9-10/KMK_1933_9-10/assets/basic-html/page69.html.

21. Filin was an odious figure who made a successful career in Stalin's time, famous for his staunch opposition to cosmopolitanism and Western influences in linguistics. He was in trouble in the early 1950s but made a comeback and lived long enough to be the editor of Lapteva (1976).

22. On the distinction between appositive and restrictive relative clauses and adjectives see, Chapter 1, note 12.

23. See an exhaustive treatment in Lapteva 1976:284–338 and references therein.

*Chapter 4*

# Scholars and Narratives from the 1950s to Today

## 4.1 A LONGER TIMEFRAME, THE ENDANGERED LANGUAGE

This chapter is quite different from the preceding ones. It covers many more decades, from the 1920s to the twenty-first century. Around 1990, it crosses a radical break that resulted, among other momentous changes, in an outpouring of available materials on the language of peasants. (Some of these materials were created after the break, while others had accumulated over the last decades of the Soviet Union and suddenly were allowed to emerge from archives and repositories.) Compared to the data used in earlier chapters, the new data is not only abundant but also different in genre: much of it involves sound recordings of *extended biographical narratives* that resulted from organized field work by linguists, sociologists, historians, and ethnographers. The present chapter thus has to address the specific issues of peasant narratives, as seen in their linguistic structure and in their treatment of biographical and historical data. While Chapter 1 presented three short examples of narratives, these do not compare either in volume or historical scope to what was recorded by very old peasants at the end of the twentieth century, when they could speak about their lives under conditions of virtually no censorship.

This chapter continues to trace the loss of the language of peasants. Neither the liberalizing historical break nor the resulting visibility of peasant speech had any impact on the steady, continuous process of its disappearance: the newly abundant wealth of data came from a small and rapidly dwindling base of old speakers whose severely endangered social dialect was about to pass away. This chapter will trace the loss through decades and disciplines, beginning with the 1930s. The overall trajectory is that until Stalin's death the socio-economic condition of kolkhozniks/peasants was terrible, but it started steadily improving in the mid-1950s and throughout the late Soviet period. Following cultural liberalization, peasants were sometimes powerfully represented in film and in the prose of "village writers" (Abramov, Belov, Rasputin, Shukshin, and others). But as subjects of scholarly attention they remained beyond what censors would allow. And in spite of material improvement, their way of life remained unattractive to young people, who left in large numbers for the more exciting and promising life in the city. At the same time, as kolkhozes became bigger and more mechanized, there were fewer available jobs, and many half-empty villages far from usable roads were declared unsupportable and resettled. Zaionchkovskaia (1999) provides an informative summary.

## Endangerment and Loss of the Language of Peasants

The process of urbanization and the concomitant loss of local languages or dialects was not, of course, unique to the Soviet Union. Nor was it unusual for linguists to collect a large sample of disappearing data from a small and dwindling base of native speakers. Russia—the Soviet Union—was only unusual in that the cause of the delay in data collection and analysis was state censorship rather than simple neglect, as in most other cases. Otherwise, the notions of language endangerment and language loss gained currency in many parts of the world in the 1970s and 1980s, when it was realized that of the 7,000 or so languages in the world about half were close to extinction. It used to be that small local languages, some of them spoken in a single mountain valley or by a small nomadic tribe, had co-existed with a larger regional or national language without being harmed. In the twentieth century, with urbanization, economic development, and encroachment by the dominant language and culture, smaller languages were coming under increasing pressure. The pressure was economic, cultural, and often governmental. In terms of numbers, the Anglo-Saxon world (Australia, Canada, and the United States) did the most damage; in terms of government violence, the Communist regimes were, unsurprisingly, particularly harsh: only in the Soviet Union and China were local clerics—shamans, mullahs, lamas—forcibly removed or simply killed to expedite the process of cultural and linguistic transition. But across the globe, native languages were constricted to the point that they were used predominantly in domestic contexts. Only the dominant language would be heard at school, and in some times and places children would be punished for speaking their own tongue. The critical point is reached when children no longer learn their language natively. Once this happens, it is only the matter of several decades before all the native speakers are gone and the language is extinct.

The 1980s saw the beginning of a massive effort to collect data on endangered and disappearing languages in the English-speaking world, continental

Europe, and Japan. That effort soon produced a substantial body of both archival data and analytical literature on documenting, preserving, and sometimes even revitalizing severely endangered languages. Displaying the familiar historical pattern, this literature is completely silent on the language of Russian peasants. The main emphasis of endangered language research has been on small languages, typically those that have been subjected to colonial oppression. As the largest social and sociolinguistic group in the country, Russian peasants were always too numerous to be considered an endangered group—until, suddenly, they weren't. The disappearance of the last generation of peasants was widely recognized, but no connection was made to the conceptual machinery of endangered language study: field methods for collecting materials; archival methods for preserving and annotating the accumulated collections; and online delivery methods for making the materials available to both scholars and interested public (see, e.g., Austin and Sallabank 2015). As a result, the collections of peasant speech published since 1990 are either on paper or in PDF files on the Web. They use different principles for transcribing and editing, and interdisciplinary communication between the fields of study (sociology, history, linguistics, ethnography) ranges from imperfect to non-existent.

With respect to documentation, the so-called minority languages (малые языки) of Russia fared better than peasant dialects: such languages as Archi in the North Caucasus, Nganasan on the Taimyr peninsula above the Arctic Circle, and Itelmen on Kamchatka were recorded and documented more rigorously than Russian peasant narratives (Kibrik et al. 2008). Russian urban speech, both educated and uneducated, was abundantly recorded, extensively studied, and reached a wide audience. From the 1960s through the 1980s recordings of educated urban speech was a popular, indeed fashionable, subject of linguistic research, while recordings of peasant narratives simply sank into repositories.[1]

As a result of this combination of attitudes, the typical questions about endangered languages have rarely been posed with respect to Russian peasants, including the crucial one on transmission. When was the decisive break between the peasant language of the parents and the more homogenized language of their children, both among migrants to the city and among the families remaining in the village? In the published material, only one researcher, working on data from a village in Siberia, observes that after 1930 the habits and patterns of peasant speech were no longer transmitted to the next generation (D'iachok 2003:104, fn. 17).[2] A similar conclusion is supported by a rigorous forthcoming study of a group of villages in the Archangelsk region (Daniel et al. 2018).[3]

Kasatkin (1993) shows that the shift was due not only to the socio-economic disruption of collectivization but also to Soviet educational policies.

He quotes an influential 1931 source: "Language teaching is part of language policy, which in our circumstances is the policy of the proletariat. [ . . . ] The Leninist stage of methodology calls for a struggle to achieve high literacy, including in oral speech. [ . . . ] This naturally follows from Lenin's general position that every cook [female] must know how to run the country, and therefore every custodian must be in command of his language well beyond his modest occupation" (p.87). Kasatkin continues: "What we see today is the result of cooks and custodians running our country" (p.87). In language-teaching policy, the result was a heavy-handed effort to eliminate all traces of local dialects (p.88). By the 1990s this had led to what Kasatkin called the degradation of Russian peasant speech: "Russian dialects are the present reality. They will not disappear in the near future, either. However, they are moving noticeably toward degradation" (Kasatkin 1993:90). His words date precisely to the time when the peasant pre-war generation was dying out, replaced by its post-war descendants.

More indirect data about the generational language change comes from the birth dates of the speakers and the time when they were recorded. It turns out that most speakers were born between 1910 and 1935, and were over 65 at the time of recording. There are exceptions. Some people were born earlier and lived very long lives; some were recorded long before publication and were thus younger at the date of the recording. Speakers who were born later in the 1930s tend to be from remote places where the language of peasants survived longer. In Kasatkin (2010), four respondents out of thirty-seven were born in 1936, three of them in Arkhangelsk province and one, an Old Believer, in Eastern Siberia. The next youngest was born in 1931. The entire distribution is shown in Table 4.1 compiled from the book's table of contents.

Lopatin and Lopatina (2006) compiled similar information in a paragraph of text. For consistency, it is represented here as Table 4.2. Most of their 149 respondents are from the Kemerovo province, but some are from the Novosibirsk province and the Altai territory. Several "typical stories from Ukraine, Belarus, etc." (p.12) are included for comparison. Note the disproportion of men and women both tables: after WWII women in villages outnumbered men 2 to 1, and they lived longer.

Table 4.1 Distribution by Dates of Birth. Kasatkin, 2010. Compiled by the Author

| Range of Birth Years | Number of Respondents |
| --- | --- |
| 1931 and later | 5 (see explanation above) |
| 1921–30 | 10 |
| 1911–20 | 15 |
| 1905–10 | 2 (1906, 1908) |
| Before 1905 | 3 (recorded in 1959–63, when they were in their 60s) |
| Total | 35 (3 men, one of whom in a group of 5 and says little) |

**Table 4.2  Distribution by Dates of Birth. Lopatin and Lopatina 2006:12–13.** Compiled by the Author

| Range of Birth Years | Number of Respondents |
|---|---|
| 1931 and later | 8 |
| 1921–30 | 72 |
| 1911–20 | 54 |
| 1904–10 | 15 |
| Total | 149, of them 29 men and 120 women |

The sharp drop in the number of respondents born after 1935 points to another difference between this chapter and the preceding ones. From Chapters 1 to 2 to 3, and chronologically from 1910 to 1920 to 1930, every decade and every chapter represents a new generation of peasant speakers, who acquired their first language in a peasant family. As this transmission of language largely stopped in the 1930s, the materials of this chapter come from speakers who belong to the same generation as the wives and younger siblings of Chapter 3, now older and less numerous.

Typically, when the youngest speakers of a language are already in their sixties, their language becomes severely endangered—contaminated by borrowings, impoverished in its vocabulary and grammar, and lacking in idiomatic nuance. This is what happened to most minority languages of Russia, surrounded by Russian or the dominant language of their region. The same general process would apply to disappearing local and social dialects. However—and this another distinctive feature of the language of Russian peasants—their disappearing remnant did not lose its language. (This may be due to the isolation of many villages and their loss of young people.) There are, of course, new lexical items reflecting new historical events or technological innovations. Some frequent words and phrases from the media unavoidably seep into peasants' speech. But the syntax, phraseology, and the narrative flow mostly persevere. This is illustrated, as much as space allows, by the examples of the next section. They are largely grouped by historical topic, but each group—indeed, each example—exhibits linguistic phenomena that go back to the observations of Chapter 1. The fact that the examples come from widely distributed parts of the country testifies to the abundance and homogeneity of the material.

The collectors were aware how little time was left to accumulate this abundance. Valerii Vinogradskii, the most prolific collector of peasant language data in Shanin's expeditions, later wrote several important books about it. Speaking of the generation born before 1930, he testified in dramatic terms to the feeling of loss (Vinogradskii 2016:136):

> The developing idea to preserve the contours and interpret the evolution of the original peasant language was propelled and accelerated by our witnessing its

final death hour. For we were, in effect, in the presence of the massive loss of the entire generation of Russian peasants whose social, cultural, and linguistic roots lay hidden in a century-old layer of history.

Berdinskikh 2011:7 takes an even longer historical view:

> We must clearly recognize that what happened in the Russia of the 1970s–1990s was not simply the natural loss of the generations born in the 1900s–1920s. With these people the thousand-year-old epoch of national life, a pattern of everyday existence that was formed over centuries, disappeared into the past.

These nostalgic observations, however accurate, need to be juxtaposed against the socio-economic conditions of the lost generations of peasantry. Even in the best of times these conditions frequently included extreme hardship; poor education, especially for women; and inefficient methods of production, also seen in examples from chapters 1–3. The biographical narratives in this chapter describe periods of hardship even more starkly. It is rare to find a happy life among people born as Russian peasants between 1910 and 1935 who lived as peasants up to the 1990s.

*Sources before 1990*

The distribution of years during which peasant texts were recorded is historically as indicative as the distribution of the speakers' birth years. Unsurprisingly, nothing of scholarly value was recorded between 1935 and 1955, in spite of some efforts at "kolkhoz ethnography" described in the next section. After Stalin's death, some aspects of liberalization were dramatic but the ideological control of the state and the party continued, especially in everything that concerned peasants and collectivization. This will be illustrated by the research projects of three scholars, the ethnographer Kushner, the linguist Kasatkin, and the historian Danilov. Kushner was by far the oldest, born in 1889, while Kasatkin and Danilov were born in the 1920s, served as young military officers in the war, and started their scholarly careers in the 1950s.

**A Kolkhoz Ethnography; the Village of Viriatino**

In 1948, Soviet ethnographers were asked to focus less on the past and more on the current condition of Soviet nationalities, including Russians. Kushner was one of the leaders in this line of research. He was well prepared. Born in 1889, by 1917 he had both some college education and a colorful revolutionary career. A private in the Civil War, he quickly rose through the ranks to become in 1920 the chief political officer of an entire army. (This was a common trajectory for young men of his profile: recall Iakovlev, the creator of *Krest'ianskaia Gazeta*, in Chapter 2.)

After the Civil War Kushner became a professor in the Sverdlov Communist University (the main school for party cadres at the time), where his interests gravitated to ethnography. Most of the time before WWII he worked as an academic and a journalist, but there were also stretches of diplomatic and possibly intelligence work. His most influential publication came out during the war, when he directed a group of ethnographers creating maps of ethnic territories and boundaries in Central Europe and the Balkans. They were pursuing questions like how far west did Belorussian populations extend, and what was the ethnic composition of East Prussia. Just one copy of the publication was produced. It was sent to the Soviet General Staff to share with the diplomats working on the post-war borders in Europe. Kushner published the theoretical underpinnings of his work in 1947 and then turned his attention to Russian kolkhozes (Alymov 2006).

In the early 1950s, against many odds, Kushner conducted an in-depth ethnographic study of a single Russian village and its kolkhoz. He first proposed such a study in 1952. The search for an appropriate kolkhoz lasted two years, hampered by the requirement that the target of study must correspond to a "typical kolkhoz" as defined in official ideology. This proved difficult: one kolkhoz chairman drank too much and had almost drowned his wife; a different village had ideologically objectionable holy springs still visited by pilgrims. Finally, the village of Viriatino in Tambov province became the object of a massive research expedition that included, in addition to Kushner, five ethnographers, a graduate student, a musicologist, an architect, and several photographers. The expedition lasted three years with several month-long stays. Methodologically, it served as a prototype for later ethnographic and linguistic fieldwork that included extended stays and immersion in local life. As scholarship, however, its outcome was practically useless. One example will illustrate. One of the ethnographers was particularly skillful in establishing close rapport with the peasants, who responded by openly sharing with her their thoughts and memories. Remembering 1929, a kolkhoz organizer recalled:

**Example 4.1 Ethnographer's record**

Собрания в основном состояли из женщин. Мужчины шли на собрание неохотно, посылали баб, мы мол не хотим колхоза и не идем. А самим интересно, о чем разговор будет, вот бабы и приходили на собрание. Начнем выступать на собрании, что межи нам мешают, что единоличное хозяйство неудобно вести, а потом осторожно о колхозе. Как скажем о колхозе, все орут: "Не желаем!"

*Translation*

Meetings mostly consisted of women. Men didn't want to go, sent their women, like "we don't want a kolkhoz, and we're not going." But they were curious what the talk would be about, so the women came to meetings. We would start our speeches about how plot boundaries get in the way, and individual plots are difficult to manage, and then carefully about kolkhoz. As soon as we mention the kolkhoz, everybody screams "We don't want it!"

This field record was preserved in the archives but did not make into the official report, where it was rewritten as follows (skipping the turgid Russian prose):

> As soon as ten-household meetings began, at which the question of organizing a kolkhoz was raised, kulaks would start a fire, setting fire to some barn or shed. Afraid to speak openly, kulaks conducted anti-kolkhoz agitation through their wives, sisters, and mothers. At the early meetings, the women of Viriatino spoke against organizing a kolkhoz, responding with the shout "We don't want it" to our calls to join the kolkhoz.

In this rendering, the "men" of the original become "kulaks" who engage in crimes. The name of the ethnographer who collected the uncomfortable materials was not included in the final report. The book based on this project was published in 1958 but preserved Stalinist censorship. It was not until 2006, when the young ethnographer Sergei Alymov revisited the same village and collected multiple interviews with two very old people, that useful data emerged from the village. Their recordings provide some of the best examples for the post-war period.

## Dialectologists at the Russian Language Institute

Soviet linguists-dialectologists started collecting peasant recordings in the late 1950s. There were several centers of this activity, including the universities at Saratov, Kazan', Penza, and Tomsk, but the most prominent one was the Russian Language Institute of the Russian Academy (RLI) in Moscow, under the leadership of L. L. Kasatkin (b.1926). Kasatkin received his degree from the RLI and was instrumental in organizing fieldwork, conferences, and a series of publications entitled *Материалы и исследования по русской диалектологии* (Materials and explorations on Russian dialectology). Kasatkin (2010) includes several recordings from the years 1959–1971. Unlike dialectal records typical of the early twentieth century that consisted mostly of phonetic observations and lists of local lexical material, Kasatkin's expeditions collected extended narratives filled with biographical detail. Theoretical justifications for this new approach—or any other discussion of peasant narratives—had to wait until much later: Gol'din's 1997 doctoral dissertation and Kasatkin's (2017:9–20) seminal article. In the meantime, going back to the list of recordings in Kasatkin's (2010) table of contents, we see a big gap between 1971 and 1986. This is because in 1974 Kasatkin was fired from the IRL for dissident activities that had provoked vicious attacks by the old Stalinist Filin (see Chapter 2), still in a position of power. From 1986 until his retirement, Kasatkin returned to his role as leader the institute's Dialectology section, operating within a much wider range of post-perestroika possibilities. The first to exploit and expand those possibilities were historians and sociologists.

## History, Sociology, Linguistics

In the years before 1990, the disciplines of history and sociology were also largely silent, or silenced, on the subject of peasants. The prominent Russian historian of peasantry, Viktor Danilov (1925–2004), had started his work in the 1950s, completing his dissertation in 1954. Reminiscing in 2002, he writes: "From the early 1930s there was a break in scholarship in the fields of sociology, economics, and history, and restarting it in the mid-1950s required a good deal of time and effort" (Danilov 2002:117). While history and economics continued in ideologically sanctioned versions throughout the Stalinist period, from the 1930s to the 1950s sociology was officially banned. In 1967, Danilov participated as a guest historian in the first-ever Soviet conference on sociology. At that conference, "the possibility of the historical-sociological study of the Russian village was completely out of the question. It took another 20 years (i.e., until late perestroika) before such a possibility was realized" (Danilov 2002:117). In the mid-1970s, Danilov's work followed a trajectory similar to Kasatkin's—in effect, the trajectory of the Brezhnev period of stagnation. Danilov's book *Советская преколхозная деревня* (The Soviet pre-kolkhoz village) had already been typeset when, at the last moment, on censors' orders, the book was "scattered"—that is, the typeset was dumped back into bins. Its material had to wait until the late 1980s, when many things became possible, including genuinely open contacts with Western scholars.

### Teodor Shanin and the First Collection of Peasant Interviews

For peasant studies, the most important Western contact was with Teodor Shanin, Chair of Sociology at the University of Manchester. The meeting between Danilov and Shanin in Moscow was transformative: they were both pre-eminent scholars of Russian peasantry, and they had shared experience of combat at the age of 18 as junior officers in their respective wars: Danilov as an artillerist in WWII, and Shanin in the Palmach—a special operations unit—in Israel's War of Independence. Between the two of them, working jointly and separately, they created the discipline of peasant studies in Russia.

Upon retirement Shanin moved to Moscow and in short order organized a series of expeditions to different regions of Russia to interview the surviving peasants. Eight interviewees, born between 1902 and 1922, are represented in Kovalev (1996). This is the first post-1990—in fact, the first ever—collection of peasant biographical narratives. At about the same time, 1995, Shanin created a new educational institution, the Moscow School of Social and Economic Sciences, commonly known as the Shaninka. For this exploit he received The Most Excellent Order of the British Empire from the Queen of England and a medal from the Russian Ministry of Education. Working from this institutional base, Shanin and Danilov organized regular seminars and produced a great number of publications, including many collections of documents, both from government archives and peasant interviews.[4]

*Kovalev, Vinogradskii and Others*

Kovalev (1996) is a large body of remarkable and at the time unprecedented material. A powerful and informative document, it is marred by a whole set of questionable editorial practices. (See Vinogradskii 2017:15–19 and references therein.) Names of places and people were changed and orthography was significantly normalized. Parts of interviews were moved around and reorganized into chronological narratives, with newly introduced subdivisions that corresponded to ethnographic topics and historical periods. Within the narratives, we don't see the questions from the interviewers, which are replaced with possibly invented "echo-questions" by the interviewees themselves, e.g., "How uncle Kondrat get to Krasnodar? I don't know that." (248) or "You said: Why did we call them 'kadets'?" (249). The resulting text cannot be properly called a transcript, and no tapes are available.

Acknowledging the importance of the book, the dialectologist G. V. Kalitkina gives a reasonable summary of the situation: "From the point of view of sociology the materials are still relevant but as a source for linguistic research texts of these kind are not valid" (Kalitkina 2006). Her verdict is certainly applicable to the study of phonetics and morphology. Here, however, we assume that at the higher levels of word-formation, sentence, paragraph, and larger units of discourse the materials are reliable. This is especially true for materials based on interviews by Valerii Vinogradskii, a professor of philosophy in Saratov.

Vinogradskii was the most prolific contributor to Kovalev (1996), responsible for about forty percent of its content. After the book came out he continued working with peasant material, publishing several books of texts and analysis. (See the summary table in the next subsection.) The books include unedited transcripts of conversations incorporated in Kovalev (1996); additional recordings from that time that had not been included in that book; and new recordings with transcripts. Since Vinogradskii's materials are more reliable, this book uses Kovalev (1996) sparingly (although some of it is unquestionably useful). Otherwise we rely on the data that Vinogradskii generously shared, including answers that he provided to multiple questions. His latest book, Vinogradskii (2017), includes interviews both with the last generation of peasants and with those of their children who did not migrate to cities but continued working the land. These will be useful in the comparison, later in this chapter, between peasants' language and the *prostorechie* of Chapter 1.

*Dialectologists*

Much dialectological data is scattered as examples in research articles. Following Gol'din (1997) those examples included excerpts from narratives and discussions of their discourse structure (see, e.g., Gol'din 2009, Bukrinskaia and Karmakova 2012b). The first substantial collection of peasant texts published as part of a book is Myznikov (2005:136–254). The introductory note (p.136) says: "Russian dialectological science, which presents fundamental works on all imaginable aspects of Russian folk dialects, has practically no large published collections of dialectal texts that would present samples of dialectal speech and also show the life, everyday circumstances, and working conditions of village people." Studies by historians and sociologists are not mentioned at all, a serious gap also seen in Kasatkin (2010). Although dialectology has opened the door to narrative discourse as a linguistic phenomenon, it has remained an island within social disciplines and even within linguistics as far as non-dialectologists are concerned. This is acknowledged as a serious problem in Gol'din (2000:54): "contemporary studies of Russian speech are mostly conducted separately for each of its social varieties." It is indeed true that dialectology remains mutually separate from, e.g., the study of *prostorechie*, even when it contains data from peasant migrants to the city. This is elaborated in the section on sociolinguistic groups later in the chapter.

## Summary of the Main Data Collections

The main data collections are brought together in the table below. There are many overlaps in content and comment between the collections from different disciplines, but few, if any, cross-references between them. In addition to the books listed in Table 4.3, many peasant narratives or significant excerpts from them are found in articles by Russian dialectologists and students of *prostorechie*.

## The Comparative Quality of the Resources as Linguistc Data

As indicated, not all of these sources are equally reliable as linguistic data. Everything from dialectologists (Kasatkin 2017 and journal articles) is typically very reliable, and the recordings are preserved in institute and university collections. However, even the transcripts in Kasatkin (2010) use standard punctuation, and, at the insistence of the publisher, were rearranged into chronological narratives and divided into titled sections (Kasatkin 2017:467 fn.1.). This is not very different from the practice of Kovalev (1996), although at the level of spelling and morphology Kasatkin (2010) is certainly more accurate.

Vinogradskii's texts in his later publications are not rearranged, and his own remarks are preserved. However, they contain less data than in Kovalev (1996), and recordings, if still in existence, seem to be kept in his private collection. Vinogradskii is not a trained linguist—none of the sociologists or historians are—but his stated policy is not to introduce any editorial changes except punctuation. Berdinskikh (2011:15fn) follows the same principles: "The narratives [published in his book—AN] completely preserve the style of speech and the particulars of the local dialect, the colloquial nature of the locals' speech." By contrast, Lopatin and Lopatina (2006:13) openly and without any regrets confess to radical surgery: removing repetitions, replacing colloquial forms with "correct" ones, and even reorganizing the order of main and subordinate clauses in a sentence. Such distinctions between sources influenced the selection of material in the remainder of the chapter. Most of the examples are from Kasatkin (2017) and other dialectologists; Vinogradskii (2017) and other late publications; Alymov (2010); Shcheglova (2008); and Berdinskikh (2011). Vinogradskii's chapters in Kovalev (1996) are included only if confirmed as authentic by Vinogradskii.

Even within these constraints, there was much more material than could possibly be included in this book, and hard choices had to be made. Many remarkable, powerful, well-told, and linguistically striking stories had to be left out. It is hoped that the included examples can give an idea of the kinds of characters and plots that informed the lives of Russian peasants in the past century. Their purpose here is two-fold: to present the peasant view of history, as reflected in their vocabulary, and to convey the peasant way of organizing and telling a story of their life.

**Table 4.3** Data Sources. Compiled by the Author

| Editor-Compiler | Date | Discipline | Title in Translation (book titles in italics) |
| --- | --- | --- | --- |
| Matveeva, T.V. | 1995 | Culture studies-*prostorechie* | *Everyday speech of a Ural city: texts* |
| Kovalev, E.I. | 1996 | Sociology | *Voices of peasants* |
| Iastrebinskaia G.A. | 2005 | History | *The taiga village of Kobelevo* |
| Myznikov, S.A. | 2005 | Dialectology | *Russian dialects of the mid-Volga region* |
| Lopatin L.N. and Lopatina N.L. | 2006 | History | *Collectivization and de-kulakization in recallections of those who witnessed them* |
| Shcheglova, T.K. | 2008 | History | *The village and peasantry of the Altai region in the 20th century* |
| Vinogradskii, V.G. | 2009 | Interdisciplinary[1] | *The tools of the weak* |
| Kasatkin, L.L. | 2010 | Dialectology | *Russian village in the stories of of its inhabitants* |
| Alymov, Sergei | 2010 | Ethnography | A non-random village (a journal article) |
| Berdinskikh, V. | 2011 | History | *Voices of the mute* |
| Shalina, I.V | 2011 | Culture studies-*prostorechie* | *Everyday speech of a Ural city: an anthology* |
| Vinogradskii, V.G. | 2011 | Interdisciplinary | *Peasants' coordinates* |
| Vinogradskii, V.G. | 2012 | Interdisciplinary | *Protocols of the kolkhoz era* |
| Vinogradskii, V.G. | 2017 | Interdisciplinary | *Voices from below* |
| Kasatkin, L.L. | 2017 | Dialectology | *Selected works, vol.2* |

[1]Vinogradskii's PhD is in Philosophy, but his preoccupations in the last 25 years have been in sociology and discourse theory.

## 4.2 BIOGRAPHIC NARRATIVES AS HISTORICAL TESTIMONY

### The Peasant Periodization of history, from Pre-Revolutionary Times to the mid-1950s

In their narratives, peasants talk about their lives against the background of Russian and Soviet history. The way they divide history into periods and the labels they use for those periods differ from what is used by people from other social classes and found in standard textbooks. This section reviews major events and the peasant nomenclature for them. In the sections that follow, boldface will be used to indicate historically significant terms both in common and peasant usage.

The main topics of peasant historical narratives are wars, state violence, and hunger. The forty years between the beginning of WWI and the death of Stalin saw ten years of major wars; a revolution; two periods of state violence, one of them in a time of peace; and three famines, two of them huge and one simply big, which together carried away millions of lives. Unavoidably, all peasant narratives touch upon those events; they were also frequent subjects of interviewers' questions.

### Wars and Revolution

The earliest distinctly remembered event in life stories is **WWI**, always called "The German war" (германская война). The central theme is whether the father of the family came back, and in what condition. **WWII**, or the **Great Patriotic War**, is usually simply война (the war). The expressions "before the war" and "after the war" invariably refer to WWII.

The term Гражданская Война (**Civil War**) is rarely used. Rather, the entire period of 1917–1921 merged into one long революция (**Revolution**), an alien word whose meaning was not entirely clear to peasant speakers. The discrete event of Bolsheviks coming to power on October 25, 1917, registered only as a vague rumor, if at all.

Alongside the Western borrowing "революция" were Russian alternatives such as переворот, literally the "overthrow" but just like "революция," a time-extended reference to the entire period of turbulence. More colloquial terms also come up. Example 4.6 shows a local word, заворох, synonymous with standard заваруха (ruckus, commotion). Shcheglova (2008), a history of peasantry in the remote Altai region, reports that "революция" never made it there at all (p.59), and only the Russian terms were used.

## State Violence and Famines

The two prime periods of **state violence** were the Civil War requisitions of 1918–1921 (продразверстка), and the twin assaults of **collectivization** and **dekulakization** (раскулачивание) of 1929–1933. The first of these was remote for the narrators of the 1990s, but the second cut deeply into historical memory: it was during the respondents' youth, it affected virtually all peasants, and it brought about a radical change that would never be undone.

**Раскулачивание** (dekulakization) is a long deverbal noun of the kind that peasants rarely used. There were thus local names for the destruction of the kulaks. In the Volga region, the verb корчевать ("uproot," like tree stumps) was common, together with the corresponding noun корчевка (**uprooting**). In some areas of the North the verb верхушить was used, from the root верх (top). (See Словарь говоров русского Севера, vol.2 and Iastrebinskaia 2005:23.) This metaphor views destruction in the opposite way: kulaks are treetops rather than tree roots, and instead of being uprooted, they are trimmed at the top.

## Famines and Hunger

Both periods of state violence ended with a famine. Russian uses the same word, **голод**, for both "hunger" and "famine." Peasant texts sometimes also use the more colloquial голодовка, which in the standard language means "hunger-strike." The period 1945–1953, from the end of the war up to Stalin's death, did not get a special name but it did have a famine of its own, in 1946–1947, and it witnessed the reintroduction of a draconian law from 1932 that did have several names: "the 7-8 law" because it was announced on 7 August; "the three ears of grain law" because that was how much you had to steal to be punished by years of hard labor; or sometimes the "handful of peas law" (Lopatin and Lopatina, p.34). The law was abolished in 1936, but a revised version was reinstated in 1947.

## Security Services

Initially both collectivization and de-kulakization were carried out primarily by local authorities but beginning in 1930 the liquidation of kulaks was taken over by the security services. There were two available designations for them. The more specific **GPU** (Главное Политическое Управление; Main Political Directorate) was the direct descendant of the Cheka. The GPU was a branch of the **NKVD** (Народный Комиссариат Внутренних Дел; The People's Commissariat for Internal Affairs). Almost without exception the narratives refer to the more widely known NKVD.

Peasant references to the NKVD are infrequent and circumspect, even syntactically. The Russian language is in general less syntactically direct than English when talking about organizations and documents. While in English organizations and documents are frequently the subject and agent in a sentence, e.g., "The CIA has finally confessed to all it misdeeds. Its official statement says [ . . . ]" The Russian translation would be more likely to say: "В ЦРУ наконец признали свою вину. В оффициальном сообщении говорится [ . . . ]." (In the CIA they finally confessed to their guilt. In the official statement it is said [ . . . ].) (Nakhimovsky 1978). In the Russian Corpus, KGB is used as the subject only eleven times, and with an active verb only three times, while the phrase в КГБ (*in* or *to* or *at* the KGB) is used 380 times. Peasant narratives go one step further in their syntactic circumspection: when the NKVD is mentioned, it is usually in the phrase **по линии НКВД** (in the NKVD line [of work]), as several examples will show.

## The Good Old Days (before the Revolution, before Kolkhozes)

A frequent question in interviews was about "earlier times" before the Revolution. Memories of traditional peasant life seem to cover the entire period before collectivization. Example 4.2 provides a clear indication. The narrator is a woman born in 1912. Her remarkable story gives a detailed account of the annual rotation of peasant work and holidays, a veritable "Works and Days" of her household. She could not have learned it all when she was five: the way of life remained the same until collectivization.

## The Individual and the Collective

To refer to the pre-collectivization period, many narratives use terms derived from the noun единоличник (individualist), translated as "individual farmer" in the dictionary but really meaning "a non-kolkhoz peasant." The term came into existence together with collectivization. Figure 4.1 shows the graph of usage for единоличник from the Russian National Corpus, with a peak around 1930, and no use at all before the 1920s.

Peasants, however, used the term retroactively to refer to the entire pre-kolkhoz condition, including the time of revolution and NEP (New Economic Policy, 1921–1928). That entire period would be called единоличество (individual-dom), even though agricultural practices were largely communal. There was no real ownership of land, either legally or conceptually in peasants' minds, even before the revolution. Each family had control over a piece of land, allotted by the number of "souls" in the family. It was called душевая land, from душа (a soul, or peasant, as in Gogol's *Dead Souls*). Every ten

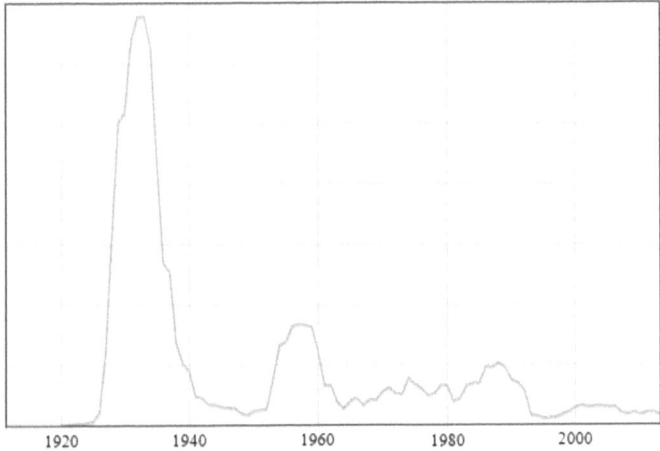

**Figure 4.1 Use of the Word единоличник from 1920.** Created by Author from RNC (Russian National Corpus).

years the land would be reallocated to account for deaths and births, and other kinds of arrivals and departures. Before the revolution only males counted as souls; Lenin was credited with adding female souls to the count. The family piece of land was usually called полоса (a strip), because that is how they were allotted, for ease of plowing and harvesting. The action of allocating land was нарезАть (slice). In a compact example, a peasant woman says: "Тогда нарезали по душам—но это было еще при единоличестве." (At that time [land] was doled out by [the number of] souls—but that was still during individual-dom [Kovalev 1996:138].)

## 4.3 EXAMPLES, GROUPED BY HISTORY

The first line of each example gives the reference, the name of the speaker, and two dates: the speaker's birth date and the date of the recording. The examples are arranged more or less chronologically by their main topic, but most of them bring in other topics, usually by association to other calamities and misfortunes. Each example is therefore additionally indexed by the topics and vocabulary presented in the preceding section.

In the first example, for illustrative purposes, all the dialectal forms are italicized. Since this is the first extended example, a few general comments on language are in order (otherwise they are reserved for the section "On peasant narratives"). Throughout the examples it is worth paying attention to the simple syntax and the narrative economy of the texts. Since English insists on a subject in every sentence, a direct object after a transitive verb, and an adjective, unless nominalized, to be followed by a head noun, translations frequently have to include additional words in square brackets.

### Example 4.2 Emel'ianova, 1912–1993. Kasatkin 2010:77

Topics: pre-revolutionary; non-kolkhoz

 Родилась я в двенадцатом году. Жили мы **единолично**, колхозов тогда *ишшо* не было, имели свою землю, лошадей, работали день и ночь. *Чижало* было. *Бывалоче* зимой мужики за скотом *ходют*, в извоз *ездиють*, *готовють* к лету сбрую. А бабы у *Хвилипповки прядуть*. Вот пост, холсты *ткуть*. Молодые *шьють*, *вышивають*, *вяжуть*, всю зиму *работають*. А летом ребятишки холсты *белють* на лугу. Там они гусей *стерегуть* и холсты *окунають* в воду, да с золою, да их *растягивають* по траве.

 *Хлебушко* доставался тяжко. *Бывалоче*, землю пахали сохой, редко у кого плуг был. Мужики спину гнули от зари до зари. Рубахи, бывало, от соленого пота *каганели*,[5] проваливались на спине. В глаза пыль комками набивается. Бывало, придеть отец с поля да и говорит: "Дочь, выкопни мне грязь из глаз." А я копаюсь, копаюсь. Сеють, бывало, с поста до самой Троицы, спешать *урвать погодку*, да и всё в свой срок: овёс в *захолодь*, а *гречишку опосля дожжыка*, когда уж *тепло-тепло* настанеть. Сеяли и просо, и *конопи*.

*Translation*

I was born in 1912. We lived individually, there were no kolkhozes yet, we had our own land, horses, worked day and night. It was hard. It used to be in winter men would look after the animals, take horses to make money hauling, prepare harnesses for summer. And women at Apostle Philip's day would spin. Come Fast, they weave cloth. Young ones sew, embroider, knit, work the entire winter. And in summer little kids would bleach the cloths in the meadow. They watch after the geese, and dip cloths in water, with ash, and spread them on the grass.

 Bread came hard. It used to be we plowed with a wooden plow, few had metal ones. The men worked hard from dawn to dusk. Their shirts would stiffen from salty sweat, stick to their backs. Bits of dust would clump up in their eyes. My father would come home from the field and say: "Daughter, dig the dirt out of my eyes." So I'm digging and digging. They would start planting at Lent and all the way to Pentecost, in a hurry to catch the right weather; and everything in its time: oats when it's cool, and buckwheat after a rain, when it's already summer-warm. Also planted millet and hemp.

## Comment

An immediately noticeable feature of this passage is the number of dialectal forms. Most of them are non-standard verb endings, but there are also phonetic phenomena, lexical items, and phraseological expressions. Phonetically, an interesting detail is the absence of the sound [f] replaced by [hv] in Filippovka, a date in the church calendar right before the long Christmas fast. Among lexical items, **хлебушко** is хлеб (bread) adorned with an emotional suffix, the way personal names can be, e.g., Иванушка from Ivan (see Ch. 3 on diminutive suffixes and Example 3.2 specifically for **хлебушек**). The Russian word for bread often means more generally "sustenance," as in "our daily bread." Other diminutive suffixes are found in the words **погодка** (weather), **гречишка** (buckwheat).

The word **бывало** (it used to be that [ . . . ]) is in the standard language. Peasant narratives use it often in telling about how things used to be. In this example, it is used five times, including twice in the dialectal form "**бывалоче**."

The noun **захолодь**, from the root холод (cold) is an old word for a cold place or period of time. This is a good example of the kind of economic word formation that was included in the Profile of Chapter 1.

The expression **гнуть спину**, literally "have your back bent often and/or for a long period of time," means "work hard," understandably originating in manual agricultural labor. The expression **урвать погодку** (literally "snatch the weather") may well be an improvised metaphor. Reduplication **тепло-тепло** is an example of a common device.

Traces of the Russian Orthodox church calendar are still remembered. Filippovka is the day (here in the extended sense of "the period") before the beginning of the forty-day Nativity Fast that ends at Christmas; it derives from the Day of Philip the Apostle.

Recall that Russia was on the "old" Julian calendar until the revolution of 1917, and the Russian Church remained on it. In today's Russia Christmas is on January 7 (corresponding to Dec 25 in the old calendar); the Nativity Fast starts on November 28, and Filippovka is November 27 (the old November 14).

Another feature of this example, previously observed both in the Profile of Chapter 1 and in the letters of Chapter 3, is the simplicity of syntax. There is only one subordinate clause. Some paratactic sequences are conjunction-less. The ratio of verbs is very high. Adjectives are all used predicatively except for "salty" in the formulaic phrase "salty sweat."

It is important to keep in mind that while this is a natural narrative by an old peasant woman, it is likely to produce a marked stylistic effect on educated readers: some may find it touching, others somewhat affected.

### Example 4.3 Litvinov. 1902–1992. Vinogradskii 2012:17

Topics: revolution as a stretch of time; pre-revolutionary

И женились в старину честь-честью, и в армию провожали. [ . . . ] Хорошо было тогда! Как ни бедно жили, а все равно – все почести выполняли [ . . . ]. А уж когда **революция** пошла, когда началась **заваруха**, – тут уж кто кого! Какой тут почет и веселье?

*Translation*

In older times whether it's weddings or seeing recruits off to the army, all was honorably done. [ . . . ] Life was good then! Even if poor, we carried out all the honors [ . . . ]. But when the revolution got going, when the ruckus started then it was all against all, no joy and honor any more.

### Example 4.4 Shishkina 1911–1992. Vinogradskii 2017:59–60. Divided in 3 parts

Topics: pre-revolutionary; WWI; non-kolkhoz; famine of 1933; WWII.

*Part 1*

Отца моего звали Шишкин, Иван Фомич. Они вместе с матерью померли в **голодовку**, в 1933 году. Я не помню точно, с какого года рождения он, отец-то, но когда он помер, ему уже много годов-то было. Я, вот, первая родилась, а он тридцати лет женился на моей матери. Я сама с 1911 года. А отец в 1914 году **на войне на германской** был. Он, мотри, был с 1877 года. Он кончил четыре или пять классов. У него уж больно хороший почерк был. Профессия у него – бедняк-крестьянин, **единоличник. С землёй душевой.** С землёй был, а землю сдавал. Семья была большая у него. Лошади не было. Потом лошадь нажил, а ее в **колхоз** пришлось отдать.

*Translation*

My father's name was Shishkin, Ivan Fomich. He died together with my mother in the hunger of 1933. I don't remember exactly what year he was born, my father, but when he died he was many years old. See, I was the first to be born, and he married my mother at thirty. I'm from 1911 myself. And my father in 1914 was at the German war. He was, you see, born in 1877. He finished fourth or fifth grade. His handwriting was very very good. By occupation he was a poor peasant, individual. With land allotted by souls. He had land but he rented it out. He had a big family. No horse. Then he saved up and bought a horse, but it had to be given up to the kolkhoz.

## Comment

This example shows good details of pre-revolutionary land ownership.

## Part 2

Мою мать звали Шишкина Евдокия Фроловна. Умерла она с голоду, в тридцать третьем году. Умерла вместе с отцом – в один дух, в один мах! А я их хоронила, сама голодная. В одночасье пять человек осталось, сирот. Мать моя помоложе отца была, лет на десять. Сорок семь лет ей было. И отец у меня был бедный, и мать он взял тоже из бедной семьи. У неё образования не было никакого. Она одно время в прислугах в Саратове жила. Потом приехала сюда, в Красную Речку. Тут она и вышла замуж за моего отца. Тут отцы их, материн и тятин, сошлися, сладились. Ну, как? Выпили и женили моих родителей. Тогда эдак было [ . . . ] Дедушку и бабушку по отцу я сама хоронила. Отец мой держал дедушку. Он его покоил до самой его смерти. Дедушку звали Фома Афанасьевич. Отец не бросал его. Он его схоронил.

## Translation

My mother's name was Shishkina, Evdokiia Frolovna. She died from hunger, in 1933—together with my father, in a single breath, in a single stroke. I buried them, myself hungry. Overnight five of us were left orphans. My mother was younger than father, by about ten years. She was forty-seven years old. My father was poor, and took my mother from a poor family. She had no education at all. For a while she was a servant in Saratov. Then came here, to [the village of—AN] Red River. It was here she married my father. Their fathers, my mom's and dad's, got together and arranged it. What's there to say? they drank a bottle and married off my parents. That's how it was then. My grandpa and grandma in father's line I buried myself. My father took care of grandpa. He sustained him till his death. Grandpa's name was Foma Afanas'evich. My father never abandoned him. He buried him.

## Comment

This narrative, like many others, goes in circles. There is also a seeming contradiction about who buried her grandparents, but she simply means that she was present when her father buried his father. There is good ethnographic detail on marriage, education, and care for the old.

## Part 3

Дедушка мой сто лет жил. Дедушка Фома меня ещё нянчил. А умер он давно-давно, ещё до **голодовки**, до тридцать третьего года. У меня братишка младший **на фронте** погиб, – он с 1924 года рождения. А дедушка его маленьким ребёнком нянчил. Помню, мать на огороде работала, а дедушка идёт, кричит: "Дуня, Дуня, скорей, скорей!..." Значит, братишка плачет, есть хочет. Дедушка Фома умер, наверное, году в двадцать шестом-двадцать седьмом. Прожил он сто лет. Мне было, когда он умер, лет пятнадцать-шестнадцать. Я его похороны хорошо помню. Я-то уж работала в то время, матери во всем помогала. Дедушка был крестьянин. Бедняк-крестьянин. Все наше потомство по крестьянству пошло.

*Translation*

My grandpa lived a hundred years. Grandpa Foma looked after me. But he died a long long time ago, before the famine, before 1933. My little brother was killed in action—he was born in 1924. And grandpa looked after him when he was a little boy. I remember mother would work in the vegetable garden and grandpa would come and call: "Dunia, Dunia, quick, quick! [ . . . ]" This means little brother is crying, wants to eat. Grandpa Foma died in about 1926–27. He lived a hundred years. I was, when he died, about fifteen or sixteen. I remember his funeral well. I already worked at the time, helped my mother in everything. Grandpa was a peasant. A poor peasant. Our entire line remained peasant.

*Comment*

Events were so crowded in those decades that every date is meaningful: her little brother was born in 1924, so he was seventeen when the Germans invaded in 1941, was drafted early in the war, and was killed in action.

### Example 4.5 Simakina 1911–1992. Vinogradskii 2012:84

Topics: kolkhoz; individual-dom; war

К нам в колхоз, в Лох, еще татары приходили молотить в уборочную. Вручную, цепами молотили, – это было еще **до войны**, как колхозы начались. Жали, молотили – у богатых людей! [ . . . ] Да и при **единоличестве** это было – и тогда татары приходили.

*Translation*

To our kolkhoz in [the village of] Lokh Tatars would also come to thresh during harvesting. They threshed by hand, with flails—it was **before the war**, when kolkhozes started. [ . . . ] But during individual-dom, Tatars used to come also.

*Comment*

При единоличестве here could equally well mean either "before the revolution" or "before collectivization, during NEP."

### Example 4.6 Тырышкина 1909–1992. Vinogradskii 2012:121

Topics: Revolution and Civil war; dekulakization

**В. Виноградский**: Баба Тоня, а вы помните что-нибудь из революции или из Гражданской войны? Здесь никто с боями не проходил?

**А. Тырышкина**: Нет, здесь никого не было, все у нас было тихо. Когда была **революция**, у нас только вот что было – перекололи царские иконы. Больше никакого **завороха** не было. И еще вот в **корчевку** было восстание. Но это уже позже, в 1929, 1930 году. А в 1917 году и позже до нас ничего не дошло, кроме того, что все царские иконы перебили.

*Translation*

***Vinogradskii***: Grandma Tonia, do you remember anything from the revolution or the Civil War? Was there fighting passing through?

***Taryshkina***. No, there was nobody here, everything was quiet. During the **revolution**, the only thing we had, all the tsar's icons [She means the Tsar's portraits in local government offices, not icons in church.—AN] were chopped up. No other ruckus happened. Also during **uprooting** there was a riot. But that was later, 1929, 1930. But in 1917 and after nothing reached us except all the tsar's icons were smashed up.

*Comment*

While some areas of the country remained untouched by the Civil War, many others, including some that were distant from the major front lines in the south and west, were deeply affected. Many simmering local conflicts were reactivated by the struggle between Reds and Whites. Iastrebinskaia 2005:21 writes about the village of Kobelevo in the Arkhangelsk province: "There was no regular army fighting, but during the war the village would be attacked by local groups, some of them red, some white. The Whites would set up vigilante justice, the Reds were also quick to kill. It was a life and death struggle." Thousands of miles to the East, in the productive agricultural area of Altai, local fighting was particularly vicious because of recent migration into the area. See the extended comment and the next two examples.

### The Civil War in Altai: Cossacks and Peasants

As part of the Stolypin reforms of the early twentieth century, the Altai region, east of Kazakhstan and near the Mongolian border, was the object of a large government-sponsored peasant migration out of overcrowded central Russia. The migration resulted in frequent tensions between the new arrivals and the older Cossack settlements, which, in turn, nursed occasional grudges among themselves. The revolution introduced yet another division between Reds and Whites, and the resulting extreme violence is still reflected in relations between families and in old people's interviews. Two examples below show the local texture of the Civil War away from the main battle lines. In the examples, the Sosnovka settlement was Red, the Charyshskaia White.

The extreme violence of these examples finds well-known parallels in the writers of the 1920s, especially Babel and Seifullina.[6] Here again, as in the case of Tolstoy, an adjustment of historical perspective is needed. The old narrators of the 1990s had never read Babel or Seifullina. On the contrary, they are, in effect, the sources for the fiction that was written many decades earlier, based on the stories and narrative rhythms that later peasant narrators preserved in their memory.

### Example 4.7 Shcheglova 2008:67. Charyshskaia (White) family

Topics: Civil War, Reds, Whites, Cossacks

Наши казаки скрылись в горах. [ . . . ] [Ворвались сосновские казаки] на конях. . . . Бабка спрятала двух внучат в сундук, сама села на него. [ . . . ] Он вошел, зыркнул на бабку, согнал. Крышку поднял, а там две головы пацанячьи в казацких фуражках. [ . . . ] Он одним взмахом сабли отсек [ . . . ] и ускакали. Наши вернулись [ . . . ] как увидели [ . . . ] по коням

*Translation*

Our Cossacks ran away to the mountains. Sosnovka Cossacks came on horseback. The old woman hid two grandsons in a chest, sat on it. [ . . . ] He walked in, took one look, chased [her] away. Lifted the top, and there are two boy's heads in Cossack caps. [ . . . ] He cut [both] off with one saber swing [ . . . ] and they left. Ours came back [ . . . ] when they saw [ . . . ] jumped on their horses

*Comment*

In two instances here (and many more in other narratives), the Russian text has a transitive verb ("chase away," "cut off") without a direct object, which is obvious from context. This contributes to the economy and energy of the narrative.

The family legend reports the retribution. All the ellipses in the example are from Shcheglova:

**Example 4.8 Shcheglova 2008:67. Sosnovka (Red) family**

Наши были в горах [ . . . ] А те прискакали [ . . . ] дядю двоюродного белые казаки закопали живьем [ . . . ] А у него оставалась одна баба дома, беременная на восьмом месяце. Они дверь входную сняли да сверху ей на живот положили [ . . . ] Встали на нее [ . . . ] Пока не выдавили [ . . . ]

*Translation*

Our men were in the mountains [ . . . ] And those came on horseback [ . . . ] white Cossacks buried my second uncle alive. [ . . . ] And in the house was his woman, alone, seven months pregnant. They took off the front door and put it on top of her belly [ . . . ] Stepped on it [ . . . ] Until they squeezed [it] out [ . . . ]

*Comment*

As in the preceding example, the transitive verb in the last sentence does not have a direct object in Russian.

Outside of inter-Cossack struggles, the majority opinion among the peasants in the region was on the side of the Reds. This is reflected in the use of the word наши (ours), a possessive pronoun that is also used as a noun meaning "those on our side."[7] According to Shcheglova 2008:63, most local people reserved this moniker for the Reds, and still do.

**Example 4.9 E. I. Dmukh, 1908–1992. Shcheglova 2008:67. "Ours" against the Whites**

Попадья у нас в Карболихе была. Выдавала красных белым. Красные пришли, босиком водили ее по Змеиногорску. Потом груди обрубили. Померла. За делом ей. Она наших белым выдавала.

*Translation*

There was a priest's wife in our village, Karbolikha. She was betraying the Reds to the Whites. Reds came, took her around the town of Zmeinogorsk barefoot. Then chopped off her breasts. She died. Serves her right. She betrayed ours to the Whites.

*Comment*

This is one of rare examples when the narrator takes sides in a long-ago conflict, but the sides are not ideological, the conflict is between local villages.

158  Chapter 4

## "Dekulakization," 1928–1933

For all the grisly inter-group violence of the Civil War, it was the state violence of collectivization that loomed largest in peasants' memory, especially when coupled with acts of state terror against kulaks. The next example again brings together the vocabulary of "revolution," "overthrow," "dekulakization," and "uprooting," highlighted in the text. It tells the story of one of two aunts; the other one appears in Example 4.11.

### Example 4.10 Tsaplin (1914–1992). Vinogradskii 2017: 65–66. The first of two aunts

Topics: dekulakization, NKVD

Старшая была у отца сестра Мария, а вот с какого года – это я не скажу. Она самая старшая была. Ее забрали **по линии НКВД**, в тридцатом году, и увезли. Вот в этом вот доме их собирали, таких вот. А у неё было семь детей. Их **раскулачили**, семью тётки Марии. [ . . . ]

*Translation*

My father's older sister was Maria, I can't tell you what year she was born. She was the oldest. She was arrested, in the NKVD line of work, in 1930, and taken away. In this very house they were brought together, people like her. And she had seven children. They were dekulaked, her entire family.

*Comment*

As noted, there is a minor anachronism in this story: in 1930, the name of the security service was GPU, not NKVD.

### Example 4.11 Tsaplin (1914–1992) Vinogradskii 2017: 65–66. The second aunt

Topics: dekulakization; revolution

А у меня не одна Мария Павловна **раскулаченная**. В Яруге жила ещё тётка – и ее **раскулачили**. Тётка по отцу. Звали ее Анна Павловна. [ . . . ] Она моложе была отца. Она была, вроде, с девятисотого года. Ее **раскулачили** и увезли на Колыму куда-то, в 1930 году. И там она, видать, умерла. Она жила в Яруге, – семь километров отсюда. А мужа у неё расстреляли, ещё раньше. Как получилось? Во время молотьбы. [ . . . ] И вот были сложены стога такие, крест-накрест. Одонья. Ну, он залез наверх. А в те поры был самый **переворот**. И ему надо бы красный флаг выкинуть, а он взял, и белый флаг поставил на одонья. Его забрали и расстреляли, как контру. Это в **революцию** было. А жену его вместе с детьми в **корчёвку** угнали [ . . . ].

*Translation*

Maria Pavlovna was not my only aunt who was dekulaked. In Iaruga there was another aunt--they dekulaked her also. My father's sister. Her name was Anna Pavlovna. She was younger than my father, born maybe in 1900. She was dekulaked and taken away, some place in Kolyma, in 1930. And she died there, I guess. She lived in Iaruga, seven kilometers from here. And her husband had been shot even before that. How did this happen? During threshing. [ . . . ] they had piled up hay stacks, cross-shaped, *odon'ias* [they were called—AN]. Well, he climbed one of them. And those days were right in the middle of rioting. He should have raised the red flag, but he got it in his head to raise the white one, on top of the hay stack. So they took him away and shot, as a contra. That was in revolution time. And his wife and children were taken away during uprooting.

*Comment*

This passage shows clearly that "revolution" covered the entire Civil War: there were no Whites or Reds in October 1917. The word переворот (overthrow) also refers to an extended period of time, with some stretches more intense than others.

Kolyma, in the Pacific North-East, was the worst part of the prison camp system; very few people came back from there. (Shalamov's *Kolyma Stories* provide a definitive account.) Large gold deposits were discovered in Kolyma in 1928. In 1931, the government decided to use prison labor to develop them. The first contingent of prisoners arrived later that year, with large numbers following in 1932 and later. The narrator may be a little uncertain about his dates, or maybe his aunt ended up at Kolyma after a spell somewhere else.

### Example 4.12 Litvinova 1902–1992. Vinogradskii 2011:32

Topics: collectivization; NKVD line

людей забирали в коллективизацию. [ . . . ] Придут и говорят: "По линии НКВД . . . " Ночью вызовут, как вроде в контору вызывают, – и без возврата!

*Translation*

At collectivization people were taken away. [ . . . ] They would come and say: "In the NKVD line [ . . . ]" They would summon you at night, as if to summon to the village office—and you're gone.

*Comment*

Judging by this example, the phrase was actually used as a formula during arrests

**Example 4.13 Литвинова 1902–1992. Vinogradskii 2011:35**

Topics: collectivization; NKVD line

Сестренка уже вышла замуж за китая. А потом, когда по линии НКВД людей подгребали, того китая тож забрали.

*Translation*

My little sister had already married a Chinese man. And later, when people were scooped up in the NKVD line of work, that Chinese man was also taken away. [ . . . ]

The Great Famine of 1932–1933

Much has been written about this event, and this chapter is not a place to provide even a sketchy history. In the barest detail, grain deliveries in the fall of 1932 were disappointing, and Stalin suspected that it was a deliberate slowdown. The government confiscated everything it could, including seed grain, to cover the needs of the cities and export deliveries. By 1933, famine began. The worst hit was Ukraine, where this deliberate famine is classified as genocide, but Volga regions, where our example was recorded, were also strongly affected.

Example 4.14 presents one story from that time. (There will be a similar one from 1946.) In its precision and power of detail it rises to the level of great literature, while remaining a deeply personal testimony of an 80-year-old woman recreating the events of almost 60 years earlier. She was 22 at the time and her husband Vania 23. The text contains Vinogradskii's text comments in italics.

**Example 4.14 Simakina, 1911–1992. Vinogradskii 2012:63–64**

Topics: famine, hunger, communal violence, cannibalism.

*Part 1*

Потом 1933 год напал, – а у нас уже всё отобрали раньше. Здесь и дедушка помер, и Ваня помер. У нас ничего ведь не осталось. Траву ели, отекли. Я вся была отеченая, как бочка. А Ваня почему-то не отеченый был. И вот у нас остался пиджак его. За печкой висел, – такой суконный, подвенечный. Я говорю ему, Ване, – он тогда еще жив был: "Ваня, ступай его продай хоть". Тут недалеко Коптовка была, деревня. Ваня пошел. Дали ему там за пиджак свеклу и молока четверть. Не за хлеб, а за свеклу кормовую продали. Вот как жили! . . . Да, вот еще чего забыла: в Коптовку-то Ваня пошел со своим дядей. Вот жду-жду, – нет и нет его. Что же это как долго нет-то?! И смерклось все, и ночь наступила. Пошла я к дядиной жене: "Кума, что, пришел, что ль, кум Донька?" – "Да нету, не пришел", – говорит. "Да что же это – как долго ходит?" Ну, нет и нет. Опять посижу, полежу ли. Снова пойду. Уж кочетья кукарекают. "Кума, пришел ли Данила твой?" – спрашиваю. "Пришел. . ." – отвечает. "Да где же Ваня-то?" – говорю. "Вон там, на Кузнецовском гумне, на канаве сидит".

*Translation*

Then 1933 hit us—and they had taken everything before that. Now both grandpa died and Vania died. We had nothing left, you know. We ate grass, got swollen. I was all swollen like a barrel. But Vania I don't know why was not swollen. And so we still had his jacket. It was hanging behind the stove, a woolen jacket, from our wedding. I said to Vania—he was still alive: "Vania, go, sell it, what else can we do." There was a village of Koptovka nearby. Vania went. He got for his jacket some beets and a gallon of milk. They didn't trade it for bread but for fodder beet. That's how we lived! . . . But I forgot to say that Vania didn't go to Koptovka alone but with his uncle. I wait and I wait, no Vania. Why is he taking so long? It got dark, night came. I went to uncle's wife: "Auntie, what's up, did your man Don'ka come home?"—"No, not yet."—she says. "What's going on, why he's taking so long?" Well, if not, then not. I sat a bit, lay down a bit, go again. Roosters are already crowing. "Antie, did your Danila come home?"—I ask. "Yes, he did"—she says. "But where's my Vania?"—I ask. "Over there, on the Kuznezov barnyard, sitting at the ditch.

*Comment*

Simakina refers to Don'ka/Danila as Vania's uncle or, generically, as кум, most commonly "godfather" but can be other remote relative.

*Part 2*

Я перелезла через овраг, пошла туды. И боюсь: поймают еще да и съедят. Ведь ловили людей и ели тогда, в голодовку-то. Ну вот, я перелезла, пошла проулком. Иду, темно. Заря чуть занялась, но не видать еще ничего. И кричать-то боюсь. Иду-иду – вот эдак вот присяду. Мне сказали--на канаве Ваня, а я смотрю – нигде не видать. Иду дальше, на зады. Опять присяду. Не видать [ . . . ] Потом кричу: "Вань, Вань . . . " Кто-то вдалеке затрепехтался. Подхожу. Он встал. Говорю: "Ты чаво же?" Он отвечает: "Я не могу больше . . . " Я говорю: "Ну ты чаво, – купил, что ль, чаво-нибудь?" А он отвечает: "У меня все отобрал кум Донька". Вот, – свой человек, а все отобрал. Пуд свеклы Ваня нес и четверть молока. И Донька отобрал все. Подлец! Ни дна бы ему, ни крышки! [*Долгая пауза, вздыхает, плачет. Потом вдруг говорит в примирительно-прощающем тоне.*--ВВ] Ну, ведь каждый сам себя спасал, что ж тут сделаешь [ . . . ] Ну, повесился тут на меня мой Ваня – идем, два тёфана. Я говорю: "Ведь я бы не дала отобрать-то [ . . . ]." А Ваня уж обессилел: он и так был худущий. А я отечная была, а он, вот, не отекал. Я наемся этих лепешков-то, из крапивы: они хорошие были, когда засохнут. И воды я много пила, потому и отекала.

*Translation*

I climbed through the ravine and went there. Scared: what if somebody grabs and eats me. People were caught and eaten then, in that famine. So I climbed through and went down a path. It's dark. Dawn is just breaking, you can't see anything. And I'm afraid to call out. So I keep walking, sit down, walk again. I was told "Vania's near the ditch," but I look and don't see anyone. I walk on, toward the back. Sat down for a bit. Couldn't see anyone. Then I called out: "Vania, Vania [ . . . ] ." Something stirred out there. I come closer, he gets up. I say: "What's up?" He says: "I can't any more [ . . . ] ." I say: "So, what happened, did you buy anything?" And he says: "Uncle Don'ka took everything away from me." Get it? one of our own, and took everything. A pood of beets Vania was carrying and a gallon of milk. And Don'ka took everything, the bastard. I wish he'd dropped dead. (*A long pause, she sighs and sobs. The she suddenly speaks in a conciliatory, forgiving tone.*--VV) Well, everybody was trying to save themselves, what can you do. . . . So, Vania clung to me, and we are walking, two goners. I said: "I wouldn't have let him take away [ . . . ]." But Vania had no strength left, he was always just bones and skin. Myself, I was swollen, but he wasn't. I ate a lot of those pancakes, from nettles: they were good when dried up. And I drank a lot of water, that's why I was swollen.

*Comment*

Evidence of cannibalism in 1932–33 is abundant, even more so than for 1921–22. Boriak (2008:28–29) writes:

> Almost all of the documents of the Communist Party and a part of the key documents of Soviet governmental agencies have already been published.

> [ . . . ] There is extensive factual material regarding the total confiscation of foods, extensive food shortages, widespread bloating [from starvation], mortality, and cannibalism. [ . . . ] The criminal files reveal the shocking truth about the total social collapse in rural regions and mental aberrations that led to the eating of corpses and cannibalism. Of the 83,000 cases launched by the NKVD in 1932-33, we have records for no more than 3,000 today (the rest were destroyed in 1956).

The government actually printed posters saying: "To eat your own children is a barbarian act" (Vardy and Vardy 2007:225).

The narratives frequently mention nettles as food, and not only during famine. In a war-time recollection, a kind neighbor is trying to give a little girl some boiled nettles. The girl is crying: "I won't eat it, there are worms crawling there." "Come, I'll just give you some liquid." The girl's mother intercedes: "Nobody in our family can eat it. We boil chives, beet leaves, cabbage leaves, but that we cannot eat." (Kasatkin 2010:203–4).

The economy of the Russian peasant narrative is discussed in the analytical section, but the mastery of example 4.14 is a good preview. It contributes to the economy that Russian can easily omit the subject of the sentence, and the present tense of the verb "to be" (copula) is a null form. Consider this passage, repeated from 4.14, with Present tense sentences in boldface, and the absence of an overt subject or the copula marked by an asterisk. The sentence with two asterisks is impersonal, has neither a subject, nor an indicative verb form, literally "nowhere to see":

> Мне сказали [*]– на канаве Ваня [*], а я смотрю – нигде не видать[**]. Иду дальше[*], на зады. Опять присяду [*]. Не видать[ . . . ] [**] Потом кричу: "Вань, Вань..." Кто-то вдалеке затрепехтался. Подхожу. [*] Он встал. Говорю: [*] "Ты чаво же?" Он отвечает: "Я не могу больше[ . . . ] "

*Literal translation, hyphenated words correspond to single words in Russian:*

> to-me they-said: on ditch Vania, but I look-nowhere to see. I-go forward, toward the back. Again I-would-sit-down. No see. Then I-yell "Van', Van'." Somebody at-a-distance fluttered. I-come-close. He got-up. I-say "So how you?" He answers: "I can't any-more."

Almost the entire passage is in the Present tense, there are no subordinate clauses, and almost every sentence has an elided constituent. Even Vania's direct speech is minimal: he simply can't. There are 42 words in the passage of which 13 are verbs, not counting the null copula. There are no adjectives.

*Part 3*

Ну, пришли домой, затащила я его на печку. Полежал он маленько и не встает. "Ты что, Ваня?" – говорю. Он: "Я не могу, я не могу . . ." Ну и я сижу тут. Нигде никакого клочка, никакого кусочка нет у нас. Потом на другую ночь он у меня и умер. Вот сколько пережила [ . . . ] (*Плачет.*) Никто сесто не пережил, а я все живу. (*Плачет, никак не может успокоиться. Долгая пауза.*) А у нас за печкой стояла соль – ящик с солью. И коптюлечка стояла на трубе. Я зажгу коптюлечку, погляжу, – а у него уже глаза дурные сделались И вот так глядит в потолок все. Я говорю: "Ваня, Ваня, да ты чего? Ваня?" А он тихо так говорит: "Я умираю [ . . . ]" Потом ка-а-к вскочит и горсть соли схватил, и говорит-кричит: "На, ешь! А то умрешь!" Я говорю: "Ваня, Ваня! Я не буду соли есть, – я и так отекаю [ . . . ]" И вот он лег опять, и я сидела все, сидела округ него. Все он это глядел, глаза остолбенели – одна с ним, одна . . . И, значит, тише, тише. И только я легла к нему – и сразу уснула. Тут кочетья уж кряковали третий раз. Я сразу вдруг очнулась, цоп за него: "Ваня, Ваня!" А он уж умер [ . . . ]

*Translation*

So we came home, I dragged him onto the stove. He lay there for a while and wouldn't get up. "Vania, how're you doing?"—I said. He: "I can't, I can't." So I'm sitting there. We don't have a shred, not a morsel anywhere. Then on the next night he died on me. That's how much I lived through. (*Crying.*) Nobody lived through that, and I'm still alive. (*Crying; can't control herself. A long pause.*) We had salt behind the stove, a box of salt. And a little kerosene light on the chimney. I would light it, take a look—and his eyes were already going weird. And he was just looking in the ceiling like that. I said: "Vania, Vania, what's with you?" And he said in that quiet voice: "I'm dying [ . . . ] ." Then suddenly he jumped, grabbed a fistful of salt and said—screamed at me: "Here, eat! Or else you'll die!" I said: "Vania, Vania, I will not eat salt, I'm all swollen as it is [ . . . ]." So he lay down again, and I was just sitting, sitting next to him. And he was just looking, his eyes stopped moving [ . . . ] alone with him, alone. And it's getting quieter and quieter. As soon as I lay next to him I fell asleep. Then roosters crowed the third time. All at once I came to, grabbed him: "Vania, Vania!" But he was already dead.

*Comment*

Any reader of Russian folklore or the Gospels would notice that the third crow of the roosters is probably a borrowing from the oral tradition. It is likely that this story was told a number of times. However, It is impossible to doubt its sincerity, and its precise observations of dying could not possibly have been invented.

### The Long 1930s and the Advent of the War

For peasants, the worst of the decade was over after 1933. The year 1937 was relatively good, with a good harvest and a few tax breaks, like (what follows is not intended sardonically): forgiveness of grain tax arrears for 1936 (March 20); lifting of taxes, both monetary and in kind, on those who were disabled because of old age (May 15); and lifting of all in-kind taxes from those lands on which crops were destroyed by natural disaster (August 14).

For the intelligentsia, these dates were precisely inverted. In 1930–1934, collectivization was generally supported, and the scope of the famine either unknown or ignored. (The poet Mandelstam, who witnessed the famine in the Crimea in 1933, wrote then "We live in ignorance of the country beneath us.") The worst of the 1930s began in 1934 with the murder of Kirov and crescendoed to the Terror of 1937–1938. These events (together with the Spanish Civil War, the Molotov-Ribbentrop pact, the start of WWII in Europe, and the Winter War with Finland) left few traces in peasant stories. In their memory, only a few short years separated the end of the famine from the German attack in 1941. From the letters of Chapter 3 we know that poverty and privation were still common. And yet, as a testimony to low expectations and the information vacuum, the peasant narratives proceed from one calamity to the next, skipping over the tolerable. The next two examples focus on the 1930s but end with the war. The first of them is by the same Emel'ianova who earlier spoke of older times in Example 4.2. Her story includes a contrast between peasant and urban life. Her long story is divided into three parts.

### Example 4.15 Emel'ianova 1912–1993.
### Kasatkin 2010:80. Life became better

Keywords: collectivization, dekulakization, Black Maria, enemies of the people, migration and life in the city, war.

*Part 1*

Ну а потом пошла коллективизация, все порушили, стали раскулачивать, из хат выгонять, постройки, церкви ломать. Много хорошего народу пострадало безвинно. Днём человек ходил, работал, ночью чёрный ворон уволок. Думаем какой это чёрный ворон? А это, говорят, машиночки чёрные приезжали.

Ну что, в колхозе долго работа не ладилась, урожаи маленькие стали, на трудодни почти ничего не давали. Народ огрубел, озлобился, стали бояться слова сказать друг другу, властям не стали верить. [ . . . ]

*Translation*

Then collectivization got going, they smashed everything, started to dekulak, kick people out of their houses, destroy barns and churches. Many good people, innocent people suffered. A man would walk around during the day, do his work, and at night the Black Raven would drag him away. We were wondering what's that black raven? And somebody explained they were black cars coming in.

Well, for a long time kolkhozes couldn't get their work organized, harvests were poor, for labordays they would give us almost nothing. People became coarse, bitter, afraid to say anything to each other, didn't believe to authorities. [ . . . ]

*Comment*

The destruction of village churches was a big part of collectivization. As with the destruction of country estates after the revolution, it was precipitated by a combination of three elements: material gain (the confiscation of property); infatuation with violence (much of that property was smashed to pieces or burnt); and a symbolic act that ushered in the new atheist era.

The "black raven," also known as the "little raven" (воронок), or "black Masha" (чёрная Маруся), was an NKVD car or van. They were black and frequently used during night time for making arrests. Some commentators insist that "ravens" were specifically vans for transportation, while "Mashas" were cars for arrests. Any connection between Soviet Black Mashas and American Black Marias is tentative, possibly based on a poem by Langston Hughes, translated into Russian in the 1930s when he visited the Soviet Union.

*Part 2*

Перед войной она, жизня-то получшела. В колхозе стали лучше обрабатывать землю, хлебушка стали собирать побольше, стали сеять пшаничку. Вот, девка, тебе расскажу, ой! Вот на праздник по Октябрьской, бывало, напекут пашаничных лепёшек на гуше, на воде, а они всё равно пышные, лёгкие, сладкие. [ . . . ] Пекли в своих печках, а потом в плетухах сносили в один двор, а там по списку раздавали, хто работает. Вот хто несёт домой три, четыре лепёшечки, а может даже хто и пять, а кто одну на пять, на шесть детей. Утрется слезами баба, кормильца её-то забрали как врага, а какой он враг!

*Translation*

Before the war life became better a bit. Kolkhozes worked the land better, harvested more bread, started planting wheat. Hey, girl, here's what I'll tell you, oy! On the holiday, the October one, they would bake wheat cakes, just flour and water, but they would still rise well, light and sweet. [ . . . ] They would bake them at home in their own ovens, then bring them in baskets to one yard and there would give them out to working members. So some would carry home three, four of those cakes, and some maybe even five, and some maybe just one—for five or six kids. The woman would be wiping tears, her breadwinner had been taken as the enemy of the people, but what kind of enemy was he?

*Part 3*

У нас одного Хведор Хвёдоровича раскулачили, мельничный ветряк отобрали, а он скрылся ночью в Запорожье уехал, там рабочим устроился на завод. Потихонечку и детишки к ему переехали, восемь кроватей стояло в одной комнате в два этажа. Ели они там одну баланду. Потом детишки подрастать стали, стали себе на уздеву [одежду—AH] зарабатывать [ . . . ] Дак он говорить, к нему как-то поехали наши деревенские, а он: "Что ж меня раньше не раскулачили? Я теперече приду с работе да хоть умоюсь, и газетку почитаю, и радиво послухаю."

Ну только стала налаживаться жизня, а тут другая беда--немец. А уж эту, деточка, горе не опишешь, не расскажешь.

*Translation*

We had a man, Fedor Fedorovich, they dekulaked him, took his windmill away, but he ran away at night, went to [the city of—AN] Zaporozh'e, and there got a factory job. One by one his kids went to live with him, there were eight bunks in one room, stacked up by two. All they had to eat was watery soup. Then the kids started growing up, making some money, at least for some cheap clothes for themselves [ . . . ]. So he says—some men from the village went to see him—and he: "I wish you had dekulaked me earlier! Nowadays I come home from work, at least I get washed, and read a newspaper, and listen to the radio."

But as soon as life started settling down a bit, comes another grief—the German. And this evil, my little child, you cannot tell, you cannot describe.

*Comment*

This Southern dialect lacks the sound [f], replaced in speech by [hv]: Хведор.

The advantages of workers' life were well known and reflected in the letters of Chapter 3. Also reminiscent of the letters is the treatment of direct speech in the end of the first paragraph: pure intonation, no syntax whatsoever.

**Example 4.16 Литвинова (1902–1992). Kovalev 1996:270. Chinese story repeated**

Topics: dekulakization; NKVD; the war.

И тут уже одна сестренка за китая вышла. И ее взял, уговорил, и восемь лет она с этим китаем жила. Потом умерла. Он ее хоронил. Хвалили: дюже хорошие похороны были. А потом его по линии НКВД забрали. У них уже двое детей было. И другая сестренка вышла за русского замуж. И ее мужа забрали, она тоже с двумя детьми осталась. А потом немец уже захватывал. Шел с Кавказа. И поразбил их жилища- -и у той, и у другой.

*Translation*

At that time one of my sisters married a Chinese man. He married her, persuaded, and eight years she lived with that Chinese man. Then she died. He buried her. People praised him, the funeral was very good. And then he was taken away in the NKVD line of work. They already had two children. And another sister married a Russian. Her husband was also taken away, she was also left with two children. And next it was already the German taking over. He was coming from the Caucasus, and smashed their houses, both of them.

*Comment*

The dates in the story suggest that the younger sister married the "kitai" around 1926 and died 8 years later, so the *kitai*, a widower with two children, was arrested around 1934. As in Example 4.15 the narrative then jumps from one upheaval to the next, in this case from mass arrests of the 1930s, skipping over the period of (for peasants) relative peace of 1935–1940, directly to the war. The last sentence probably refers to a specific historical event: on July 31, 1942 the 4th German tank army was redirected from the Caucasus toward Stalingrad, and passed through the village in the Krasnodar region where the sisters had lived.

**The War: Under Occupation**

The next example picks up the story in the same August 1942, a couple of hundred miles to the North East, toward Stalingrad. As a background: the Germans invaded the Soviet Union on June 22, 1941. The Soviet Army liberated all Soviet territory by mid-1944. In between, large numbers of Soviet citizens lived under German occupation that lasted, depending on where you lived, from a few months to more than two years [ . . . ] Atrocities committed during that time have been intensely studied but everyday life, with its gradations from resistance to passive acceptance to shades of collaboration, remains a difficult topic in Russia. However, a recent book, Kovalev (2011) has examined the issue and advanced its acceptance for study and discussion. Peasant testimonies, mostly devoid of ideology, bring a special contribution to such a discussion. The following narrative takes place in an area around Stalingrad, the deepest point of German penetration. (The village of Golubinskaia, Kalachevskii districts, Volgograd province.) There were no Jews and no Einsatzkommandos there, only the Wehrmacht.

Even with some omissions the story is long and divided into three parts.

**Example 4.17 Pelageia Romanenko, 1924–2000. Kasatkin: 2010:81**

Keywords: war, occupation

*Part 1*

В сорок втором пришли в августе месяце немцы к нам, тут были до двадцать второго ноября. Ну немцы тоже заставляли работать. Им ходили миндажи рыли и окопы рыли. Чо скажут, то и рыли. И там какой хлеб остался, ходили граблями гребли, собирали, молотили там в одном дворе. Ток был, расстилаешь, молотилка была, с молотилкой гоняешь лошадь, а потом эту зерно сгребали граблями, вон там веяли руками. Ну потом там по котелку давали домой, хто работает. [ . . . ]

*Translation*

In 1942, August, Germans came to our village, stayed here until 22 November. Well, Germans also made us work. We went to dig bunkers for them, and also trenches. What they tell us, we would dig. And whatever grain was left, we would go rake up, collect and thresh in one courtyard over there. We had a threshing floor, spread [the grain] out, and there was a thresher, we'd get a horse to pull the thresher, then rake in the grain, and winnow by hand. Then everyone would get a potful, to take home, those who worked.

*Comment*

The most important word in this passage is "also": "Germans also made us work." Female labor in the Soviet Union during the war is a big subject. (See the next example.)

The Russian word for "bunker" is a French borrowing, блиндаж (blindage). The narrator, in a typical dialectal way, says миндаж (mindage), simplifying the initial consonant cluster. Technically, she uses the place of articulation of the first consonant, [b], and the manner of articulation of the second consonant, [l].

*Part 2*

У нас домик там был и кухонька, мы в кухне жили: отец--это вот свекор, я у кого жила, и мать, и девчонка. А немцы в доме жили, они все занимали. Как идут: "Курку, яйки" и все это топором, варили, ели, все позабирали. И коров резали, забирали все. [ . . . ]

А у нас тогда какой-то там старший стоял в хатке, и кухня стояла в дворе, немцы это готовили, часть какая-то там. И вот придут часовые в хату суды, зайдут и "Гитлера в капут, Сталина капут. Всё, война капут. И мы бы к мамам, к папам поехали бы все, и ваши, и мы бы. А то война, война вот." Оно видишь как. А мы сидим, отец и мать тут. [ . . . ]

*Translation*

We had a little house with a small kitchen, and we lived in the kitchen: the father—that's my father in law, I lived with them—and mother and the little girl. The Germans lived in the house, they occupied the whole place. When they come: "Chicken, eggs," and all to the axe, cooked, ate, they took everything. Cows were slaughtered also, everything they took. [ . . . ]

We had some kind of a commander staying in the house, and their kitchen was in the backyard, Germans cooked there, their unit of some sort. And their guards would come into the house and: "Hitler go kaput and Stalin kaput, and that's it, war—kaput! We'd all go back home, to mamas and papas, your lot and us lot." So it goes. And we're just sitting there, father and mother, all here. [ . . . ]

*Comment*

German soldiers apparently all knew some Russian words, and mispronounced most of them. In all war novels, their first demand is "chicken, eggs," mispronounced in exactly the way that the narrator remembers, perhaps from oral tradition. Conversely, all Russians knew how to say: "Hitler kaput." In the narrative, the guards spoke broken Russian that the narrator reproduces fifty-eight years later.

*Part 2*

Bukrinskaia and Karmakova (2015:7–8) report a very similar story from an old woman in the Pskov region, 1,500 miles away. They note that this is an old folkloric motif, reflected in the proverb: "When landlords are fighting peasants' hair gets pulled."

Ну, были - хто?- были финны очен плохие. Финны, чахословаки, я их не люблю по севодняшний день. Очен вредные были. А немцы – нет! Вот, бывало . . . мы их уже понимали, по-и́хному. Они со словариком. Один и ɣоворит: "Пусть бы ваш Сталин, наш Υитлер вышли на дуэль, хто коɣо победи́л – тоɣо и власть! "Што мы, – гъврит – хочем ɣоло́вы ложи́ть здесь, у России? Конечно, нет. Ну, застаýляют как ваших солдат, так и наших, а мы вот воюем".

*Translation*

Well, who was here? Finns were, very bad. Finns, Czechoslovaks—I don't like them to this day. They were mean. But Germans-no! Sometimes it would happen [ . . . ] we could already understand them, when they speak. They would be with a dictionary. One of them said: "Let your Stalin and hour Hitler have a duel, who wins he has the power. Do we want—he says—lay down your heads here, in Russia? Of course not. They make us, your soldiers and our soldiers, so we're fighting.

*Part 3*

А это мать пойдёт соли попросить, там один молодой повар такой был, он насыпить в кружку консервную, дасть. Глядишь, кусок хлеба дасть. [Следует абзац про немецкий хлеб--АН] Раз пошла мать (это свекровя), и соли он ей насыпал в банку консервну. [Следует абзац про свекровь--AN] Ну и, значить, приносить она соль, ну варить туды-суды. Варит там, какой-то травы кидает, ну йисть-то надо было чой-то там. А в печке русской в чугунке варили, на рогачах пхали тоды. Говорить: "Солила-солила щи--они не солоны. Уполюшка, покушай щи." А я говорю: "Мам, чо же щи будут солёны--они с сахаром." Она: "Как с сахаром? Какой же это сахар? Ты чо же?"--"Щи-то сладкие",--я говорю. "Он мне сахару насыпал, а я думала--соли, думаю: это же свежий соль, солю--они сладкие." Это заместо, она просила, соли он сахару дал.

*Translation*

Mother would sometimes go ask for salt, there was a young cook there, he would pour some into a can and give [her]. Sometimes he would give a piece of bread. [A digression on German bread follows—AN] One day mother went (that's my mother in law) and he poured some into a can. [A digression about the mother-in-law follows.] So she brings the salt and starts cooking, messing around. She's cooking, and adding some greens, we had to eat something. And we cooked in the Russian stove, in an iron pot, we had an oven fork to push it in. And she says: "I added more salt, and more salt, but the cabbage soup is still not salty. Uliushka [the woman's name—AN], you try. And I says: "Mama, why would the soup be salty, it has sugar in it." And she: "What do you mean, sugar? What kind of sugar is this? What are you saying?"—"The soup is sweet,"—I said. "So he poured me sugar, and I thought it was salt, so I'm thinking it's fresh salt, and I'm adding, but they're sweet." So instead of, she asked for salt, he gave her sugar.

*Comment*

What makes this episode somewhat poignant is that sugar was even more scarce that salt in many households, even before the war. A mother's letter of Nov 30, 1939 says: "Вася у нас живется тихо ничего нет сахара нет живем без сахару 4-ай месец сейчас белова хлеба нет молоко 3 рубля литр мясо 15 руб. кг. картошка 8 руб. мера очень все дорого ись совсем нечего затем досвидание известная твоя мать." (Vasia, life is quiet here [but] there's nothing, no sugar, we've been without sugar for four months, there's no white bread, milk is three rubles a liter, meat is fifteen rub. a kilo, potatoes are 8 rub. a bag, everything is expensive, there's nothing to eat, with that good by, your mother.) The letter is not even from a kolkhoz but from a provincial town; the writer is a recent peasant.

**The War: Women's Labor**

There were few able-bodied men left in the villages during the war. While industrial workers were needed for the war effort (the "labor front"), almost everything men did in the countryside was put on women's shoulders, including back-breaking physical work. In kolkhozes women plowed and harvested (using cows or themselves, because most horses were also drafted for the war effort). Example 4.18 is from outside the kolkhoz.

**Example 4.18 K. Gus'kova, 1924–2007. Kasatkin 2017:599**

Topics: First months of the war. Women labor.

    В сорок первом году мне двадцать первого сентября исполнилось шестнадцать лет[8] и меня, хоп, на трудовой, на лесоповал. Дали мне коня хорошего лес возить. Я за ним и хожу, и пою, и кормлю, и работаю на нем. Проработала на нем месяц или два--прислали моему коню повестку в армию, на войну забирают. Говорят: "Нюрка, твоего коня Володю берут в армию, завтра гони его, на работу не выезжай." Ну что ж, запрягла, покормила. "Ну Володя, милый, поехали со мной." Пригнала на конный двор коня, я его поцеловала, он у меня был добрый конь. [ . . . ]

Одну ночь я ночевала, опять стучат у дома. Мама выходит: "Кто?" "Нюрке повестку на торф."

*Translation*

In forty one, September 21, I turned sixteen, and off you go to labor duty, felling trees. They gave me a good horse to cart trees away. So I look after him, and water and feed him, and work him. I worked him a month or two, then he gets a draft summons, he's taken to the front. I'm told "Niurka, your horse Volodia has been drafted, tomorrow take him there, don't come to work." Well, so be it, I harnessed, I fed. "So, sweet Volodia, come with me." I took him to the horse yard, gave him a kiss, he was a good horse. [ . . . ]

That one night I spent home, and again there's a knock on the door. Mother comes out: "Who's there?"—"Summons to Niurka for peat work."

*Comment*

The Russian original of the first sentence uses many fewer words than the translation. It literally says: "I turned sixteen, and me, off, to labor, to tree-felling." Here "me" is in the Accusative case, i.e., the direct object of some verb; and the verb is expressed not even by a real word "off" but by an interjection indicating a jumping forward movement: "They—hop-hop—me to labor." Furthermore, the destination of hopping is in Russian described by a preposition followed by an adjective without a noun: in the context, the preposition clearly indicates that the noun is "front": "[they] hop-hop me to [the] labor [front]." The number of square brackets in this gloss is a good measure of the economy of the original.

The economy continues with the already familiar omission of direct objects for "harness" and "feed," as in 4.7, 4.8.

In the last paragraph, the completely a-syntactic integration of direct speech into narrative is one of many such examples, reminiscent of the way direct speech is integrated in the letters of Chapter 3.

The rest of the excerpt describes peat work. It is divided in three parts.

## Example 4.19 A. A. Gus'kova, 1924–2007. Kasatkin 2017:599–601. Women labor

*Part 1*

Жили в палатках, по 50 человек в одной палатке В этой палатке была одна маленькая печка. [ . . . ] В палатках развелись блоха, клоп, вошь.

Хлеба на на торфу давали по килограмму, и давали килограмм шпику на месяц. И давали карточки, все в карточке указано. И работала столовая с шести часов утра. И вот мы с шести утра стояли все с котелками в руках и ложка. Вот подходишь к кассе, дают тебе килограмм хлеба, отрезают от карточки кусочек, и котелочек подаешь. В котелочек первого наливают и на второе давали или картошечки ложечка, или кашки какой-нибудь ложечка. Если картошка, то бывает и хвост рыбки какой-нибудь. И вот мы с этим котелком отправлялись в палатку и садилися покушать пока горячее. Сядем на табуреточку, у нас у каждого была тумбочка.

А половина седьмого--вышка стоит, стоит парторг на вышке, выступает. [ . . . ] Потом говорит: "Все, отбой, все на работу." [ . . . ]

Вот работаем с полседьмого и пока нам не поставят флаг на вышке на обед, это было полпервого. Если с вышки флаг сняли, значит обед кончился, все на работу должны идти.

*Translation*

We lived in tents, fifty to a tent. The tent had on little stove. [ . . . ] In all tents were fleas, bedbugs, lice.

The peat works gave us one kilo of bread per day and a kilo of salted pig fat for a month. And also ration cards, everything was written on the ration card. There was a canteen, opened at six a.m. So at six we all stood there, with our metal bowls, and a spoon. You walk up to the cashier, get a kilo of bread, they cut off a piece from your ration card, you give them a bowl. They would pour some soup in the bowl, and also a spoonful of potatoes, or a spoonful of some porridge. If potatoes, then sometimes a fish tail of some fish. And so we would take our bowl to the tent and sit down to eat while hot. We would sit on a stool, and each of us had a nightstand.

At 6:30, the tower, and the party boss on the tower giving a speech [ . . . ] Then he says: "That's it, the end, go to work."

So we work from 6:30 and until the flag comes up on the tower for lunch, that would be 12:30. If the flag is down, this means lunch is over, we all must go back to work.

*Comment*

Historically, peat for fuel had been extracted in Europe as early as the thirteenth century. By the late nineteenth century, coal had largely replaced peat as an energy source, but peat fuel was still produced as needed. With Donbass occupied by the Germans from 1941 to late 1943, peat production became essential for the Soviets. Even in the post-war reconstruction plan, 1946–1950, peat-fuel production loomed large.

## Part 2

Отмеряли нам по десять ар на человека сделать змейки. Торф был разливной. Он сначала как крахмал наливается, а потом он садится на низ, а сверху воду сливали. А когда вода сойдет, посылали трактор резать торф на кирпичики. А его чтобы поднять, надо по локоть в землю влезть. Он же там грязный такой, и сырой, и тяжелый. И вот ставишь вперед в одну сторону, потом в другую сторону, в одну сторону, потом в другую сторону. И вот так каждый день работаешь, каждый день одно и то же, никаких выходных не было. [ . . . ]

## Translation

They measured 1,000 square meters for us, to do little ridges. The peat was thick liquid. It would at first thicken like starch, they settle down, and water was drained from the top. When water was gone they would send a tractor to cut the peat in bricks. But to lift it [for the ridges—AN], you had to get in it up to your elbow. It is dirty down there, and wet, and heavy. And so you put [some] first on one side, then on the other side, on one side, on the other side. And so you work every day, every day the same thing, no days off ever. [ . . . ]

## Comment

The work Gus'kova describes had been automated many years ago but the Soviets did not have enough tractors for peat work or kolkhoz work, so female labor was used.

Throughout her narrative Gus'kova uses the Russian grammatical construction that has no subject and the verb in the third person plural: "[They] measured 1,000 square meters for us." "[They] would drain water from the top." "[They] would send a tractor." The effect is sometimes similar to English Passive (water would be drained) and sometimes conveys the impression of an impersonal force that does things to people and nature.

## Part 3

Теперь идем с работы, шесть часов вечера, опять вывеска на вышке: флаг--конец рабочего дня, все домой. Пришли домой, расположились поесть, попить. Очень бывает хочется после сухомятки пить, потому что первое давали только утром, а весь день-то мы на сухом хлебе, по кусочку брали с собой шпику, нам кусочки отрезали на месяц. Пить очень хочется. Пили прямо из канавы. [ . . . ] Вперед тряпки стлали, потом платки стали стлать, а потом как придется стали пить.

Приходит вечером этот опять начальник [ . . . ] и говорит: "Сейчас в ночь кабель таскать." Я говорю: "Мы ж только с работы пришли, у вас совесть есть или нету."—"Совесть у всех есть, а что надо, то для фронту всё надо, всё для фронту. Кабель таскать и всё."

*Translation*

Now we're going back from work, six in the evening, again there is a sign on the tower: a flag, the end of workday, everybody [go] home. We would come home, settle down to eat and drink. We were very thirsty after a day of only dry food, because we had soup only in the morning, and the whole day we would be on dry bread, we also took a piece of pig fat, they cut a piece for us for a month. We were very thirsty. Drank straight from the ditch. At first we would put a piece of cloth down [for filtering—AN], then we would use a kerchief, and then we just drank from the ditch.

One evening that boss comes again and says "Tonight we have to carry cables." I say: "We just came back from work, have you any shame or have you no shame."—"We all have shame, but whatever the need, it all need for the front, everything's for the front. Go carry cables, and that's it."

*Comment*

The workday was 11.5 hours a day with a half-hour break, no days off. The only organized meal was in the morning. There was no drinking water. In emergencies, there could be additional labor at night.

The boss quotes the official, omnipresent slogan: "Всё для фронта, всё для победы." (Everything for the front, everything for victory.)

**The Post-War Years, 1945–1953**

The years 1945–1953, from the end of the war to death of Stalin, were exceedingly bleak. There was one last famine of 1946–1947 in which almost a million died.[9] Even in the absence of famine, there was wide-spread hunger, combined with the draconian laws that meted out harsh punishments for stealing a little food for your family. The job of kolkhoz rangers (объездчики) was to inspect the pockets and baskets of kolkhozniks returning from the fields, most of them women. (After the losses of the war, kolkhoz women outnumbered men two to one, but men dominated administrative positions.)

The next example was recorded in 2006, from a speaker born in the mid-1930s. The narrative time is soon after the war. The place is the familiar village of Viriatino that was the locale of Kushner's 1950-era study. There are interesting similarities in technique between this man's story and the one analyzed in Bukrinskaia and Karmakova (2012b): a similar quick sequence of visual episodes, often described by sentences without any predicates at all or with a verb replaced by an interjection.

## Example 4.20 No birth date, recorded 2006. Alymov, 2010

Тогда мы горох поехали молотить. Приехал объездчик Андрей Иванович. Говорят, приехал проверять, чтобы никто не взял. А с бочкой, с водой, я-то маленький. А у женщин у всех, может, по пригоршне этого гороха, и они туда, в воду, у меня там полбочки воды — бух-бух. Говорят: ехай, ехай. А он видит, что я на лошади сижу, у меня ничего нет. Сижу на бочке. Сюда на конный двор приехал, они все туда, достает каждая из воды — домой. Домой придет — горох сварит ребятишкам.

*Translation*

We went to thresh peas then. A ranger came, Andrei Ivanovich. They say he came to inspect, to make sure nobody taking. I was with the barrel, with the water, just a little boy. And the women, all of them, had perhaps a handful of those peas, and they all ping-ping them into the water—I had maybe half a barrel of water. And they say: go, go. And he can see that I am sitting on the horse, I don't have anything, I'm just sitting on the barrel. [When I] came here to the horse yard, they all [go] there, each gets [her peas] from the water, and [goes] home. [When she] comes home she'll cook some peas for her kids.

*Comment*

This passage illustrates the syntactic economy and what Bukrinskaia and Karmakova (2006) call the "expressivity" of peasant narratives." Note that to obtain a minimally grammatical English translation the translator has to insert several verbs and a missing direct object for a transitive verb that actually is in the text. The Russian uses interjections and adverbs, including deictic elements (*here*), to indicate action and movement. A translation also needs conjunctions for subordinate clauses. The switching of tenses, reproduced in the translation, contributes to the economy and dynamism of the story.

This passage, recorded by an ethnographer, also illustrates the meta-issue of the principles of transcription. The word for ranger (объездчик) has a cluster of three consonant letters that would all be pronounced by a single sound. A linguist would replace those three letters with one, [щ], or, depending on the dialect, with double [шш].

The situation of this passage is relatively benign. In some parts of the county, including newly acquired territories, 1946 was as bad as 1933. Kasatkin (2017:568–70) provides a powerful testimony, recorded in a Ukranian village that was in Romania between the wars, until 1940, when it was occupied by the Soviets as part of the Molotov-Ribbentrop division of Eastern Europe. In 1941 Romanians were back together with a few German units, but the

Soviets re-occupied the area in 1944. Their policies in such double-occupied areas were extremely harsh, intended to terrorize the population that was on the enemy side or under occupation during the war, and suspected, rightly or wrongly, of nationalism and collaboration with the Germans. Ironically, the village was settled in the eighteenth century by Russian Cossack Old Believers who ran away from Russia to practice their faith without religious persecution in what was then the Ottoman Empire.

**Example 4.21 Daria Gorshkova, 1931–2003.**
**Kasatkin 2017:565–583. Primorskoe, Ukraine**

*Part 1*

Война закончилась девятого мая, ну и почали нас шарабу́ить — всё выбирать, забирать. Ну, повыгребли всё, по хатам ходили, даже родители у лежаночку закапывали зёрнушко, они отрывали, забирали всё, что было что съедобное. Вот всё вези, сдавай, всё вези, сдавай. Всё забрали. [ . . . ] Во так было в сорок пятом, под сорок шестой год осенью. Но это быстро всё прошло, они за месяц всё протрусили, оставили только пустое всё. И тут люди уже спужалися. И тут холод как раз, Бог морозу такого дал, ой. [ . . . ]

Ну и начался голод, нигде нема чего есть. Это я буду рассказывать, как у нашем селе. Зима сорок шестого года и зима ужасная. Ещё и Бог такую зиму дал, что страсть, сорок градусов, больше сорока. [ . . . ]

*Translation*

The war ended May 9, and right away they started shaking us down—take everything out and away. [They] raked out everything, went from house to house, parents would even bury a little grain under the stove bench--they would dig it all out, take away everything you could eat. Whatever you have, bring it, turn it in, bring it, turn it in. That's how it was in 1945 in the fall going to 1946. But this passed very quickly, within a month they had shaken out everything, left everything just empty. And then people got really scared. And then, right there, God sent such cold, oy [ . . . ]

And so hunger began, nothing to eat anywhere. I will tell you how it was in our village. The winter of 1946, a terrible winter. On top of it all God sent such a winter, a horror, minus forty, below forty [-40 C, which is also -40 F—AN].

*Part 2*

Буду говорить про свою семью. Отец, мать и нас трое деток. А гляди по всех полках, по всех ку́тиках — не найдёшь что-нибудь, чтоб у рот можно было покласть. [ . . . ] Сразу умер отец с голоду. Умер — закопали. Потом и девочка, моя сестра. И там люди все по селу мруть, даже рядом соседи опухают, умирают. И на санки кладуть их и везуть на кладбище. По селу идёшь, а люди лежать, той упал, той лежить уже, той доходить. Хоронить нема кому же, взять и закопать, бо все бессильные. [ . . . ]

*Translation*

I can tell about my family. Father, mother and three of us, children. But look on every shelf, in every corner, you won't find anything to put in your mouth. [ . . . ] Father died from hunger right away. Died, got buried. Then also the little girl, my sister. And out there in the village people die, even next door neighbors get swollen and die. So they put them on a sled and take to the cemetery. Walking in the village you see people lying, one falling down, one already lying, one near death. There's nobody to bury, to take and to dig, for nobody has any strength. [ . . . ]

*Part 3*

На нашей от вулице вам час расскажут. Коло нас две семьи все умерли. Пять детей и матка, и батька умерли. Сбоку тоже, так само умерли. И собак люди ели, и крыс ели, и даже люди людей ели. [ . . . ]

*Translation*

Others in our street will tell you. Two families next door all died. Five children and mother and father died. A bit to the side also, died the same way. People ate dogs, and rats, and some people even ate people. [ . . . ]

*Comment*

On a village scale this reproduces the conditions of the siege of Leningrad, on rich agricultural land in Ukraine, soon after the V-Day.

The text has several Ukrainian lexical items but otherwise is completely in line with texts from Russia.

*The Post-Stalin Decades*

After Stalin's death, life immediately became easier. Stalin died in March 1953; in September, the Central Committee passed a resolution that increased state payments for agricultural products, slashed taxes on individual plots by eighty percent, and wiped out all accumulated tax arrears. By 1956 the system of labordays became more flexible and generous, though it was not until 1966 that it was abandoned altogether, replaced by regular monetary payments. The size of individual plots was increased, and agricultural products from them flooded "kolkhoz markets" in all major cities. In areas of better soil and climate, kolkhozniks became quite rich by Soviet standards: a car, better housing, new furniture, a television set. Some better-managed kolkhozes also became rich and passed some of the wealth to their members. Even so there were typical Soviet problems, illustrated by two vignettes from a kolkhoz-millionaire, with annual profits in the millions of rubles. The first is about shortages of consumer goods and popular food staples, unavailable even if you had money. The setting is a visit by a delegation from Poland, brought by the authorities to show off the successful kolkhoz:

**Example 4.22 Recorded 2006. Alymov 2010.**
**Polish delegation at a kolkhoz**

Давно, еще при Ожогине польская делегация приезжала. Дорога на Перкино — оттуда ехали, а тут на вышке сидят: едут, стукнули в колокол. Тут подготовились. В магазин тут привезли все: баранки, и батоны, и селедки, все. А все лезут покупать. А они говорят: не лезть, как бы у нас тут все это есть. Тут выстроили всех пионеров, концерт для них сделали.

*Translation*

A long time ago, under Ozhogin [kolkhoz chairman—AN] a Polish delegation came. The Perkino road—they came from there, and here people were on a tower: [when they saw the Poles were] coming, [the villagers on the tower] rang the bell. Here [in the village] they were ready. Everything had been brought to the store: bagels, white bread, herring, everything. And everybody's pushing to buy. But they [the authorities] say: stay out, [it should be] as if we have it all. Then they [the authorities] lined up all the young pioneers, gave a concert for them [the Poles].

*Comment*

The square brackets in the translation testify to the brevity of the original. To a remarkable extent, there are very few subject noun phrases with head nouns: they are either pronouns or totally absent. The meaning of the predicates makes the references clear: the Polish delegation, the villagers on the lookout, the villagers pushing to buy scarce food staples, the authorities pushing them back.

The food staples listed in the text would have been more easily available in the city—another stimulus for leaving the kolkhoz behind. The word "bagel" in that list may startle readers. Russian has four words for a round piece bread with a hole in it: бублики, баранки, калачи, сушки. Both бублики and баранки share with the bagels brought to the West by Jewish immigrants the unusual detail of being boiled before they are baked. Бублики are softer. The баранки in the excerpt are less airy and have a less distinctive crust.

The second vignette is about democracy. The kolkhoz chairman of the story (we are still in Viriatino!) was a major reason for its success. However, he had constant fights with the district (county) administration. The district, like everybody else, had quotas. If one kolkhoz produced less than its quota, the district had to take more from a successful kolkhoz. Ozhogin, who was chairman from 1935 to 1963, with a break for four years of war from which he returned a much-decorated hero, sometimes successfully resisted the district's demands. At some point the district decided it was time to remove him. By law this could only be done by the kolkhozniks' vote, but Ozhogin was, understandably, very popular. This explains the highly unusual open conflict between "the people" and the administrator from the district center who came to call the meeting and get the vote. Ordinarily such a meeting would be a boring affair of a couple of hours, but this one lasted three days. The story of the confrontation is again very concise; the translation uses a lot of square brackets to supply words that the original leaves out.

**Example 4.23 Recorded 2006. Alymov 2010. A vote in the Soviet Union**

Ну, дело дошло, Сепелев этот приехал, говорит: будем собирать. Трое суток собрание, никак его не освободят. Он говорит: буду собирать общее собрание, на общем ничего — буду цеховые, бригадные, по одному буду опрашивать, но я приехал, чтобы его снять и все. Спорите вы, шумите, не шумите — я приехал его снять. А грамотный, говорит — хороший у него язык. А тут народ шумит, говорит: ты тут, снять! Как народ скажет, народ, дескать, его избирал. А он прямо в открытую говорит: народ — это мухи, насажаются много, а махну — ни одной нет.

*Translation*

So the time came, that man Sepelev arrived, [and] says: "We're calling [a meeting]." The meeting [was] three days, [and] no way he [Ozhogin—AN] can be removed. He [Sepelev—AN] says: "I will keep calling a general meeting; [if] the general gets nothing, I will [call] shop [meetings], team [meetings], I will talk one on one, but I came to remove him and that's it. Whether you argue, whether you shout or don't shout, I came to remove him." And [he was] well-educated, [when] he spoke he had good language. But the people are shouting, saying: who are you, "remove"? [It will be] what the people say; the people, they say, elected him. And he openly said it straight: people are flies, [when] they land, they're many, but [if] I wave [my hand] there isn't a single one.

*Comment*

In this confrontation both sides understood that if the peasants crossed a certain line the repercussions would be severe. Just a year earlier, a labor strike in the city of Novocherkassk was suppressed by regular troops, with twenty-six killed and scores wounded. This was carefully concealed, but rumors spread, and even without rumors, barely ten years after Stalin's death nobody had any doubts about the lines that could not be crossed.

In the sentence before last, the phrase "they say" translates an old parenthetical Russian word, дескать, that means something like "as they say." Russian has three such words, дескать, мол, якобы, the first two neutral, the last casting doubt on the veracity of what is being said.

### Demographics and "Soviet Persons"

Increased prosperity did not stop massive migration to the city, especially by the young. According to official data published in the media until 1979, every year from 1951 to 1979 1.7 million people migrated from the village to the city (Koester-Thoma, 1994:20).

This adds up to fifty million people, on top of at least twenty-five million who had migrated before the war. The reasons usually cited are the boredom of village life, isolation, bad roads, and lack of opportunity for social advancement. (The Soviet-Russian notion of культурность [culturedness] is frequently invoked as well: village life was much less 'cultured' than urban life.) In addition to these reasons, there were also massive streams of involuntary migration from the village to prison and labor camp, whose survivors usually ended up in cities. The millions who came back alive from WWII also in large numbers settled in cities instead of going back to their villages.

The summary demographic figures for the peasant-urban population are given here from Kozlova (1996:12), based on Zaionchkovskaia (1991:20).

> In old Russia, more than eighty percent were peasants, and only 2.7 percent did intellectual work. By the end of 1926, the urban population of the USSR was eighteen percent, the same as before WWI. Only in the beginning of the 1960s did the country's share of urban population (fifty-six percent) approach the level of most so-called developed countries. By the mid-1980s, the USSR's agricultural sector employed twelve percent of the population, industry almost sixty percent, and intellectual work close to thirty percent. *Most of those*

*Scholars and Narratives from the 1950s to Today* 183

*who belonged to the last two categories were of peasant stock.* (Emphasis added—AN)

The last sentence above supports Kozlova's main thesis:

> Russia is a country of former peasants. The *sovok* (a derogatory label for a "Soviet person") is mostly a former peasant who became "not-a-peasant." (p.12) The history of a peasant becoming 'not-a-peasant' and the history of our country in the twentieth century are two twins. (p.13)

Continuing the metaphor, we can say that a little brother of those two twins is the history of peasant language becoming 'not-peasant-language,' changing into one of two possible outcomes: standard educated Russian or the familiar *prostorechie* (henceforth called Urban Vernacular), the uniquely Russian phenomenon of a spacially homogeneous urban social dialect defined by the educational level and speech attitudes of its speakers. Acknowledging this development is the first step in creating a sociolinguistic map of Soviet society around the time when it was about to fall apart--and when, by historical coincidence, the surviving speakers of Russian peasant language were entering the last decades of their lives.

Even in their dwindling and disappearing condition, Russian peasants preserved their vitality, as shown by the last example of this section. Zinaida Fedotova was born in 1936, in a village about 300 miles south of Leningrad. She remembers how, in the summer of 1941, her village was overrun by the Germans. "However, they didn't touch the people, only took away all the food" (Kasatkin 2010:284). When the Germans moved on, some people from surrounding villages were evacuated, by truck and train, all the way North to a village on the White Sea, in the Arkhangelsk province. Zinaida lived the rest of her life there. "My childhood was hard. I had almost no school. We had to work, we went to work very young. [ . . . ] I only finished two grades" (p.287). At twelve, she started kolkhoz work. Her story was recorded when she was relatively young, sixty-seven years old. Its last section is about her life in retirement.

### Example 4.24 Zinaida Fedotova. (1936–2003). Kasatkin 2010:289–90. Forest, nature

И в лес в летнее время хочется сходить. Хочется--радость такая. Сходишь, как будто и жизнь другая. Как хорошо в лесу, еще с чайком-то когда дак. Чайку-то согреешь да попьешь, ой прелесть. Костерок зажгём, затушим. Я люблю в лес ходить. Я одна--мне и никого не надо. Уйду одна, брожу--места знаю дак, лишь бы от дороги никуда не уйти.

Мне уж не первый раз, я всё одна почти в лес хожу. Внучку вот когда возьму. Они здесь живут-то, приходят ко мне, чаю-то попить приходят.

Другой раз я с медведем встретилася, и с волком встречалась. Бойся-не бойся, встретишься дак--куда денешься-то. Такой азарт получиться! С волком-то встретилась тагды, дак азарт получился. Думаю: "Я ему сейчас! Он на меня нападёт, дак я ему в живот ножиком!" Нет, он потом свернул в сторону, я пробежала скорее.

Дедко даве повалился отдохнуть, а я говорю: "Нет, я пойду в лес схожу. Принесу, не принесу, а всё равно сброжу." Вот так. И грибов принесла на варю, черники много. Но только очень сыро, я все сапоги залила и всё. Дожжа-то утром-то много было. Я вязанье бросила, вот в лес пошла. Не отдыхаешь, всё время крутишься, всё чего-то делаешь.

*Translation*

In the summer I like to walk in the forest. I like it very much--a big happiness for me. You take a walk, and it's like your life is different. It's so good in the forest, especially with tea. You make some tea, you drink it, so lovely. We'd light a fire, then put it out. I love going to the forest. I go alone, I don't need anybody. I go, wander along—I know all the places, just trying not to go too far away from the path. It's not the first time, I almost always go alone. Sometimes I would take my granddaughter. They don't live very far, so they come visit, they come for a cup of tea.

The other day I ran into a bear, and I ran into wolves, too. Scared or not scared, once it happens, what can you do. A great thrill comes over you. When I ran into a wolf that time, a great thrill. I was thinking: "I'll show him! If he jumps, I'll stab him in his belly with my knife." But no, he turned the other way, and I ran faster.

Lately my old man went to rest, but I said: "No, I'll go to the forest. Bring something back or not, I'll go anyway. So I did. I brought mushrooms for soup, and a lot of blueberries. But it was wet, my boots were full of water, and everything. There had been a lot of rain in the morning. I left my knitting to go to the forest. No time to rest, one thing after another, something to do all the time.

*Comment*

The text shows typical dialectal features of the North, not of the region she left when she was 5. The Northern features include:

- post-position particle -то, as in "с чайком-то" (with tea), "чайку-то" (tea)
- conjunction дак in the end of a clause, as in "еще с чайком-то когда дак" (literally "especially with tea when then")

In a throwback to the 1920s letters, the borrowing азарт (thrill) is used with a wrong Lexical Function: азарт получился, literally "thrill happened."

## 4.4 THE LINGUISTICS OF PEASANT NARRATIVES

The accumulated material of this chapter—a small but representative sample of a large body of recorded interviews—testifies to multiple commonalities in peasant narratives across regions and dialects. Many such commonalities are extra-linguistic as they reflect deeply etched shared historical experience. This was the subject of the preceding section. The current section is about shared *linguistic* features that are specific to peasant narratives, separating them from other varieties of spoken Russian. The first step is to identify those varieties.

### Sociolinguistic groups and their backgrounds

A simple but convincing scheme of sociolinguistic divisions of Russian is laid out in Krysin (2003). His suggestions are sometimes criticized as too rigid, imposing hard-and-fast boundaries on fluid gradations. These criticisms are addressed below, together with additional considerations that mitigate them.

Krysin's four sociolinguistic groups are shown in Table 4.4. The labels attached to them are familiar from earlier chapters: "Colloquial Russian" for the educated speech of those who use the literary language; "Dialectal Language" for speech of peasants, and "Urban Vernacular" (UV), the *prostorechie* of earlier chapters, for less-educated varieties of urban speech. Krysin's main innovation (first suggested in Krysin 1989) is to divide UV in two distinct subgroups, defined as follows:

Quote 4.1 Krysin 2003 on UV-1 vs. UV-2

Two groups of speakers of the present-day vernacular are clearly identified: older urban dwellers, with no, or only primary, education, whose speech shows clear links to dialect or semi-dialect ([ . . . ] urban vernacular-1), and young or

Table 4.4 **Social Groups of Speakers.** Compiled by the Author

| Speaker Group | Social Dialect |
|---|---|
| 1 Peasants who grew up in a traditional peasant family and remained peasants/kolkhozniks to the end of their lives. | Dialectal Language |
| 2 Peasants who grew up in a traditional peasant family but migrated to the city as grown-ups. (These were identified as "recent peasants" in Ch. 3.) | Urban Vernacular-1 |
| 3 Mid- to low-educated urban speakers who were born and grew up in the city but did not learn the standard language. | Urban Vernacular-2 |
| 4 The educated urban class. | Colloquial Russian |

middle-aged urban dwellers who have unfinished secondary education and have not mastered the norms of the literary language. Their speech has no traces of dialects but to a great extent is influenced by jargon (urban vernacular-2).

It is important to place Krysin's distinctions in the context of the earlier discussion of endangered dialects. The defining feature of both Dialectal and UV-1 speakers (rows 1 and 2) is that their first language was acquired in a peasant family that still maintained traditional peasant language and culture. Apart from small linguistic islands in remote places, by the late 1930s and especially after the war that traditional peasant language was no longer passed from parents to children. By the early twenty-first century, both Dialectal and UV-1 were severely endangered dialects that have since passed from the scene. By contrast, UV-2 and Colloquial Russian (rows 3 and 4) were dynamic, growing, and increasingly inter-penetrating. For younger generations of the twenty-first century, the line between UV-2 and Colloquial Russian seems more blurred, while the line separating both of them from the disappearing peasant dialects is quite sharp. At the same time, the line between Dialectal and UV-1 (the top 2 rows) is much less pronounced and also rarely discussed because of how the discipline of linguistics is practiced in Russia.

*Diverging Peasants, Isolated Disciplines*

Peasants in rural areas have always been studied by dialectologists, whose fieldwork would take them to villages in search of ever more precise documentation of localized speech variants. There was no such thing as a dialectologist doing fieldwork in a city, studying either an established city dialect or the fluid dialects of recent arrivals from the countryside. As a result, UV-1, a close relative of dialectal language, makes no appearance in Russian dialectology. Conversely, students of Urban Vernaculars have been recording urban speech primarily for cultural analysis, not linguistic detail. The most extensive collection of urban texts is Shalina (2011); an earlier analysis of that material (Shalina 2009) is organized around what she calls "cultural scenarios:" Life in the Village, Path to the City, and Life in the City. As these names indicate, Shalina accepts the division into UV-1 and UV-2, and although her anthology contains both kind of material, her main interest is in UV-1.

There is very little communication between rural dialectologists and urban culturologists even when their data show remarkable similarity.[10] Part of the problem may simply lie in the principles of transcription: urban linguists (and also ethnographers) tend to show fewer dialectal features, which deprives dialectologists of the phonetic detail that constitutes an important component of their data. For that reason, they may not see these transcriptions as representing anything dialectal.

The self-confinement of dialectologists to rural areas made sense for most of the twentieth century, when peasantry was the largest, albeit shrinking, demographic group in the country. Over that time Russian dialectology accumulated a wealth of material, including two geographical atlases of Russian dialects. Work on the first atlas began before the revolution and continued, without a proper conclusion, up to the Terror when several key participants were executed. Work on the second one started soon after the war but really took off only after Stalin's death. It continued through the three post-Stalin decades, the last volume coming out in the early twenty-first century, in a new country that had very few peasants left. However, the annual rhythm of fieldwork and research continues in dialectology, even if it is sometimes difficult to find dialect speakers in semideserted villages.

Against this background, in the late 1990s dialectologists branched out from villages into small provincial towns, where they found an unexpected presence of dialectal features in what otherwise would be the standard literary language. Since the generalized sets of dialectisms that they uncovered extended over larger geographic regions than the more local dialects of earlier times, a new term, *regiolect*, was coined for the new phenomenon.[11] There is relatively little regiolect data currently available, and what exists is not entirely consistent. Gerd (2000:48) says that most speakers of regiolect are local intelligentsia, in which category he includes "teachers, doctors, librarians, [and] local government officials." However, some samples in Bukrinskaia and Karmakova (2012a) show a much less educated language that is reminiscent of the speech of peasant migrants of the previous generation. The relationship between UV-1 and the regiolects of the next generation has not been studied. The reason for this probably lies in the boundaries between disciplines discussed earlier: regiolects were discovered and studied by ethnolinguists and dialectologists, who were, for the first time, examining the speech of peasants' children, people who were not themselves peasants and lived in urban environments. Until that time, the language of urban environments had been the preserve of "cultural linguists" and sociologists.

## Features of Peasant Narratives in Contrast and Comparison

With all this background in place, our central claims can be stated more precisely: (1) the corpus of peasant narratives contains diagnostic features absent from narratives by other sociolinguistic dialects; (2) the corpus of peasant narratives does NOT contain some diagnostic features (lexical, syntactic, phraseological) present in narratives of those other dialects. With respect to Colloquial Russian specifically, the claim is that there are only three possible kinds of features: those found in Colloquial Russian but not in Dialectal; those found in Dialectal but not in Colloquial Russian; and those found in both, which are general features of Russian found in all sociolinguistic varieties.

UV-1, which uniquely overlaps with Dialectal, needs a separate discussion based on its own set of examples. UV-2 is largely left out of consideration because it is so alien to Dialectal, but it does make a couple of minor appearances.

Features of Dialectal speech emerging from the narratives of this chapter contain and extend the peasant language profile established in Chapter 1. In this chapter, some profile features are grouped together and simply restated with minor elaboration, but some are substantially expanded because of abundant additional material in the later sources. In section headings below numbers in parentheses refer to the sections in the profile.

## 1. Phonetic and morphological features; local vocabularies

The first and most obvious feature of peasant narratives is that they contain many dialectisms (see, e.g., Example 4.2 and discussion). The precise details of local dialects vary from one area to another, but all peasant narratives have some dialectal elements that would be uncommon in urban speech, except as a conscious imitation by an intellectual, or in a passage by a UV-1 speaker who has not completely lost her mother tongue in the city.

As noted in the Profile, many dialectal words have narrow specific meanings, designating details of peasant life and work. Many of them go back centuries, as recorded in older texts and dictionaries.

## 2. Abstract and deverbal nouns; present active participles

There are relatively few abstract and deverbal nouns. Nouns with the Church-Slavonic suffixes—ени(е)/–ани(е)/- ити(е) are extremely rare. Even the religious term Заговенье (the day before a major fast) comes out with a Russian suffix, Заговины (Kasatkin 2017:541).

Russian Present active participles also use Church-Slavonic suffixes and are practically non-existent in peasant narratives.

## 2a. Lexicon in UV-2

UV-2 is also easily identified by its lexical peculiarities, but they belong to a totally different universe. UV-2 is not local. It does not invent local words with specific narrow meanings. In one of its several strands it is prone to solecisms, using abstract and deverbal nouns where concrete nouns are called for. Priiatkina (2000:235) cites such examples as: "кормим сахарной свеклой всё животноводство" (we feed sugar beets to the entire animal husbandry—i.e., all animals); "научный потенциал института уже три месяца без зарплаты" (the scientific potential of the institute has been without pay for three months—i.e., the staff of the institute). There is no irony in these uses, they are completely serious misappropriations of sophisticated vocabulary.

## 3. Adjectives and verbs

Adjectives are relatively low frequency words in most texts. In peasant speech they are quite rare and used only as predicates or as restrictive adjectives in stable adjective-noun combinations. Appositive adjectives are practically absent. The verb ratio is, on the contrary, quite high. These quantitative observations are fairly obvious from the data, but can also be confirmed by Zhuravlev (1988)[12], where several social dialects and speech genres are statistically compared. For verbs (p.113) the index for Dialectal narrative is 0.20 while for Colloquial Russian it is 0.16, and even lower for public presentations and lectures. For adjectives (p.117) the ratio is reversed: the indices are 0.05 and 0.08 respectively.

## 4. Word formation

As mentioned in the Profile, Dialectal word-formation is energetic and economical. Example 4.2 illustrates with the word заxoлодь that adds one-syllable prefix to the word холод (cold) to describe "a cold stretch or spell in space or time."

One area where Dialectal word formation is generous is in the use of diminutive suffixes. (Example 4.2 has three.) According to Sveshnikova (2007), Colloquial Russian texts show [diminutive suffixes] in 1.7 percent of nouns while the lowest ratio in dialects is 2.5%, and in the North-West (Pskov, Novgorod) it is much higher, close to 10%. In 4.25 below, the suffix added to the borrowed word грамм (gram): "А зярна-то ведь не давали в колхозе ни граммочки" (The kolkhoz didn't give us even a single little gram of grain). Even so, the overall index of "derivational complexity" in Zhuravlev (1988:103), calculated as the average number of derivational suffixes per word, shows that dialectical narratives exhibit almost one-third fewer such suffixes than Colloquial Russian.

## 5. Syntactic simplicity and narrative economy

Both in the letters of Chapter 3 and the examples of this chapter, the syntax of peasant narratives is very simple. Complex sentences with subordinate clauses are rare. The range of subordinate conjunctions is narrow and their use infrequent: the syntactic structure is indicated by intonation. To some extent this is also true of Colloquial Russian *conversation*, where syntactic units, which may or may not be properly formed sentences, are shorter and simpler.[13] However, Colloquial Russian *narratives* often exhibit syntactic complexity that would never be found in Dialectal narratives. Consider an example from an older woman who was born before the Revolution and lived her entire life in St. Petersburg-Leningrad. The story is about a famous turn-of-the-century writer whom the speaker visited as an adolescent. The interviewer asked whether she had met any famous people there.

**Example 4.25 Recordings of the 60s–70s. The speaker is 75 years old. Barinova 1978:107**

Я только ходила/ потому что я слушала как он читал/ и я упивалась // Потому что у него замечательный голос/ и мне было очень интересно / а так я не бывала когда у них были [ . . . ] там какие-нибудь приемы или что//

*Translation (subordinate conjunctions are highlighted)*

I only went **because** I listened to **how** he read [his works--AN] / and I relished it // **Because** he had a splendid voice / and [the content--AN] was very interesting to me / but otherwise I never visited **when** they had [PAUSE] some kind of receptions or something

 *Comment.* A more natural translation of the first sentence would be "I only went to listen to him reading [his work]." The more literal translation illustrates the syntactic complexity of the original: a subordinate clause within a subordinate clause, both properly outfitted with conjunctions. Not a single example like that would be found in peasant narratives.

Conversely, in contrast to 4.22 and 4.23, Colloquial Russian does not tend to drop syntactic constituents like subjects and direct objects. Recall the sentence in 4.22, glossed here with all the gaps shown in brackets:

Дорога на Перкино — оттуда ехали, а тут на вышке сидят: едут, стукнули в колокол.

The Perkino road—[the Poles] were coming from there, and here, on a tower [some villagers] were sitting: [when they saw the Poles] coming [they] rang the bell.

Contrast this narrative with a passage from a video recording by Liliana Lungina. Lungina grew up mostly in Europe, where her father was a Soviet trade representative. At some point he was summoned to Moscow and not allowed to leave. Lungina and her mother returned to Moscow years later, in 1934. In the 1990s, just as Russian peasants were recording their memoirs, the film director Oleg Dorman videotaped Lungina telling her own life history. Dorman made the tapes into a hugely popular television series and later into a book, Dorman (2009). The excerpt in Example 4.26 describes Lungina's first day in Moscow, when her father took her to Red Square. The example gives the book page as reference, but the text has been corrected (or rather un-corrected back to the recording).[14] The words and phrases that indicate Colloquial Russian provenance are in boldface.

**Example 4.26 Lungina 1920–1997. Dorman 2009:137, corrected from recording**

Красная площадь была еще полна первомайских украшений. Меня поразили, конечно, все эти плакаты красные с лозунгами "Социализм победит", "Трудящиеся всего мира, объединяйтесь" и прочее, но больше всего меня поразило возле Лобного места **была сделана** огромная фигура, кукла Чемберлена, и эту куклу жгли все время, поджигали, а вокруг **люди, взявшись за руки,** плясали. И это произвело на девочку, **приехавшую из Европы, впечатление** вообще какого-то [ . . . ] ну варварства какого-то. У меня было какое-то чувство, что я в Африку попала. Жгут живого как бы **человека**, а кругом [ . . . ] на радостях пляшут **люди**!

*Translation*

Red Square was still full of May 1st decorations. I was of course struck by all the red banners with the signs "Socialism will be victorious," "Worker of the world unite," and so on, but I was struck the most, near the Lobnoe Mesto[15] there was a huge figure, an effigy of Chamberlain, and this effigy was being burned all the time, they kept setting fire to it, and all around it people were dancing, holding hands. For a girl who had just come from Europe this looked like, I don't know, some kind of barbarity. I felt like I suddenly was in Africa. They are burning something like a live human being, and all around people are dancing from joy.

*Comment*

In a peasant narrative, the Passive verb form "was made" would be a subjectless active plural form. The adverbial and the participial phrases would be verbs phrases paratactically arranged in the narrative. The nouns человек and люди would simply be omitted. The result would be much shorter; the second sentence would be similar to: возле Лобного места сделали куклу огромную Чемберлена, и эту куклу жгут все время, а вокруг взялись за руки и пляшут.

### 5a. The Stylistic and Emotional Impact of Syntactic Simplicity

As in Chapter 3, we observe here the inclusion of a striking detail in a context of uniform syntax and narrative rhythm. The effect can be startling, though likely unintentionally so. In the next example, a woman imprisoned for an argument with kolkhoz organizers digresses to tell the story of a female prison guard:

### Example 4.27 Simakina 1908–1992. Vinogradskii 2012:69

Потом допрашивать взялись – два раза на день допрашивали. Конвоиром была женщина. Сама осуждённая: сделала ребенка и в смородину его закопала, а сосед доказал. Ну, донес, ей дали три года за него – за ребенка-то. Вот она при тюрьме там помогала . . . Идет она, отпирает: "Пошли, Симакина, на допрос . . ."

*Translation*

Then they started interrogating me—two interrogations a day. The escort was a woman. She was a convict herself: made a baby and buried it in cranberry bushes, but a neighbor reported. He informed [on her—AN], she got three years—for the baby. So she was helping out in prison. [ . . . ] She would come, open the door: "Let's go, Simakina, interrogation."

*Comment*

Note the total absence of any "trigger warnings" or value judgements in this sequence of simple sentences. The treatment of direct speech adds to the maximal economy of the passage.

The next example is, by contrast, about making and keeping babies but the effect is similar. The time is soon after the war. The husband comes back alive but severely wounded, one arm just hanging by tendons. She wanted to move to the city, he didn't think he could:

### Example 4.28 Aleksandra Min'kova, 1915–1999. Kasatkin 2:469

Ага, ну не схотел: "Давай тут останемси". Ну один дитё, другой дитё, третий дитё, четвёртый дитё, пятый дитё, шастой дитё. Да ишо по два. Угу. Ну он го(вори)т: "Ну куда ехать с этой оравой. Тут мы то с зямлёй, то содим, то косим, то так (в)о(т) (в)от с зямлёй". А зярна-то ведь не давали в колхозе ни граммочки. Шерсть отдай, мясо отдай, яички отдай, картошк(у) отдай. Да. А иде её брать: одна корова и шес(т)ь душ детей. Иногда сяду вот, грешница, Господи, може(т), Сталин эт(о) виноват, а може(т), своя влас(т)ь.

*Translation*

Yeah, he didn't want to: "Let's stay here." So one baby, another baby, a third baby, a fourth baby, a fifth baby, a sixth baby. Some of them in twos. Yeah. So he says: "Where would we go with this crowd? Here we're with land, we plant, we mow, that's how it is with land." But in the kolkhoz they wouldn't give us any grain, not a gram. They take wool, they take meat, they take eggs, they take potatoes. Yep. And where would I take it all: one cow and six kids. There were times I would sit down, a sinner: "Oh Lord, maybe it's all Stalin's fault, or maybe it's our local bosses."

*Comment*

Min'kova's syntax is maximally simple but her narrative is skillful, with rhythmic repetitions interspersed with direct speech, in two out of three cases inserted without a syntactic frame.

In saying "six kids" she actually uses "soul" as a counting noun: "six souls of kids," as in land allocation in the village commune.

*6. Formulaic expressions*

Formulaic expressions are a rich source of comparison and contrast between Colloquial Russian and Dialectal. Consider again Example 4.2. The expressions "bend their back from dawn to dusk" common to both, but in the Colloquial (or written literary) Russian they would be stylistically marked, almost pretentious.

Also in 4.2, the expression урвать погодку (catch the right weather) would be understood in Colloquial Russian but unlikely to be said: the corpus gives only one example of "урвать в погоду" (get some work done in that spell of good weather) from a nineteenth century book describing agricultural work.

Many expressions quite unmarked in Colloquial Russian would not be found in Dialectal: понятия не имею (I have no idea); произвело впечатление (made an impression).

The concentration of Dialectal-specific formulaic expressions seems lower in post-1990 recordings than in the early collection of texts, admittedly too small for valid comparisons. However, in the late narratives the impression of formulaic speech often emerges from rhythmic repetitions and occasional rhyming. Here is a typical example from the same Fedotova who was thrilled to run into a wolf in the forest (Example 4.24). Remembering her difficult life after the family was resettled in the North, she writes:

**Example 4.29 Fedotova 1936–2003. Kasatkin 2010:287**

Дак всё вновь, всё заживались вновь. Ни тряпок никаких, ничего нет, ни постельного, ничего-то нету, всё-то надо было как-то самим. И вот стали поживать-то, наживать-то ложки поварежки.

*Translation*

So everything from scratch, everything we had to start from scratch. No clothes of any kind, no nothing—no bedding, no anything, everything we had to somehow [acquire] ourselves. And so we started getting by, saving up on pots and pans.

*Comment*

Many decorative details are lost in translation. The phrases "ничего нет" and "ничего-то нету" say the same thing twice but the second time with two added alliterative syllables. The verbs translated as "settle down, getting by, saving up" are all from the same root meaning "live." The last two of them rhyme and are immediately followed by a rhymed formulaic expression translated as "pots and pans"; it literally means "spoons and ladles" but is intended to convey kitchen utensils in general. The whole passage is very tightly knit together.

**Comparisons with Urban Vernaculars**

Comparisons of Dialectal with UV-1 and UV-2 could be the subject of a separate study, but a few examples give the flavor of the material.

*UV-1 Gradations*

Example 4.30 from Shalina (2011) is another memory of peasant childhood, a story about the speaker's grandmother. Shalina's in-text comments are in italics.

**Example 4.30 A. B. 1932–2007. Shalina 2011:30–31. Peasant grandparents**

А шутники они были большие / дед-то Антип с Парасковьей // [*улыбается*] Бывало / лето / деревня зелёная стоит / как щас помню / ту-у-у-чи комаров // [*показывает руками*] Представь себе / идём втроём по тропинке / по просеке / а комары просто заедают // Бабы тада / может не все / конечно / ходили без штанов // Вот баушка Парасковья идёт / всё отмахивается веткой / а потом ка-а-а-к поднимет подол да как закричит / "У-у-у собаки" // Попа голая / и грит / Ешьте / собаки! // Это на комаров-то она. [*смеется*] [ . . . ]
   Старые-то женщины лет в шийсят юбки длинные носили / до самых пят почти // Длинные / да в складку / да широкие // И вот **если баушка ходила куда-то в гости / а придет домой /** ищет в своих складках / то пряники / то конфеты вытаскиват // [*вытаскивает*] Любила меня очень //

## Translation

They were very funny, grandpa Antip and Paraskov'ia. [*smiles*] It used to be, summer, the village is all green, I remember like it was yesterday, CLOUDS of mosquitoes. [*shows with her hands*] Imagine, we're walking, the three of us, down a wide path through the woods, and mosquitoes are killing us. The women then, maybe not all, walked around without underpants. So grandma Paraskov'ia chases them away with a branch, and then she lifts her skirt and yelled "YOU, bitches." Her butt naked, and she says: "Eat, bitches!" [*laughs*] It's at mosquitos she [is yelling]. [ . . . ]

Older women of about sixty wore long skirts, almost to their heels. Long, with folds, and wide. And so **if grandma went visiting somewhere—she comes home** and starts rummaging in her folds, either it's a gingerbread or candy she pulls out. She loved me very much.

## Comment

Syntactically this is a typical peasant narrative, e.g., there is a typical syntactic incongruity in the sentence that starts with a subordinate conditional clause, including the conjunction если (if), but then the main clause starts with a coordinate conjunction. Lexically, the phrase "представь себе" (imagine) is unusual in a peasant text but otherwise the vocabulary is traditional. Yet the speaker, seventy-five years old, left the village when she was 20 and worked at a factory until she retired. The language of other parts of her story shows the urban influence.

### Example 4.31 A. B. Shalina 2011:32. Father during the war. Talking to her granddaughter

Он [отец] работал у нас мастером на заводе / в формовочном цехе / где делались изделия для сталелитейного завода / для нижнетагильского // Ковшовые кирпичи / розетки / воронки всякие / сифоны / в общем всякая всячина // Все было для фронта / все для победы // Щас это никто не понимает / особенно нынешняя молодежь // Какие же тяжелые дни пережило наше поколение! И не дай вам Бог узнать / что такое война! Да даже твои родители воспитывались в этом послевоенном духе // Ну да ладно / всё равно меня трудно понять // [ . . . ]

А если у отца и останется када свободное время / он шел в колхоз какой нить // [ . . . ] Мужиков-то в колхозах было мало / вот отец и уходил / ремонтировал сеялки / веялки / трактора да комбайны / и ему за это хорошо платили // И он привозил домой то флягу молока / то капусты // Некоторые семьи траву ели или сено / умирали // Сено в кишки впивалось / сразу смерть // А что было делать?! Есь-то [*есть-то*] хотелося, жить-то хотелося // Скотину забивали / продавали / ее нечем кормить было // А мы за всю войну ни ра-а-зу травы с сеном в рот не брали! // Хоть и жили небогато / но всегда было у нас и молоко / и даже мясо //

*Translation*

He [father—AN] was a foreman at the factory, in the molding shop where they produced various items for the steel factory, the one in Nizhnii Tagil [a city in the Urals—AN]. Specialty bricks, sockets, funnels, siphons, in general all sorts of things. Everything was for the front, everything for victory. Nobody understands this nowadays, especially today's young people. Our generation lived through such difficult times! And may the Lord spare you from learning what war is like! Even your parents were being brought up in that same post-war spirit. Oh never mind, all the same it's hard to understand me. [ . . . ]

And if my father had any free time, he would go to some kolkhoz. [ . . . ] There were very few men in kolkhozes, so my father would go there, repair seeders, winnowers, tractors, combines, and he was well paid for this. And he would bring home now a flask of milk, now some cabbage. Some families ate grass or hay, died. Hay would puncture your gut, instant death. But what could you do? Everybody wanted to eat, everybody wanted to live. They slaughtered animals to sell, there was nothing to feed them with. But not once in the entire war did WE put any grass or hay in our mouths! We lived modestly but we always had milk and sometimes even meat.

*Comment*

Several items of vocabulary and phraseology separate this text from the Dialectal language. Most obvious and least interesting is the terminological jargon, the names of goods produced by the factory. These are not in principle different from peasants' jargon for their tools and produce. More important are Passive phrases "делались изделия" (items were produced) and "твои родители воспитывались в этом послевоенном духе" (your parents were being brought up in that post-war spirit," where the intended meaning is probably "remembering the war spirit"). These immediately tag the text as non-peasant. This is not to suggest that older peasants did not complain about "today's youth," but those complaints were mostly cultural: we worked hard and they are lazy; we drank only on holidays, they drink every week, and worse yet, take drugs; we danced beautiful dances and they just shake to some crazy music.

The notion of children being brought up in some spirit or another is part of Soviet vocabulary that peasants were generally immune to. In Chapter 3 not a single letter was marked as both "peasant" or "SovYaz" (i.e., contains obvious Soviet language). The narratives of Chapter 4 occasionally express gratitude to Lenin, e.g., because before Lenin only boys/males were counted as "souls" in allocating communal land but Lenin ordered the inclusion of girls as well. In more recent events, the government is praised for giving peasants pensions, embarrassingly small, but much better than nothing.

In summary, UV-1 materials frequently have passages that are indistinguishable from Dialectal, especially in reminiscences of childhood and adolescence in the village. In all of them there are also traces of vocabulary and phraseology that are alien to Dialectal. The frequency of such traces and the starkness of their contrast with Dialectal depend primarily on the speaker's level of education and degree of involvement with city life.

## UV-2 contrasts

UV-2 is very different in its linguistic manifestations from both Dialectal and UV-1. It is a very dynamic social dialect, and several directions of change are quite recent. One has already been mentioned: the preference in some groups for abstract nouns, frequently resulting in solecisms. Other solecisms result simply from sloppy use of language. Also very common are the discourse-level lexical items that serve as fillers or hedges. Well-known examples in English are "you know," "I mean," and, of course, "like." Example 4.32 from a current corpus of everyday Russian conversations[16] contains some Russian equivalents, shown in boldface. Solecisms, in italics, are explained in square brackets in the text.

### Example 4.32 Recorded 2009-11-09. A young woman talks about her driving lesson

меня дядька/посадил **короче говоря** *за машину*//и спросил /ну **типа** умеешь **вообще** кататься или нет ? сидела за рулем ? я говорю/ну(:) как/пару раз было дело конечно//

*Translation*

That man put me, in short, behind the car [i.e., "behind the wheel"] and asked, like, do you, basically, know how to ride [i.e., "drive"]? have you been at the wheel? I said, well, you know, a couple of times it came to that, of course.

In two lines of 4.32 there are three fillers. Neither Dialectal nor UV-1 use those. Occasionally, Dialectal and UV-1 speakers would use an expletive (e.g., Kasatkin 2017:468) but always with an emotional impact, not as a filler frequently found in UV-2—mostly among working-class men but increasingly—and this is a recent phenomenon--among women and the better educated.

## CONCLUSIONS: THE UNITY OF PEASANT LANGUAGE

The life stories of Russian peasants are dramatic and eventful. They are also well told. The examples in this chapter were selected for historical context and linguistic detail. If they also show narrative skill it is because most of the accumulated material is like that. An anthology of peasant stories makes a powerful read.

This book has traced records of peasant language from the turn of the twentieth century to the turn of the twenty-first. From our initial limited view of the lost speech of a hundred million to the abundant records of their descendants, now dispersed and few in number, we can see an underlying unity. This unity is found in the economy and local distinctiveness of vocabulary; in the radical simplicity of syntax; in tightly structured phraseology with alliteration and rhythm; and in a tradition of story-telling. It is further held together by the shared historical experience that left the same scars on millions of people. The cumulative record of Russian peasant speech, in all its prejudice, wisdom, and artistry, remains a treasure to study and learn from.

## NOTES

1. According to L. L. Kasatkin (personal communication), the Russian Language Institute of the Academy of Sciences collected hundreds of peasant recordings in those decades, and similar collections accumulated in other research institutions, but little was published.

2. The statement is in note 17. The same note says: "The results of this investigation have not yet been published."

3. M. Daniel et al. (2018).

4. On June 20, 2018, the Russian College Accreditation Agency (RosObrNadzor) abruptly withdrew accreditation from Shaninka, even though it was considered one of the best educational institutions in Russia. As of this writing (July 2018) the story is still unfolding.

5. The word cannot be found; possibly "коженели," http://www.nffedorov.ru/d ialect/str/str12.html#str12.

6. See especially the last page of Seifullina's 1923 novella *Перегной* (Humus), which features Cossacks, peasants, and a pregnant woman in a village in the southern

Urals. Gorham (1993:74–77) discusses the novella at some length but misidentifies the time and place of the action, in addition to several other inaccuracies.

7. In 2005–2012 this was the name of the pro-Kremlin youth movement.

8. The date of birth is given as 1924. If this is accurate then she would have been seventeen, not sixteen in September 1941.

9. According to Zima's (1996) definitive history, the harvest of 1946 was poor but famine was avoidable. As in 1932–1933, the government sold grain abroad. See Ganson (2009) for an English-language account.

10. At a 2018 conference of dialectologists, the audience was presented with a narrative passage and asked to identify whether it was dialectal or "urban." The common judgement was that it was dialectal; in fact, it was recorded from an older UV-1 speaker who had been away from her village for decades.

11. The phenomenon was first identified and given a name by Trubinskii (1991), Gerd (1990). Interesting examples and discussion in Bukrinskaia and Karmakova 2012a.

12. Zhuravlev investigates eleven varieties of written and spoken Russian including Colloquial Russian, Urban Vernacular, and Dialectal, each of the three divided into "monolog" (narrative) and "dialog" (conversation) varieties. Eighteen parameters are chosen, five of which are adopted from Greenberg (1960). While Greenberg's approach was developed for the typological comparison of languages, Zhuravlev successfully applies it to comparing social dialects. We quote his figures for the "monolog" varieties of Colloquial Russian and Dialectal. Zhuravlev's results completely support our observations.

13. Zhuravlev 1988:132 shows the average length of conversation sentences to be about half the length of narrative sentences, both for Dialectal and Colloquial Russian.

14. The text is at the very beginning of Episode 4 of the series, https://www.youtube.com/watch?v=1K1t5SVaxHg.

15. A stone platform on Red Square in front of Saint Basil's Cathedral.

16. See Bogdanova-Beglarian N., et al. 2016 "Sociolinguistic Extension of the ORD Corpus of Russian Everyday Speech." In Ronzhin, A. et al. (eds.) *SPECOM 2016, Lecture Notes in Computer Science*, Springer, pp.659–666.

# Bibliography

Alymov, Sergei. 2006. *P I. Kushner i razvitie sovetskoi etnografii v 1920-1950-e gody.* (P. I. Kushner and the development of Soviet ethnography in the 1920s–1950s.) Moscow: In-t etnologii i antropologii RAN.

———. 2010. "Nesluchainoe selo." (A non-random village.) *Novoe literaturnoe obozrenie*:101. http://magazines.russ.ru/nlo/2010/101/alk7.html, accessed May 27, 2019.

Austin, Peter and Julia Sallabank, eds. 2015. *The Cambridge Handbook of Endangered Languages.* Cambridge: Cambridge University Press.

Avanesov, R. 1964. *Dialektologiia.* (Dialectology.) Moscow: Nauka.

Belikov, V. I. and L. P. Krysin, 2017. *Sotsiolingvistika* (Sociolinguistics), 2nd ed. Moscow: Urait.

Berdinskikh, V. 2011. Речи немых. (Speeches of the mute). Moscow: Lomonosov.

Bol'shakov A. 1930. *Kraevedcheskoe izuchenie derevni.* (Ethnographic study of the village.) Leningrad: Rabotnik prosveshcheniia.

Boriak, Hennadii. 2008. "Holodomor Archives and Sources: The State of the Art." *The Harriman Review.* 16:2, 21–36.

Borkovskii, V. ed., 1978. *Istoricheskaia grammatika russkogo iazyka. Sintaksis. Prostoe predlozhenie.* (A Historical Grammar of Russian. Syntax. The simple sentence.) Moscow: Nauka.

Bourdieu, Pierre. 1991. John B. Thompson, ed. *Language and Symbolic Power.* Cambridge, MA: Harvard University Press.

Boyd, Brian. 1991. *Vladimir Nabokov: The American Years.* Princeton, NJ: Princeton University Press.

Bukrinskaia, I. A. and O. E. Karmakova. 2006. "Ekspressivnost' kak norma dialektnogo teksta" (Expressivity as a norm in dialectal texts.) In *Russkii iazyk segodnia.* Vypusk 4. (The Russian language today. Vol. 5.) Moscow: Azbukovnik. 93–103.

———. 2012a. "Iazykovaia situatsiia v malykh gorodakh Rossii" (The language situation in the small towns of Russia.) *Issledovaniia po slavianskoi dialektologii.* (Studies in Slavic dialectology.) Moscow: Institute of Slavic Studies, the Russian Academy. 15: 154–155.

———. 2012b. Opyt analiza narrativnykh dialektnykh tekstov. (An analysis of dialectal narratives.) In Rozanova, N. N., ed. *Russkii iazyk segodnia. Vypusk 5.* (Russian language today. Vol. 5.) Moscow: Azbukovnik.

———. 2015. "Kommunikant v prostranstve dialektnogo monologa." (The speaker in the space of the dialectal monolog.) St.Petersburg: LARNG (Lexical Atlas of Russian Dialects-2015), 110–121.

Chomsky, N. 1965. *Aspects of the Theory of Syntax.* Cambridge, MA: The MIT Press.

Chukovskii, Kornei. 2012. Дневники (Diaries), Vol. 1. Moscow: PROZAiK.

Daniel, M. et al. November 2018. "Dialect loss in the Russian North." Submitted for publication.

Danilov, V. 2002. "Istoriki v sotsiologicheskom issledovanii rossiiskoi derevni." (Historians in the sociological study of the Russian village.) In *Рефлексивное крестьяноведение* (Reflexive peasantology). Moscow: ROSSPEN, 115–140.

Danilov, V. et al., eds., 1999. *Tragediia russkoi derevni.* (The tragedy of the Russian village. Collectivization and Dekulakization. Documents and Materials In 5 volumes 1927–1939.) Vol. 1. Moscow, ROSSPEN.

D'iachok M. T. 2003. "Russkoe prostorechie kak sotsiolingvisticheskoe iavlenie." (Russian prostorechie as a sociolinguistic phenomenon.) Izdatel'stvo Sibirskogo Federal'nogo Universiteta (Siberian Federal University Press) Humanities Series, 21: 102–113.

Dorman, Oleg. 2009. *Podstrochnik. Zhizn' Lilianny Lunginoi, rasskazannaia eiu v fil'me Olega Dormana.* (Literal translation. The life of Lilianna Lungina told by herself in the film of Oleg Dorman.) Moscow: Astrel'.

Fenomenov, M. Ia. 1925. *Современная деревня* (The contemporary village). Moscow: GIZ. Vol. 1–2.

Filin, F. 1936. "Новое в лексике колхозной деревни," Литературный критик (Literary critic), 3:135–160.

Freed, Stanley, Ruth S. Freed and Laila Williamson. 1988. "Capitalist Philanthropy and Russian Revolutionaries: The Jesup North Pacific Expedition (1897–1902)." *American Anthropologist,* New Series, 90/1: 7–24.

Ganson, Nicholas, 2009. *The Soviet Famine of 1946–47 in Global and Historical Perspective.* New York: Palgrave Macmillan.

Gerd. 2000. "Neskol'ko zamechanii kasatel'no poniatiia 'dialekt.'" (A few observations regarding the concept of 'dialect.'). In Krysin 2000:45-52.

Gol'din, V. E. 1997. *Teoreticheskie problemy kommukativnoi dialektologii.* (Theoretical problems of communicative dialectology.) Saratov: Saratov University.

———. 2000. "Vnutrenniaia tipologiia russkoi rechi i stroenie rusistiki." (The internal typology of Russian speech and the structure of Russian language scholarship.) In Krysin 2000:53–65.

———. 2009. "Povestvovanie v dialektnom diskurse" (Narrative in dialectal discourse). *Izvestiia Saratovskogo Universiteta. Novaia seriia. Filologiia. Zhurnalistika.* (Proceedings of the Saratov University. New Series. Philology, Journalism. 1:3–7.

Gorham, Michael. 1993. *Speaking in Soviet tongues.* De Kalb: Northern Illinois University Press.

Gorkii, Maksim. 1953. *Собрание сочинений в тридцати томах, 27: Статьи, доклады, речи, приветствия* (1933–1936). Moscow: GIKhL.
Graziosi, A. 1996. *The great Soviet-Peasant war. Bolsheviks and Peasants, 1918–1933*. Cambridge, MA: Harvard Ukrainian Center.
Greenberg, Joseph H. 1960. "A Quantitative Approach to the Morphological Typology of Language." *International Journal of American Linguistics*. 26:3, 178–194.
Iakovlev, Ia. 1923. *Derevnia kak ona est'*. (The village as it really is.) Moscow: Krasnaia Nov'.
———. 1924. *Nasha derevnia*. (Our village.) Moscow: Krasnaia Nov'.
Iastrebinskaia, Galina. 2005. *Taiozhnaia derevnia Kobelevo*. (The taiga village of Kobelevo.) Moscow: Pamiatniki istoricheskoi mysli.
Inkeles, Alex. 1968. *Social Change in Soviet Russia*. Cambridge, MA: Harvard University Press.
Karinskii, N. M. 1935. "Iz nabliudenii nad iazykom sovremennoi derevni." (Observations on the language of the contemporary village.) *Literaturnaia kritika* 5: 159–175.
———. 1936. *Ocherki iazyka russkikh krest'ian*. (Essays on the language of Russian peasants.) Moscow: Sotsekgiz.
Karpovich, Michael. 1946. "Review of *Vstrecha s Rossiei: Kak i chem zhivut v Sovetskom Soyuze: Pis'ma v Krasnuyu Armiyu*, 1939–1940. by V. Zenzinov." *The American Slavic and East European Review*, 5/3–4:237–239. http://www.jstor.org/stable/2492111, accessed May 27, 2019.
Kasatkin, L. L. 1993. "Russkie dialekty i iazykovaia politika." (Russian dialects and language policy.) *Russkaia Rech'*, 2: 82–90.
Kasatkin, L. L. 1999. *Sovremennaia russkaia dialektnaia i literaturnaia fonetika kak istochnik dlia istorii russkogo iazyka*. (Phonetics of contemporary Russian dialects and of the literary language as a source for the study of the history of Russian.) Moscow: Nauka.
———. 2017. *Izbrannye trudy, t.2*. (Selected works, vol. 2.) Moscow: Iask.
Kelly, Catriona. 2002. "A Laboratory for the Manufacture of Proletarian Writers: The Stengazeta (Wall Newspaper), Kul'turnost' and the Language of Politics in the Early Soviet Period." *Europe-Asia Studies*, 54/4: 573–602.
Koester-Thoma, Z. 1994. "Sfery bytovaniia russkogo sotsiolekta. (Sotsiologicheskii aspekt)." (The geographic distribution of a Russian social dialect.) *Rusistika*. 1–2:18–28.
Kibrik, Aleksandr, A. Arkhipov, M. Daniel (eds.). 2008. *Malye iazyki i narody: sushchestvovanie na grani. Vypusk 2. Teksty i slovarnye materialy*. (Minority languages and peoples: On the verge of extinction. Issue 2. Texts and lexical materials.) Moscow: Jazyki slavyanskoy kultury.
Kolesov, V. V. (ed.). 1990 *Russkaia Dialektologiia*. (Russian dialectology.) Moscow: Vysshaia shkola.
Kotkin, Stephen. 1997. *The Magnetic Mountain*. Oakland: University of California Press.
Kovalev B. N. 2011. *Povsednevnaia zhizn' naseleniia Rossii v period natsistskoi okkupatsii*. (The everyday life of the Russian population during the Nazi occupation.) Moscow: Molodaia gvardiia.

Kovalev, E. M. (ed.). 1996. *Golosa Krest'ian* (Peasant Voices), Moscow: Aspekt Press.
Kozlova, N., and Irina Sandomirskaia. 1996. *"Naivnoe Pis'mo": Opyt lingvo-sotsiologicheskogo chteniia*. Moscow: Gnozis.
Koznova, Irina. 2106. *Stalinskaia epokha v pamiati krest'ianstva Rossii*. (Stalin's era in the memory of Russian peasants.) Moscow: ROSSPEN.
Kriukova, S. S. (ed.) 2001. *Krest'ianskie istorii: Rossiiskaia derevnia 20-kh godov v pis'makh i dokumentakh*. (Peasant stories: the Russian village of the 1920s in letters and documents.) Moscow: ROSSPEN.
Krysin, L. P. 2000. *Russkii iazyk segodnia. Vypusk 1*. (Russian language today. Vol. 1.) Moscow: Azbukovnik.
Lakoff, George and Mark Johnson. 2003. *Metaphors we live by*. Chicago: University of Chicago Press, 2nd edition.
Lapteva, O. A. 1976. *Russkii razgovornyi sintaksis*. (The syntax of spoken Russian.) Moscow: Nauka.
Markasova, E. V. 2002. "Sel'kor pod obstrelom: stereotipy vrazhdebnogo okruzhenija i zhertvennosti v 'kommunikacionnom zavoevanii' derevni." (Sel'kor under fire: stereotypes of hostile environment and victimhood in the 'communicational occupation' of the village.) https://www.academia.edu/2384428/, accessed May 27, 2019.
Matveeva, T. V. (ed.) 1995. *Zhivaia rech' ural'skogo goroda. Teksty*. (The live speech of a Ural city. Texts.) Ekaterinburg: Ural University Press.
Mel'chuk, I. A. 1974. *Opyt teorii lingvisticheskikh modelei "Smysl ⇔ Tekst'*. (An essay on the theory of linguistic models Meaning ⇔ Text.) Moscow: Nauka.
Meromskii, A. 1930. *Iazyk sel'kora*. (The language of the village correspondent.) Moscow: Federatsiia.
Mokienko, V. M. and T. G. Nikitina. 1998. *Tolkovyi Slovar' iazyka Sovdepii*.(The explanatory dictionary of the language of 'Sovdepiia' [the Soviets—AN]). St. Peterburg: Folio-Press.
Myznikov, S. A. 2005. *Russkie govory srednego Povolzh'ia*. (Russian dialects of the mid-Volga region.) St. Petersburg: Nauka.
Nakhimovsky, A. 1978. "Organizations and documents in Russian syntax." *Papers from the 14th Meeting, Chicago Linguistic Society*, 297–306.
———. 2015. "Toward a history of the 'Soviet Language' (SovYaz): archival documents, electronic sources, and the National Corpus." *Slavic and East European Journal* 59:2: 270-289.
———. 2017. "Krest'ianskii iazyk i Revoliutsiia: Pis'ma vo vlast' do i posle 1917 goda." (Peasant language and the Revolution: letters to power before and after the Revolution.) *Revue des études slaves*, Philologie et Révolution, tome LXXXVIII, fascicule 1–2:113–34.
———. 2018. "The transcripts of the JAFC Trial as an Extended Conversation: Words, Sentences, and Speech Acts." *East European Jewish Affairs* 2:210–232.
———. 2019. forthcoming. "20th century peasant letters as background to 19th century Russian literature." *Cardinal Points*.
Naumov, V. P. 1994. *Nepravednyi Sud*. (Unrightous Tribunal.) Moscow, Nauka.

Nefedov S. A. 2011. *Istoriia Rossii. Faktornyi analiz*. t.2. (History of Russia. Factor analysis. Vol. 2.) Moscow: Territoriia budushchego.
Orlov, Igor' B., Aleksandr Livshin. 1998a. "Revoliutsiia i sotsial'naia spravedlivost': Ozhidaniia i real'nost' ('Pis'ma vo vlast'' 1917–1927 godov)." In: *Cahiers du monde russe: Russie, Empire russe, Union soviétique, États indépendants* 39: 487–513.
———. 1998b. *Pis'ma vo vlast: 1917–1927*. Moscow: ROSSPEN.
———. 2002. *Pis'ma vo vlast*: 1928–1939. Moscow: ROSSPEN.
Paperno, I. 2009. *Stories of the Soviet Experience: Memoirs, Diaries, Dreams*. Ithaca, NY: Cornell University Press.
Platonov, Andrei. 1983. *Potaennyi Platonov: povest' i rasskazy*. (Hidden Platonov: a novella and short stories). New York: Tret'ia volna.
———. 1987. *Potomki Solntsa. Rasskazy i povesti*. (Descendants of the sun. Stories and novellas.) Moscow: Pravda.
Pomerantseva, E. V. 1971. "Fol'klornye materialy 'Etnograficheskogo biuro' V. N. Tenisheva" (Folklore materials in the "Ethnographic bureau" of V. N. Tenishev). Sovetskaia Etnografiia 6:137–147 https://www.booksite.ru/etnogr/1971/1971_6.pdf.
Schneider, Edgar W. 2013. "Written data sources." In Christine Mallinson, Becky Childs & Gerard Van Herk (eds.), *Data collection in sociolinguistics: Methods and applications*, 169–178. London: Routledge.
Seifullina, Lidiia, 1923, 1989. *Peregnoi*. (Humus) Novonikolaevsk, Sibirskie ogni. Reprinted in *Chetyre glavy*. (Four chapters.) Moscow: Sovremenik.
Selishchev, A. 1928. *Russkii iazyk revoliutsionnoi epokhi*. (The Russian language of the revolutionary era.) Moscow: Rabotnik prosveshcheniia.
Senchakova, L. T. 1994. *Prigovory i nakazy russkogo krest'ianstva 1905–1907 gg*. (Resolutions and petitions by Russian peasants, 1905–1907.) Vols.1–2. Moscow: Rossiiskaia akademiia nauk.
———. 1999. *Prigovory i nakazy russkogo krest'ianstva 1905–1907 gg*. (Resolutions and petitions by Russian peasants, 1905–1907.) Moscow: Editorial URSS.
Shafir, Ia. 1923. *Gazeta i Derevnia*. (The newspaper and the village.) Moscow: Krasnaia Nov'.
Shalina, I. V. 2009. *Ural'skoe gorodskoe prostorechie: kul'turnye stsenarii*. (Urals urban vernacular: cultural scenarios.) Ekaterinburg: Ural University Press.
———. 2011. *Zhivaia rech' ural'skogo goroda. Khrestomatiia*. (The live speech of a Ural city. An anthology.) Ekaterinburg: Ural University Press.
Shmelev D. N., ed. 1989 *Iazyk i lichnost'*. (Language and identity). Moscow: Nauka.
Shpil'rein, Isaak. 1928. *Iazyk krasnoarmeitsa*. (The language of the Red Army soldier.) Moscow-Leningrad: Gosudarstvennoe izdatel'stvo.
Sokolov, A. K., ed. 1998a. *Golos naroda. Pis'ma i otkliki riadovykh sovetskikh grazhdan o sobytiiakh 1918–1932 g.g*. (Voice of the people. Letters and responses by ordinary Soviet people about the events of 1918–1932.) Moscow: ROSSPEN.
———. (ed.) 1998b. Obshchestvo i vlast'. 1930-e gody. (Society and power. The 1930s.) Moscow: ROSSPEN.
Stonov, D. M. 1926. "Po zaraiskim derevniam." (In the villages of Zaraisk district.) *Izvestiia*, May 16, 1926, 1. (Continued from the May 9 issue.)

Sveshnikova, N. V. 2007. "Modeli diminutivnogo slovoobrazovaniia v russkikh govorakh." (Models of diminutive word formation in Russian dialects.) In *Dialektnoe slovoobrazovanie, morfemika i morfonologiia.* St. Petersburg: Nauka; Vologda: VGPU, 289–298. https://www.sgu.ru/archive/old.sgu.ru/files/sveshnikova_modeli.doc.
Tan-Bogoraz, 1905. Novoe krest'ianstvo. (The New Peasantry.) Moscow: Knigoizdatel'stvo E. D. Miagkova Kolokol.
———. 1924a. *Staryi i novyi byt.* (Old and new ways of life.) Leningrad: Gosizdat.
———. 1924b. *Revoliutsiia v derevne.* (Revolution in the village.) Leningrad: Gosizdat.
———. 1925. *Obnovlennaia derevnia.* (The rejuvenated village.) Leningrad: Gosizdat.
Tarkhova, N. S. 2006. *Armiia i krest'ianstvo: krasnaia armiia i kollektivizatsiia sovetskoi derevni, 1928–1933.* (Army and peasantry: the Red army and the collectivization of the Soviet village.) Moscow-St. Petersburg: Letnii Sad.
Tenishev, V. N. 2004–2009. *Materials of the Ethnographic Bureau of V. N. Tenishev. Vols. 1–8.* St. Petersburg: The Russian Ethnographic Museum.
Trubinskii, B. I. 1991. *Sovremennye russkie regiolekty.* (Contemporary Russian regiolects.) Pskov: Izdatel'stvo Pskovskogo Universiteta.
Ushakin, S. and A. Golubev (eds.). 2016. *XX vek: Pis'ma voiny.* (XX century. War letters.) Moscow: NLO.
Várdy, Steven Béla and Agnes Huszár Várdy (2007). "Cannibalism in Stalin's Russia and Mao's China." *East European Quarterly.* 41: 2,223–238.
Vinogradskii, V. G. 2011. *Krest'ianskie koordinaty.* (Peasant coordinates.) Saratov: Izdatel'stvo Saratovskogo instituta RGTEU.
———. *Protokoly kolkhoznoi epokhi.* (The protocols of the kolkhoz era.) Saratov: Izdatel'stvo Saratovskogo instituta RGTEU.
———. 2015. "Krest'ianskii mir v diskurse pokolencheskoi pechali." (The peasant world in the discourse of inter-generational sadness.) *Sotsiologicheskie issledovaniia* 12, 82–91.
———. 2016. "Golosa krest'ian v ikh diskursivnoi proektsii." (The voices of peasants projected on their discourses.) *Przegląd wschodnioeuropejski. East European Review* 7/2: 135–151.
———. 2017. *"Golosa snizu": diskursy sel'skoi povsednevnosti.* (Voices from below: discourses of everyday village life.) Moscow: Izdatel'stvo Delo.
Wanner, Leo. 1996. *Lexical Functions in Lexicography and Natural Language Processing.* Amsterdam, Philadelphia: John Benjamins.
Wood, David. 2015. *Fundamentals of Formulaic Language.* London: Bloomsbury Academic.
Yokoyama, Olga. 2008 *Russian Peasant Letters: Texts and Contexts.* Vols. 1, 2. Wiesbaden: Verlag Otto Harrassowitz,
Zaionchkovskaia, Zhanna. 1991. *Demograficheskaia situatsiia i rasselenie.* (The demographic situation and the distribution of population.) Moscow: Nauka.
———. 1999. "Vnutrenniaia migratsiia v Rossii i v SSSR v XX veke kak otrazhenie sotsial'noi modernizatsii." (Internal migration in Russia and the USSR in the twentieth century as a reflection of social modernization.) *Mir Rossii.* 4: 22–34.

Zemskaia, E. A. 2004. "Russkoe prostorechie kak lingvisticheskii fenomen." In *Iazyk kak deiatel'nost'* (Language as activity), 354–362. Moscow: Flinta.

Zemskaia, E. A. and D. N. Shmelev (eds). 1984. *Gorodskoe prostorechie: Problemy izucheniia*. (Urban vernacular: problems of studying.) Moscow: Nauka.

———. 1988. *Raznovidnosti gorodskoi ustnoi rechi*. (Varieties of urban speech.) Moscow: Nauka.

Zenzinov, V. M. 1914. *Starinnye liudi u kholodnogo okeana*. (Ancient people by the cold ocean.) Moscow: Tipografiia Riabushinskogo.

———. 1916. *Ocherki torgovli na severe Iakutskoi oblasti*. (Notes on trade in the North of the Iakutiia Province.) Moscow: Tipografiia Riabushinskogo.

———. *Vstrecha s Rossiei: Kak i chem zhivut v Sovetskom Soyuze: Pis'ma v Krasnuyu Armiyu*, 1939–1940. New York: published by author.

Zhuravlev, A. F. 1988. "Opyt kvantitativno-tipologicheskogo issledovaniia raznovidnostei ustnoi rechi." (A quantitative typological study of varieties of oral speech.) In Zemskaia and Shmelev 1988:46–147.

Zima, V. F. 1996. *Golod v SSSR 1946–1947 gg. Proiskhozhdenie i posledstviia*. (Famine in the USSR 1946–1947: origins and consequences.) Moscow: Rossiiskaiia akademiia nauk, In-t rossiiskoi istorii.

Zubov, A. (ed.) *Istoriia Rossii. XX vek*. (History of Russia. 20th Century.) 2 vols. Moscow: Astrel'.

# Index

biographical narratives, 133; as historical testimony, 146–49; editorial policies in publishing, 142, 144; main data collections, 143–45; speakers' birth dates, 136–37
Bogoraz, Vladimir: biography of, 9–10; in 1905, 11–14; in 1920s, 48, 99
Bolshevik language. *See* SovYaz
Bolsheviks, 42–45
Bukrinskaia, I. and O. Karmakova, 170, 176–77, 187

calendar, Julian and Russian Church, 82, 92, 151
censorship, 139–41
collectivization and dekulakization, 67–68; and destruction of churches, 165–68; in post-1990 recordings, 155–68
Colloquial Russian syntactic complexity, 189–91
Conceptual Metaphor, 35–37, 62
contaminations in syntax and phraseology, 50, 55, 62–64

Danilov, Victor, 140–41
dialectology, 1–2; and other linguistic disciplines, 143, 186–87
dialects: social, 1, 185–87

edinolichnik (non-kolkhoz peasant, единоличник), 68, 148–50, 152, 154–55
Emancipation of 1861, 29
Ethnography, Soviet, 139–40

famine of 1891, 29–30
famine of 1921–1922, 47
famine of 1932–1933, 47, 160–65
famine of 1946–1947, 176, 178–79
Fenomenov, Mikhail, 11, 18–19, 21–22
Fitzpatrick, Sheila, 88
forms of address, 75–77; comparison of nineteenth- and twentieth-century examples, 77–79; levels of formality in, 76; pronouns in, 75–76; role of suffixes in, 76

Gol'din, I. E., 141, 143
Gorky, Maksim, 5, 9, 32, 46
GPU-NKVD, 43, 60, 74, 130n3, 163, 166, 168; in peasant narratives, 147–148, 158–60, 165

Iakovlev, Ia. A., 8, 21, 40, 46–49, 51

Kasatkin, L. L., 135–36, 138, 144, 145, biography of, 140–41

kolkhoz: impact on peasant language and society, 124–25, 166; post-Stalin, 179–82
Krest'ianskaia Gazeta, 26, 49, 139
Krysin, L., 22n2, 185–86
Kushner, P. I., 8, 138–39, 176

laborday (Russian трудодень), 87, 89, 91, 109, 166, 179
language of peasants, 1–2; as endangered language, 133–35, 137–38; periodization of history in, 146–49; and prostorechie, 2–4, 194–98; simplicity as style, 100–101, 192–93; SovYaz influence on, 52, 54, 60–62
letters 1939–1940: designations of the enemy in, 105, 116–17; from schoolchildren and a schoolteacher, 111–13; gradations of literacy, 89, 110–11; historical background to, 83–84; social composition of, 85–87; SovYaz in, 105; typical components of, 90–92; unique features of, 82–83
letters, personal, 75–76
letters to power (leaders and newspapers), 7, 26; 1905–1917, 30, 33–35; lexical features of, 54, 61–62; peasants vs. landlord in, 28; pre-1905, 26–32; syntax and style of, 52, 60; wrong Lexical Functions in, 62
Lexical Functions, 35–37, 62–63
Lungina, Liliana: biography and an example, 190–91

Meromskii, A., 20, 37, 48–49, 54
migration of peasants to cities: in letters of 1939–1940, 88–89; post-Stalin, 182–83

NEP (New Economic Policy), 41, 47, 131n18, 148, 155; unfair pricing in, 40–41, 51–52
non-peasant letters, 1939–1940, 114–23; names for Finland and its people, 116–17; playful openings and ditties, 120–22; SovYaz in, 115–16, 117–20

Old Believers, 81, 136, 178

peasant history, 7–8, 146–49
peasant language: periodization of history in, 146–49
Peasant Letter Profile, 88; an example of conformance in letters of 1939–40, 97; first deviations from, 39; in letters of 1939–40, 123; in a letter by a "recent peasant," 101; in post-1990 recordings, 151, 188–89
peasant letters, 1939–40: diagnostic lexical items in, 79, 94–95; direct speech in, 85, 92–93; discourse features in, 113–14; echoes of 1920s letters to power in, 127–29; orthography in, 109–10; and peasant content (poverty, hunger, powerlessness), 108–9; and vocabulary, syntax, phraseology, 123–29
peasant migration, 107
peasants: in early collectivization, 74; in old age, 97–99, 100–101, 183–85; and passports, 70; and recent urban migrants, 102; as second-class citizens, 70, 87–88, 96; young and optimistic, 104
post-war years, 176–80
prostorechie, 2–4, 89, 183; examples of prostorechie 1, 194–97; example of prostorechie 2, 197–98; prostorechie 1 vs. prostorechie 2, 185–88, 194, 197

regiolects and local dialects, 187
Revolution of 1905, 32–33
Revolution of 1917 and Civil War, 37–38
Russian National Corpus (RNC), 10, 14, 23, 31, 35–36, 39, 43–45, 60, 65n4, 148–49, 152–55, 158–59
Russo-Japanese War, 138–40, 176, 181

sel'cor, 49–50
Selishchev, A., 8, 22, 41–42, 44–45, 47–48, 55, 124
Shalina, I., 157, 186, 194–97
Shanin, Teodor, 141–42
sources for examples, ix, 7, 143–45
Soviet Army: social composition of, 73; and political officers, 73–74
Soviet-Finnish War, 83–84
Soviet Person (sovok), 182–83
SovYaz, 25, 37–41, 43–46, 49–50, 54, 83, 105, 128, 130, 197; 1917–1928 vs. post-Stalin, 40; and army service, 38, 40, 65, 89; an example of deverbal nouns in, 59; neologisms in, 43–44; syllabic abbreviation in, 17, 37, 41, 43, 45, 57–58, 80; and use of the word "mood," 73–74, 84, 130n3
syntax: and conjunction-less subordinate clauses, 9, 18, 32, 126–27, 151; economy of, 34, 177

Tan, N. A. *See* Bogoraz, Vladimir
Tenishev, Prince, 10, 16–18

Urban Vernacular. *See* prostorechie

Vinogradskii, V., 137, 142–44, 145
Viriatino, village of, 138–40, 176, 181

War Communism, 1917–1921, 46–47
World War I ("the German War"), 146, 152
World War II ("the Great Patriotic War"): after June, 1941, 6, 8, 11, 75–78, 88, 93, 109, 114, 123; before 1941, 81–82, 177; and occupation, 154, 168–76, 177–79

Yokoyama, Olga, 6, 8, 11, 75, 77–78, 88, 93, 109, 114, 123, 131n16

Zenzinov, Vladimir, 8, 9, 78, 81, 82
Zhuravlev, A. F., and frequency analysis of dialects, 189, 199n12,13

# About the Author

**Alexander D. Nakhimovsky** completed a tour of duty in the Soviet army before receiving an MA in mathematics from Leningrad University (1972) and a PhD in linguistics from Cornell University (1979). For 15 years he taught and published in general and Slavic linguistics and language pedagogy. Beginning in 1985 he taught at Colgate University, first in the Department of Computer Science, and then, from 2015 until his retirement in 2018, as director of the Linguistics Program. He is the author, coauthor, or editor of books and articles on computer technologies and on Slavic and general linguistics. From 2006 to 2011, he was director of an NSF project on documenting endangered languages. Since 2013 he has been working on the history of the Russian language in the twentieth century. He has published several articles on the topic, most notably on the impact of Bolshevik propaganda on the language of peasants in the 1920s, and on the language of the testimony in the 1952 secret trial of the Jewish Anti-Fascist Committee, whose members had endured three years of interrogations before the trial and expected, accurately, that they were going to be executed. He is currently at work on peasant autobiographical narratives as testimonies of war, occupation, and the Holocaust.

www.ingramcontent.com/pod-product-compliance
Lightning Source LLC
Chambersburg PA
CBHW050904300426
44111CB00010B/1374